IT'S WORTH IT

A Fresh Perspective on Faith, Religion and Relationships

PRAISE FOR *IT'S WORTH IT*

"I have never read such a heartfelt and inspiring perspective on the potential of the local church and the importance of each person's role within it. Pastor Jeff Little is a man with a purpose—a purpose that builds up the lives of others and brings transformation to his community. Here is a man who leads by example; through integrity and dedication he has shown what it means to embrace the calling that God places on each of our hearts. *It's Worth It* will encourage the reader to live their life as an expression of Christ's love, constantly growing in their faith and strengthening their values. The Lord is raising up a new generation of leaders who are making an impact on the world, and this book will make you excited to be a part of that."

MATTHEW BARNETT, Co-founder of The Dream Center, Senior Pastor of Angelus Temple

---

"I spend a lot of time with people and leaders from all over the body of Christ, but I'm a local church girl. I truly believe the local church can transform lives and impact culture.

"In *It's Worth It*, Jeff Little clearly communicates the divine relationships and God-given purpose available to all of us through the church. As someone who has had the privilege of ministering with Jeff and his team, I can tell you these aren't unproven ideas or hypotheticals, they're the kind of hard-learned insights that can only come from seeing God change real people. If you're looking for a fresh perspective on faith and relationships, you'll find it here!"

CHRISTINE CAINE, pastor, author, co-founder of *The A21 Campaign*

"*It's Worth It* is a beautiful picture of the local church—colored with faith-filled wisdom, fiery passion and rich humor. Having known Jeff for almost twenty years this book is literally his heart on a page. You will never regret picking up this book—it's completely worth it!"

STEVE ROBINSON, Senior Pastor, Church of the King, Mandeville, LA

"One has to be around Jeff Little to realize how he loves and values people – and to experience his passion to connect people with the work of God's Kingdom. His new book, *It's Worth It: A Fresh Perspective on Faith, Religion and Relationships*, is practical, inspiring, and a great resource for anyone who wants to live the kind of life God created them to live. This book is a must read for those who love people and the Kingdom of God."

TOMMY BARNETT, Co-Pastor, Phoenix First Founder, LA & Phoenix Dream Centers

---

"I had the opportunity to meet Jeff before he planted Milestone Church and I've watched as God has done something truly special through him. I believe God has given us a unique partnership with churches in cities right next to each other who learn, glean and benefit from one another to advance the Kingdom in our region. His new book, *It's Worth It*, communicates life-changing biblical insights in a fresh, conversational way. I highly recommend it."

ROBERT MORRIS, Founding Senior Pastor, Gateway Church
Bestselling author of *The Blessed Life*, *From Dream to Destiny*, and *The God I Never Knew*

"I'm proud to call Jeff Little my friend and I'm convinced God is doing something incredible at Milestone Church. God's hand is on Milestone because it's a church that cares about people who don't know Jesus. That matters to God. *It's Worth It* is more than the story of Milestone — it will inspire you and give you fresh insights into the things that God values."

RICK BEZET, Lead Pastor, New Life Church, Arkansas

"I am proud to call Jeff Little a friend and ministry partner. He has a contagious passion for the local church that not only comes through in his book *It's Worth It*, but even more so in his day-to-day love for God and people."

TOM MULLINS, Founding Pastor of Christ Fellowship

"God has placed in the church uniquely gifted, anointed leadership to build up the church into the fullness of Christ. In God's kingdom every member is valuable and vitally important to His purpose. Pastor Jeff Little is a leader who inspires and instructs the church family in righteousness, and stimulates believers to good works and compassionate action. I have witnessed up-close and personal Christ revealed in Jeff's life and relationships with others. Both his life and message profoundly impact all who know him and hear his messages. As you read about his journey, you will be encouraged to find your part in God's heart and in His family. Every member is important!"

JAMES ROBISON, President, LIFE Outreach International, Fort Worth, TX

"Walking alongside Jeff Little in spiritual family, I have seen him demonstrate his willingness to give whatever it takes to lead those around him into something extraordinary. As a brother in the Lord, Jeff is always there supporting me, continually modeling the very same principles he discusses in *It's Worth it!*

"I strongly encourage you to experience Jeff's journey through the pages of this book, where he shares his story and highlights values that are truly 'worth it.' Take another look at some key concepts, live the life you were meant to live and open your heart to embrace what God is passionate about. It's time for this fresh perspective!"

ERIK LAWSON, Senior Pastor, Element Church

"It has been my privilege to walk with Pastor Jeff Little for almost twenty years. I've seen him grow from being a communicator and a teacher of God's Word, to someone who has become a world-class leader and master builder.

"It is without hesitation or reservation that I can endorse not only what Jeff Little communicates in this book but the very person who communicates it. The greatest message any of us will ever communicate is not what is written or spoken but what is lived. Jeff Little is a man of God and that qualifies him to speak on God's behalf."

JACOB ARANZA, Pastor, Our Savior's Church, Broussard, LA

"When you're in the middle of a challenging struggle it's difficult to see the other side. In his book *It's Worth It* Pastor Jeff Little will infuse you with encouragement through his own trials and triumphs as a pastor, husband, father, church planter and leader of a growing church. No veneer. No façade. No platitudes. An awesome reminder—It's Worth It!"

SAM CHAND, Leadership Consultant and author of
Cracking Your Church's Culture Code (www.samchand.com)

"Jeff's new book, *It's Worth It*, shows again how God's mighty power works through leaders yielded to God's leading, even when the way seems illogical. If you are a pastoral leader that has ever thought 'I must be crazy', then this book is for you. You are probably not crazy but dreaming dreams of what God is calling you to and in leading a church that can be used for God's glory."

DAVE TRAVIS, Chief Executive and Chief Encouragement Officer, Leadership Network

---

"Pastor Jeff is an exceptional leader because he leads by example. His humility and exceptional character are evident when you meet him and watch him lead. And one of his most admirable qualities is his humor. He lifts you and inspires you to love life and live with integrity. It is an honor to know Jeff and be his friend."

GREG SALCICCIOLI, President Coachwell Inc., Author of *The Enemies of Excellence*

IT'S WORTH IT

A *fresh* PERSPECTIVE ON
FAITH, RELIGION, AND RELATIONSHIPS

JEFF LITTLE

IT'S WORTH IT *is dedicated to the faithful people*
of Milestone Church who honor Jesus, live for His mission, dream,
serve, give, get over offenses, care, grow, and love.

Thank You,
PASTOR JEFF

TABLE OF CONTENTS

INTRODUCTION

Jesus told a story about a man who stumbled upon a treasure buried in a field.[1]

From a distance, it looked like a typical plot of land. People passed by it all the time. But when the man found the treasure, the field was no longer ordinary. In a moment—everything changed. In his joy, in his excitement, he sold everything he had to buy the field.

This wasn't one of those decisions he labored over. He didn't take the time to write a pros and cons list. It's an impulse buy...but not one he'd regret later. The man acts immediately because he knew what he was gaining was worth far more than what it cost.

Like many people today, the original audience loved the idea of this man unexpectedly hitting the jackpot. But this wasn't the idea Jesus was communicating. He was describing what happens in the heart of an individual who sees the Kingdom of God[2] as it truly is.

Not religion. Not trying to be a better person. Not the faith of your culture or your parents. Not a generic spirituality that helps you get what you want.

---

1   Jesus tells the whole story in one verse: Matthew 13:44.
2   Matthew uses the phrase, "Kingdom of Heaven," where all the other Gospels choose the phrase, "Kingdom of God." Bible scholars call this a "circumlocution"—intentionally avoiding the term "God" out of reverence. This makes sense when we realize Matthew's audience was primarily communicating to a Jewish audience who would have chosen this approach.

When Jesus uses the phrase, "*Kingdom of God*" He's not so much talking about a physical place or a future era.[3] What He's actually describing is *reality as it was intended to exist. The life you were created to live.*

When you catch a glimpse of *that*…you're immediately willing to sell everything to get it.

The price you're willing to pay is a direct result of the value you place on the item you're considering. If you don't see its worth, you leave it alone. For many, faith and religion are impractical and largely unhelpful.

But what if we've missed something? What if there was something more to them? Faith and religion frame the way we view the world, and largely, our approach to the relationships in our lives.

What if we thought we understood the whole "*Jesus thing*" but what we saw was the empty field instead of the treasure buried there?

A new perspective on the priceless value of these three things could change everything.

I heard a story recently that may help you see what I'm describing.[4]

A brother and sister were cleaning out their parents' home in England not long after they died. These moments are difficult. As an emotional default, some of us shift into administrative mode and try to get everything done as quickly and efficiently as possible. For others, we move forward by sentimentally reflecting upon the memories we shared.

---

3   What makes heaven so spectacular is the same thing that made the Garden of Eden paradise. It's more than streets of gold or perfect creation—it's everything functioning the way God designed it to be.

4   http://www.telegraph.co.uk/culture/art/artsales/8128244/Chinese-vase-sells-for-53m-the-ultimate-cash-in-the-attic.html accessed on 10/20/2014

As the siblings were packing everything up, they found an old vase that wasn't included in the will. It wasn't really impressive but they wondered if it was worth something, so they decided to take the artifact to an expert in antiquities for an appraisal.

To their surprise they learned the vase was from an 18th century Chinese dynasty and could be worth as much as between eight hundred thousand and 1.2 million pounds.[5] While they were finishing all the details of the estate they set the vase on top of a bookshelf while they waited for the auction. They weren't sure what they'd actually get when the bidding finally started.

What happened next would forever alter their lives. A bidding war broke out and near the end of the proceedings, each alternating bid was a million pounds. The sister nearly passed out. The winning bid of 43 million pounds ($69 million) is believed to be the highest sum ever paid for a Chinese piece of art.

> THAT'S WHAT JESUS IS SAYING
> ABOUT HIS KINGDOM.
> MOST PEOPLE HAVE NO IDEA
> **HOW TRULY PRICELESS IT IS.**

We don't know how their parents got the vase. We don't know if they ever considered selling it. It's safe to say no one in the family realized the incredibly valuable treasure sitting in the open in their home. They may have admired the vase or thought it was nice, but they had no idea how valuable it truly was.

---

5   The conversion rate from British pounds to American dollars is about 1:1.61 so in our currency the range would be between $1.28 million to $2 million.

That's what Jesus is saying about His Kingdom. Most people have no idea how truly priceless it is.

////////////////////////////////////

I'm passionate about the things of God. I've joyfully traded everything for the Kingdom of God.

Go ahead, call me crazy, but I think it's still possible for you and I to experience reality as God intended it to exist. We can actually live the life we were created for.

And here's the craziest part: *I believe the place we find this is in the local church.*

I know you've been hurt. So have I. I know what it feels like to have your hope crushed when people who called themselves Christians showed self-righteous judgment in a moment that called for forgiveness and mercy.

I've met the hypocrites, the fakes, the flakes and the *"spooky-spiritual."* I've seen the guy with the fish on his car who cuts you off and gives you the hand gesture that doesn't mean "Hello!" I know about the numerous leaders who've had moral failures. I've seen the pain caused by poor leadership and the human propensity to control and criticize those who disagree.

But it doesn't matter. I still believe in the church.

As a young preacher, people often told me that my only future in the ministry was as a traveling speaker; I was way too direct to stay in the same pulpit week after week. I was like hot sauce—a little bit added flavor and spiced things up, but take too much and you end up sweating and feeling queasy.

A lot of these people were right. Over time, I've added different tones and approaches to my communication. I've tried to refine my message, improve my articulation, and broaden my appeal. People matter to God—I believe this message is more important than the messenger.

But my passion wasn't for effect...it's at the core of who I am. I can't help but get excited when I think of God's heart for people and His plan for the world. And I can't think about either one of those things without thinking about the church.

Where other people see an empty field of dirt, I see something worth far more. I see a buried treasure. After more than twenty years as a pastor, my love for the local church continues to grow.

We live in a time when so many in our current generation are open to investigating the claims of Jesus. Although they enjoy a good debate and interesting banter, they are genuinely searching at a deep spiritual level.

I believe these are just a few of the things they want to know:

- Who was the real, historical Jesus of Nazareth?
- What does He have to do with us today?
- Did Jesus have the answers to life's deepest questions?
- Can we best understand Jesus as a great moral teacher who summarized the deepest truths of the world's great religions?
- Or was He more than a man—did He claim to be God and if so, was He right?

Often this genuine passion and interest all but disappears when the subject turns to the church. Maybe you've seen the bumper sticker: "*I love Jesus, but I hate his followers.*" One of the easiest ways to make new friends, sell books or raise page views on your blog is to talk bad about organized religion in general, but specifically, about the church.

Somehow I don't think this pleases God.

The Bible calls the church *"the bride of Christ"*[6]—most people have respect and admiration for Jesus, they're just not too into His wife. And believe me, I've had more than my share of run-ins with some of the most embarrassing and troubling parts of the body of Christ.

Despite my personal nightmarish experiences, the numerous scandals in the newspapers, the goofy guys on TV we've all seen and the countless bad clips on YouTube, I still believe the book of Ephesians when it says God's wisdom will be made known to the world through the church.[7]

God hasn't given up on His Church. The local church is the hope of the world.[8]

AND ONCE YOU FIND
THAT TREASURE BURIED IN
THE FIELD...YOU WANT EVERYONE
ELSE TO FIND IT TOO.

I'm convinced Jesus believes in His Church too. Ephesians 5 says He loves her so much He gave His life for her and He's continuing to sanctify her—a word that literally means, *"to be set apart for sacred use."*

In His entire life He promised to build one thing: His Church. That's it. He told a rag-tag group of followers who were afraid to be in a strange city

---

6   For starters check out Ephesians 5:25-27, Revelation 19:7-9, 2 Corinthians 11:2, and Matthew 25:1-18. It's not an exhaustive list but it helps to illustrate the point.

7   Ephesians 3:10. Stay tuned...we'll be coming back to this verse.

8   This phrase comes from the fantastic book *"Courageous Leadership"* by Bill Hybels. (p.12) But while Hybels may have phrased it that way, the idea long predates him. One of the greatest preachers who ever lived, Charles Spurgeon, in a message he preached in 1863 said, *"The Church is the world's hope!"* (p. 2 http://spurgeon.server310.com/vols49-51/chs2952.pdf accessed 11/6/14).

near a cave where sketchy things went down that He was going to build His Church and He said nothing would be able to stop it.[9] The local church is His Plan A and He doesn't have a Plan B.

//////////////////////////////

I wrote this book for several reasons.

First, I want to provide a new perspective for anyone who can only see an empty field of dirt. I understand why you've looked at the church or at Christians in the past and decided, *"There's nothing there."*

But I want you to take another look.

It's tragic when people pass by something of incredible worth and completely miss what has been there waiting for them all along. Jesus is worth it. His Church is worth it. Becoming who God created you to be is worth it.

I don't have all the answers and I'm not perfect, but I know where to find the treasure. And once you find that treasure buried in the field...*you want everyone else to find it too.*

Second, I want to inspire and encourage those who haven't given up on the beautiful idea of the church, the bride of Christ, a genuine community of real people who aren't perfect but who genuinely love God and love people.

Listen, there are no perfect people, and so it follows that there are no perfect churches, but when you find this contagious atmosphere that cultivates the biblical truth and unconditional love that we're all desperately seeking, there's nothing like it.

---

9   This story comes from Matthew 16. But stay with me. We're going to spend enough time there that you'll know it by heart by the end of the book.

It takes courage, a willingness to risk, and more than a little trust to look for this kind of church, but if you're looking, DON'T GIVE UP. God is still making His home in the midst of those who love and obey Him.

I meet people all the time who theoretically believe that this could work, but somewhere along the way they lost hope that they'll ever find it. They decided that the cost of investing their time, making themselves vulnerable in relationships, and risking disappointment was just too high. It was more than they were willing to spend.

> ALL THEY CAN SEE IS AN EMPTY FIELD OF DIRT. I WANT THEM TO FIND THE TREASURE THAT'S BURIED IN IT. HIS NAME IS JESUS. HE'S BUILDING HIS CHURCH. **AND HE'S WORTH IT.**

It breaks my heart every time I hear that gifted people have checked out a local church and decided that there was nothing there for them. Many times, serious leaders who want to make a difference in their community end up deciding this is not something the church cares about.

Several years ago one of these couples visited our church. They'd had so many challenging experiences with church in their past they were ready to give up on not only a particular congregation, but the idea of a church as a whole.

Sometimes it hurts to hope. If you've been there, you know exactly what I mean. As long as you believe what you're longing for is out there, you live with the painful reality of what you're missing.

But if you decide it's not real—it doesn't exist anywhere—it becomes far easier to let go. You stop thinking about it. Those hopes and dreams fade away until they're ultimately gone.

This is where this couple found themselves. After their first visit they said it all seemed too good to be true. The people were too friendly, the children's ministry volunteers were too considerate, and the guys in the parking actually seemed to care. They were unsettled by the experience. Why were these people behaving this way? There had to be an ulterior motive.

But they kept coming. We just tried to patiently love them as they worked through what God was doing in their hearts.

I'll never forget what the wife told me: *"When you tell me that the church can work, even after what we've been through, I find myself WANTING to believe you."*

We've seen this story repeated over and over. There are tens of thousands of people in our region who've had a bad experience with church and religion and right now they're wondering whether they're going to give up on God.

I can't stop thinking about these people. They keep me up at night.

All they can see is an empty field of dirt. I want them to find the treasure that's buried in it. His name is Jesus. He's building His Church. And He's worth it.

It's my prayer that God would allow Milestone to be the kind of community that repairs injured faith and restores lost confidence in the value of the local church. The purpose of this prayer is not to make us famous or to give us a great reputation to build our pride. Instead, it's our hope that through this community of people, God would be loved and honored in our city, our region, our nation and throughout the earth.

What God has been doing in our community has caused us to see the local church from a fresh perspective. It's not a dirt field any more; it's a buried treasure. And when you're in this kind of environment, it leaves a mark. Like a cup of coffee that leaves an impression on a napkin.

God hasn't stopped telling stories. Each of us has our own story, our own walk with God, and there are moments in life when God is doing something special, something sovereign, innocent and pure and it's absolutely inspiring. When we're fortunate enough to be involved in these moments, God wants us to tell our story.

For the last several years the church that I have the privilege to pastor has been experiencing one of these moments. As our church continues to grow, I want everyone who comes in contact with us to have access to the story so they too can experience the love and goodness of God. There have been so many times where we could relate to the church in Acts 2:43—"*Everyone was filled with a sense of awe...*" We don't want to ever lose this.

Communication is an interesting thing, and the larger a community grows, the more intentional we have to be. I want to continue to include others in this family while maintaining what Jim Collins describes as "*a humble resolve.*" This notion balances an unshakable belief in who you are and what you're doing with an extraordinary value for others.

We believe that God has given us a mission, values, tools and resources to empower this church and to train and release leaders. It's our goal that this book will become a valuable resource in this process.

Honestly, as a leader I do have a fear that by writing and publishing our story it could somehow take away the humility, the grace, and the focus on serving others that's found in the culture of our family. Our hope in sharing our story is not to promote my ministry, Milestone Church or to build our brand. We want to inspire and transform others with the unstoppable love of God and the mission of His Kingdom, which is available now and can be experienced through, the local church.

Finally, I know God uses ordinary people who have all kinds of weaknesses and fears. A tragic misperception of too many people says a great church is only full of gifted people with no problems who never make mistakes. We've all been tempted to feel that way, even though the idea is ridiculous.

I recently heard the story of a man who drove to Milestone and sat in his car in the parking lot several weeks in a row. He wanted to come inside but he was nervous and afraid—he didn't think he'd fit in. Each week he came with the intention of walking through the doors, but instead each week he drove off without setting foot inside. On the sixth week, he came in and was overwhelmed by the love and acceptance he experienced.

The first time I heard this story, tears started to well up and even as I'm writing these words now I can feel them returning. The purpose of the church is not for self-righteous religious types to remind themselves of how much better they are than everyone else.

If I'd been sitting in the car next to him, I would have simply said: *"You're welcome here. Not a better version of you, just as you are today. I know it's not easy. But there's a treasure for you. It's buried in a field...but it's worth it."*

The church is a place where anyone—no matter how old they are, where they live, who their parents were or weren't, what they've done or what they know or don't know—can meet God through Jesus and be supernaturally transformed.

I can't tell you how much it comforts me that God didn't hire a PR firm to write Scripture. If He had, there would have been way more "spin"; they would have edited out the mistakes, the blunders and all the bone-headed moves that make the characters of the Bible so real. These aren't simple, one-dimensional Sunday school stereotypes who can't relate to the complexities of modern life—they're messed-up people just like you and me that God used to change the world.

I have seen faithfulness outdo talent with my own eyes and I've witnessed passion for God outshine superior knowledge and tradition. The Apostle Paul had it all—faithfulness, talent, passion, and knowledge and tradition and he said God used him more through his weaknesses than his strengths.

Jesus is still using fisherman, shepherds, and ordinary sinners that have been radically changed by His grace. He hasn't given up on His Church and He hasn't given up on you.

It's not perfect. It's not easy. But *it's worth it.*

It is my prayer that as you read the Milestone story you'll be filled with new passion and love for God, a renewed hope and confidence in the local church, and a child-like excitement to be a part of what God is doing in the earth.

The truth is, it's not just a prayer I'm praying for you. This prayer is for me, for our team, for our children, for your children, for our neighbors, our city, and for all those who hear our story.

> I HAVE SEEN FAITHFULNESS
> OUTDO TALENT WITH MY OWN EYES
> AND **I'VE WITNESSED PASSION
> FOR GOD** OUTSHINE SUPERIOR
> KNOWLEDGE AND TRADITION.

CHAPTER ONE

THE CHURCH IS WORTH IT

Jesus never promised to build a religion. He never promised to build compassionate, creative non-profit organizations. He never promised to promote one particular denomination, or to even pick one country at the expense of the rest.

And no matter how many athletes or rock stars give Him a shout-out after their latest triumph, Jesus never promised to build anyone's career or make their dreams come true.

Each of these in their own way can accomplish a great deal of good and can be a wonderful benefit to many. But they're not what Jesus is after. They're not His primary mission. They're not what He gave His life to build.

The only thing Jesus ever promised to build is His Church.

His Church is not insignificant, an afterthought, or an anachronistic symbol of old-time religion lingering on the margins of a progressive culture.

Despite what we may have seen, His Church is not petty, small, impotent, myopic, safe or self-serving.

He told His disciples, *"the gates of hell"* would not overcome it.[1] We'll come back to what He meant by this strange little phrase later.

Peter wrote the early churches and told them that they were a chosen people, a royal priesthood, a holy nation, a people belonging to God so that they would declare the praises of the One who called them out of darkness and into His marvelous light.[2]

The author of the book of Hebrews believed that it was absolutely critical for followers of Christ to meet as the church no matter how much opposition they faced in the process. He challenged his audience not to give up on the church, as many are inclined to do, because the church is where we encourage each other—where we motivate fellow Christ followers towards love and good deeds.[3]

Paul told his young partner in ministry, Timothy, that the church was God's Household, the pillar and the foundation of the truth.[4]

Paul had a lot to say about the importance of the church in his letter to the large, thriving church in the culturally significant city of Ephesus. He told them that Jesus loves the church so much that He gave Himself up for her to make her holy, blameless, and radiant.[5]

There have definitely been points in my life where I didn't feel like the church was worth it. You've probably had an experience somewhere along the way that made you question whether or not the church is worth it too.

---

1   Matthew 16:18
2   1 Peter 2:9
3   Hebrews 10:24-25
4   1 Timothy 3:15
5   Ephesians 5:25-27

> # MOST PEOPLE DON'T VALUE THE CHURCH. THEY DON'T THINK **IT'S WORTH IT** BECAUSE ALL THEY'VE SEEN ARE FIELDS OF DIRT.

Eventually, all of us end up investing our lives, our talent and our energy into something. For some of us it's a business, for others it's their family and for some it's their own reputation and accomplishments. The question is: what kind of return are we going to receive from our investment?

Jesus told the story of a man who found a treasure buried in a field.[6] Once he saw the treasure, it changed his perspective completely. No price was too high. He sold everything in order to gain the field.

Most people don't value the church. They don't think it's worth it because all they've seen are fields of dirt. They've never been able to dig down deep enough to find the buried treasure.

You can find so many people who will tell you that they like Jesus; they just can't stand His followers.[7] Ghandi, a favorite of people who are vaguely spiritual, famously once said: *"I like your Christ, I do not like your Christians. Your Christians are so unlike Christ."*

---

6   Matthew 13:44

7   A pastor named Dan Kimball actually wrote a book called, *"They Like Jesus But Not The Church"* from his own experience of hearing non-Christians say this to him over and over. We don't share the same philosophy of ministry but I respect the fact that Dan didn't give up on the church in favor of a different approach. Unfortunately, many pastors do.

But that's not how Jesus feels about it. He doesn't love His perfect followers who are as mature, strong and righteous as He is—He doesn't have any. He loves and uses broken people who make mistakes but put their trust in Him. He believes by His Spirit they can do great things. He calls them His own, His family, His Church.

And Jesus believes His Church is worth a lot…it was worth His *life*.

He has never regretted His decision. He's not re-thinking His approach. Through all the mistakes, all the pain, all the terrible ways people have let Him down— from snake-handling to selling indulgences, He refuses to change His strategy.

There is no Plan B—Jesus is all in with His Church.

He designed the church to show the world what He's really like through a community of believers characterized by grace, peace, forgiveness, re- demption, encouragement, power and transformation.

And whether or not the church does a good job, God hasn't given up on that part of the church's responsibility.

An Early Call

I grew up going to church with my family every Sunday. I never struggled to believe in God and I didn't mind going to church. I actually liked listening to the messages and learning about the Bible. The people there were nice enough and they were polite and treated me well. But after a while, I started to wonder what the point was.

We just showed up each week because we were supposed to. I knew what we were against—no smoking, no drinking, no cussing, no chewing and definitely NO SEX before marriage. But I couldn't really tell you what we were FOR. I didn't see any clear intentionality, an over-arching purpose or a measurable goal.

And most of all, I never saw any of the kind of people of influence and significance I hoped to one day become at church. I wanted to be a leader, I wanted to do something with my life—run a successful business, play offensive line in the NFL, or win dramatic cases as a powerful and compelling attorney.

But then I had one of those defining moments.

JESUS BELIEVES
HIS CHURCH IS WORTH A LOT...
IT WAS WORTH HIS LIFE.

I was 12 years old. I was in my bedroom, sitting on the floor next to my unmade bed that showed my NFL pennant sheets. If you were a boy and you grew up in the '80s, you either had that matching set or one of your friends did, and you wanted one. They were awesome! Tampa Bay had that crazy old bright orange pirate as their mascot and the Bengals had just put stripes on their helmets. Those were simple times with simple pleasures.

With each year that goes by I realize how blessed I was to grow up in my home. It was a loving and stable environment that forged character in me. I can vividly remember sitting in church as a young boy and hearing the Gospel message. It captured my heart and my imagination. Just a few months before that day in my room, I sat around my family's kitchen table, prayed and gave my heart to Jesus—I wanted Him to be the Lord of my life and I promised to serve Him forever. I was baptized a week later.

But as I sat in my room that day, I heard a clear, distinct message: *"I am calling you to ministry."* The impression was unmistakable and I immediately knew without a doubt that it was God who was calling me. I didn't know what to do next so I jumped up and ran out and told my mom and dad. I figured they would know how to handle this kind of situation.

Their balanced response further demonstrated God's goodness and wisdom at work in my life as an impressionable young man. My mom immediately started rejoicing and breaking out into a spontaneous, Charismatic worship service.

My dad wasn't quite ready to party. He's an engineer, a deeply practical and rational thinker. He got out a pen, a piece of paper and a calculator and began to ask me how I planned to provide for myself (and eventually a family) while pursuing this call to ministry. In his own way I know he was excited about it and he was joking with me—which was often his way—but in hindsight I appreciate his reaction. I've actually used it on others who've shared a sense towards the same call. He was being a good dad—he simply wanted to make sure I understood the magnitude of this decision. This was not something I was to take lightly.

In the moment, I had no context for what my dad was saying. My twelve-year-old brain could barely grasp what my plan was for the rest of the summer, much less the rest of my life. I did know I didn't call myself—God had called me. I figured if He wanted me to do it, He'd provide a way to make it happen.

Looking back I'm incredibly grateful for the way both of them responded. I needed both the encouragement and joy my mom gave me, along with the strategic discipline from my dad. In the months and years that followed, I wrestled with what "*being called*" actually meant. How do you respond to this kind of thing as a kid? Do you drop out of school and join a monastery? Do you try to get a good preacher to coach you along and give you some help?

I didn't know what to do, but I was pretty sure that I didn't want to be a pastor. I didn't think I fit the pastor mold. I liked excitement and adventure too much to stay tied to a local church. It seemed pretty boring. Whenever I saw people who were passionate and excited about God who were also strong leaders it was usually a dynamic speaker who held big events, an outspoken athlete, or an influential leader involved in some sort of specialized ministry.

When I left home to go to college at Baylor University—for those of you who don't know, it's what we call *"Jerusalem on the Brazos"*—I planned to pursue one of those roles in ministry. I wanted to be anything but a local church pastor. However, while I was at school, I began to see the strong, dynamic Christian leaders I'd hoped were out there. Seeing them in action moved me—I wanted to get in the game, I wanted a chance to lead.

I was a college student attending Baylor University studying to become an effective Christian leader, but little did I know that decision was like enrolling in my own personal ministry school of hard knocks.

The School of Hard Knocks

I went to college to get trained and to begin my career…not to find a wife. So you can imagine how surprised I was when God supernaturally orchestrated a situation to cross my path with a beautiful young lady named Brandy.

Our moms knew each other—they'd spent a season walking and praying together in the mornings. Let me tell you, something miraculous happens when a mom prays—and the Bible says when two or more come together and agree about anything they'll receive it—and if those two are moms? Forget it.

I may be a little slow to catch on, but I'm not stupid. Before long, we were engaged to be married.

During this time I was busy doing all kinds of youth events—speaking at camps, youth rallies and retreats—but as the date continued to draw closer, I started to think about how I would make a living and provide for my new bride. My mentor/ministry leader at Baylor was a former president of the Southern Baptist Convention. Not only did he approach me about applying for a job, but he wrote my parents a letter describing in detail how he saw the call of God on my life through my gifts and talents. I wasn't expecting that—it's not like I'd ever had a college professor write a letter to my parents before.

I still had all the same fears and hesitations about being trapped into a local church situation. I feared that would suck the life out of me as it slowly suffocated my goals and dreams until I ended up looking like the deflated and defeated leaders I'd seen growing up around church.

But I did what any 20-year-old kid who was soon to be married and in need of a job would do. I reluctantly said, "*Okay.*" My name went into the school's ministry guidance and placement center where churches with job openings searched to find candidates they were interested in.

The two job leads that came back to me were similar in some ways and very different in others. The first opportunity was at a large, established church with a well-developed youth program, a decent salary and even a nice expense budget. To a college kid living off student loans and the spare change he could find in couches, payphones (remember those?), or Coke machines, this looked like the big leagues.

The second offer was at an older, smaller church that needed a lot of help and was offering a robust salary of $50 per week. Looking back, I know why God wanted me to choose this option, but I'm amazed I actually obeyed. I took the tougher job at the smaller church for less money.

I am deeply competitive and sometimes this gets me into trouble—but I would need every ounce of fight I had in me to survive what was waiting for me around the corner.

The "Temporary Interim" Pastor

There I was, the youth director at this little church with lots of "*seasoned*" members. That's a nice way of saying some of these guys went to high school with George Washington. A few might have even hung out with Moses.

Not exactly the same crowd as my youth circuit. I had to get some new material—but I had all the confidence in the world…which didn't always work out so well.

The first week I was there, they asked me, "*Can you do music?*" I may be wrong sometimes, but I'm never in doubt. How hard could it be?

All I knew about leading music was that I should wear a suit coat. I'm not exactly sure why I thought wearing a jacket was all I needed to pull it off considering that my musical skills lie somewhere between tone-deaf and dog torturer.

I guess that's one of the perks of being a leader—sometimes you're not scared when you should be.

I got up there the first week and a wave of panic hit me. I had no clue what I was doing. I told the people to open their hymnal to the proper page so we could sing verses one, two and four (*insider tip: you never sing three*). I started waving my arms in a rhythmic motion like the guy leading an orchestra or the band leader at a football game. I tried to sing low enough so that no matter how bad it sounded, at least I sounded like a man. I was pleasantly surprised nobody laughed out loud or got up and walked out. With such modest expectations among the congregation, it made me wonder how bad the guy before me was.

After leading the youth and the music department for a little more than six months, the pastor came to me and told me that he didn't want to be there anymore. He told me he'd felt this way for a while—he wanted to go back to school and get a master's degree in history. He said he'd already talked to the deacons and they'd agreed to make me the "*temporary interim pastor.*"

I ignored the fact that this was the most tentative job title in the history of ministry—and maybe the most redundant. "*Temporary*" is fairly clear. It means "*not for long.*" But just in case there was any doubt in the uncertainty of my position, they threw the interim in there too. As in, *"we're stuck with you until we get the person we want."*

It didn't stop me. I was ready to roll. After all, I was a seasoned, mature, 21-year-old engaged guy who had all the answers. I didn't have much, but I did have a passion for God's Word and that's enough to shake things up.

I started to preach every Sunday morning, and when you preach God's Word, people's lives begin to change. It was an exciting time as some good things were really beginning to happen.

We started small groups, people were excited, and our services were over-flowing...we felt unstoppable. The church was growing—both in numbers and in diversity. This wasn't the same old church crowd...there were people from both sides of the proverbial tracks, from different neighborhoods, different backgrounds, different ethnicities, all coming together united in worship of the God who made each of them unique.

I thought it was awesome. So when the leadership of the church called me in for a meeting on a Sunday afternoon, I thought I was getting a raise or at least a more permanent title. Maybe they'd just tell me how much they loved and appreciated us and the hard work we were doing.

Not so much—they were leaning in a slightly different direction.

"We want you to resign."

You could say I was a little surprised and a little upset. Back then, I wasn't the most diplomatic guy...more fire-starter than peacemaker. After I got over the initial shock, I threw down the gauntlet. I'd like to say I was filled with righteous fervor, but the truth is my competitive side kicked in.

I looked them in the eye and said, *"You didn't call me here, God did. I'm not leaving until He tells me to!"*

They weren't intimidated—after all, I'd committed the unpardonable offense of bringing in the "*wrong crowd.*" It wasn't like I was busing in people from the next town over or another city. These were their neighbors. Some of the "*wrong crowd*" were even their own children.

One guy smoked in the fellowship hall after a recovery meeting and one of the old-timers blew a gasket. You would've thought the offending party was worshipping Satan, not smoking a Marlboro.

Somebody else wanted to run me out because I actually let people into the church's library and encouraged them to read any of the books they found there. You know…the kind of shocking moral failures that get pastors kicked out of churches all the time.

It turns out we had very different ideas about who the "*wrong crowd*" was. I thought the wrong crowd meant people who were resistant to God, who didn't want to see lives transformed, or were unwilling to change or be inconvenienced so others could come to know and love Jesus.

But I was willing to fight over the idea of who the wrong crowd *was not.* People who were far from God, people who were lost, people who thought the church didn't understand them or didn't care what they were going through…these weren't the wrong crowd. In my Bible, these were the people Jesus went looking for. So I tried to go looking for them too.

That was the final straw. I was no longer fit to be either temporary or interim. The title they wanted for me was "former."

So when they said, "*We'll vote you out!*" I fired back, "*Then start voting!*"

I gotta admit—it felt really good. But it was only the beginning of a cold war that would last several months.

A Messy Break-Up

Even the smallest things became a battle. One Sunday morning I began to take up the offering; in the course of a worship service this is about as routine as it gets. Everybody called the deacon who handled this job "Snappy." I'm not sure where his nickname came from—but on this morning he resembled one of those old, nasty turtles.

He stood up and defiantly declared, *"I'll never take up the offering as long as you're the pastor."*

My church wasn't afraid to kick people out. A few decades earlier they ex-communicated a struggling young musician and his sister. Something about him bothered them so they sent him packing. He crossed the street and started playing at the Methodist church, less than a football field away.

I can't say for sure but I always wondered if this experience inspired him to write a song you'll probably recognize: *"On the Road Again."*

Yep. My church booted Willie Nelson—now they had their sights set on me.

They'd shake their keys at me from the pews if they thought I'd been preaching too long. I saw every version of their best "stink eye" and heard them muttering under their breath and whispering to each other. Brandy would come home and cry, and I'd just try to laugh it off. I called my regional support from the denomination, and they told me to just be patient—when something new opened up, I'd be first in line to get the spot.

Promises like that can encourage you for a moment, but they don't help so much when people start showing up at the parsonage, looking to pick a fight. I literally almost got in a fist fight in my front yard. I'm not a small guy, so somebody's got to be seriously angry to be fired up enough to come take a run at me. But they came anyway.

And not just the men.

One woman in the church was really upset with me, and I'd been studying in Proverbs to respond to people who are angry with you by loving them. So we mowed her lawn and told her how much we cared about her. The more we did for her, the angrier she got. One day she grabbed Brandy and shook her as she said, "*You...don't...love...me!*"

Now when mean old church ladies freak out, grab your wife and toss her around like a salad, most people would bail. But I've been known to be both a little stubborn and a little competitive. I wasn't going to let them force me out—I wasn't going to let them abuse my wife either, but if I ran, they'd win. And I wasn't going to let that happen.

Our lives had become the nightmare of most seminary students and new pastors. But believe it or not, looking back, I know God was doing something in our hearts that would last a lifetime.

In the midst of all this drama, I went to a Promise Keepers event, which was a large movement of men's gatherings in the mid to late '90s. The leader of Promise Keepers was Bill McCartney, a great football coach and a strong man of God who was also the father of one of my friends from school. I got invited to go and be with a bunch of the leaders—it was like going to the Super Bowl for pastors.

I'll never forget hearing these men of God talk about how God desires unity in the body of Christ. Jesus told his disciples that people would know we loved and followed Him by the way we loved each other. As I heard these words and thought about the train-wreck of a little church I was leading, I decided I had to do something. The speakers kept talking about how deeply God desires unity among His people. I couldn't get past the idea I was pastoring the single, least-unified church in the entire body of Christ.

I had been studying what Paul says in 1 Corinthians about communion and how if we have anything against each other it would be better if we didn't gather than if we tried to go on acting like nothing was wrong. I'd also been thinking a lot about how Jesus said that if we don't forgive, we'll be tormented.

So that next Sunday morning I took those two passages and went to church ready to do whatever it took to make it right.

I didn't just preach that morning—I poured my heart out over those two passages. When I came to the end, I told the church I was sorry for the mistakes I'd made as the pastor, and I wanted to forgive and do whatever needed to be done in order to reconcile the situation.

Nothing happened. Total silence.

For what felt like forever, no one said anything; no one even moved. Then a lady got up and said she'd harbored some unforgiveness against some of the leaders who were making things hard on me. The chairmen of the deacons immediately stood up, looked at her and said and in a cold, harsh tone: "*Sit down lady. We don't need your forgiveness.*"

In that moment, I felt God say, "*Enough.*" I looked to the people whose hearts were good and who'd been saved in that church, and I told them to go to another church in town I trusted.

And then I turned to the people who were running me out and said, "*If you guys want this building back so badly you can have it, but based on your perspective, I don't think you can call this a biblical 'church.'*"

I went to church that morning fully expecting to reconcile. I believed things were going to work out. I wasn't planning what came out of my mouth next. I hadn't even talked about it with Brandy, but the following statement changed our lives forever.

"*Effective immediately, I officially resign as pastor.*"

They gave me a standing ovation. That will do a lot for your self-esteem.

Later that day they killed my dog.

After the adrenaline wore off, I went back to clean my office and knelt down and cried. I was fully committed to that little church. I wasn't looking for a way out or a reason to quit. I wanted to see God do incredible things in the community—and He was. I never imagined it would end that way.

You could say it was a messy break-up. By Tuesday of that week, I'd packed everything we owned (which wasn't much) and moved in with my in-laws.

This was a defining moment for me. Three passages of Scripture guided me through the process and to this day, I believe it's why I can look back and laugh instead of wanting to punch something or cry.

If God hadn't guided me through this, I could have easily given up on the church.

The first came from Matthew 18.[8] Jesus is telling a parable about a man who was forgiven a debt so exorbitant he never could have repaid it. The same man demands to be paid back for a small loan. When the Master learns about this, the King James says the man is turned over to "tormentors." Jesus finishes the parable saying, *"This is how my heavenly Father will treat each of you unless you forgive your brother or sister from your heart."*[9]

This helped put this experience into perspective for me. I was mad, frustrated and I wanted God to deal with "Snappy," the chairmen of the deacons and whoever killed my dog, but I didn't want to be turned over to the tormentors. I knew I had to forgive them—my willingness to forgive wasn't about them.

It was about my relationship with God.

When I was praying that morning, I was reflecting on 1 John 4:20: *"If someone says, 'I love God,' and hates his brother, he is a liar; for the one who does not love his brother whom he has seen cannot love God who he has not*

---

8   No, not that passage from Matthew 18. I've wondered if things would have been different if I would've known how to follow the pattern Jesus gave there.

9   Matthew 18:35 (NIV)

seen."[10] After what the chairmen of the deacons had pulled, I was convinced you might call this group of people an organization or a club, but it wasn't a church, not by even the most general, biblical standards.

By the time I'd finished cleaning my office and was heading out of town, my heart and my mind were focused on what Jesus told his followers in Luke 9. *"If people do not welcome you, leave their town and shake the dust off your feet as a testimony against them."*[11]

I loved this idea.

I had it all planned. I was going to leave a pair of my shoes at the city limits as a righteous testimony to what they'd done. Like an Old Testament prophet or an early Christian martyr, I was going out in a blaze of glory.

Brandy talked me out of it. She thought it wasn't a great idea and maybe a little immature. I told her I was just obeying Jesus and doing what the Bible said.

She didn't see it that way. She was right…she almost always is. But you gotta admit, they deserved it and it would've made a better ending.

---

10   NASB
11   Luke 9:5 (NIV)

CHAPTER TWO

"SOME WERE SENT...SOME JUST WENT"

If you believe greeting cards, they say life is defined by significant moments—high school graduation, your wedding day, the birth of your children, and walking in the door of your first home.

I knew this was definitely a moment...it just didn't feel too significant.

I was in a poorly decorated hotel off the Meacham exit of the I-35 freeway near Fort Worth, worshipping with an assorted collection of 32 other followers of Christ. We were a variety pack. We weren't seeker-sensitive, we weren't cutting edge, and we weren't an emerging church; we were just a group of people desperate to obey God and see Him do something great.

We had to be. Otherwise, as a group, we would have made a quick decision to quit.

Our drum kit looked like the worn-out display model on clearance at *Toys-R-Us*. We could have used a garden rake on the shag carpet that hadn't been cool since the late '70s. If we had brought in a couple of lava lamps and thrown up some beads in the doorways we could have completed the look.

As we were trying our best to worship, I stared into the groovy, gold-trimmed hotel mirror and wondered if I had made a big mistake. This wasn't the first time I questioned a life-changing decision, and it wouldn't be the last. I bet a lot of people would have second-guessed some of my choices; after all, I hadn't always done church in an obscure and antiquated hotel room.

Before I moved my family to Keller, I had been the Senior Pastor of a growing church in Abilene, Texas. Sure, Abilene's not exactly a major metropolitan center, but God was doing great things there; we had a functioning budget, an established presence in our community, and we were experiencing the kind of success young pastors dream about. But I knew that God spoke to me about planting a new church in Keller, a growing suburban area in the Dallas-Fort Worth metroplex. Honestly, when God first began to speak to me about it, I didn't even know where it was.

After my wife Brandy and I prayed about it, we received counsel from some trusted mentors and leaders that we looked to for guidance. All of us agreed that the direction was from God and we should obey. Within a couple of weeks, we shared the vision with a few people. To our surprise, families and young people whose lives had been changed came forward and said they believed God was calling them to go with us.

This seriously upped the ante. Families actually sold their homes and relocated. People quit their jobs and were willing to take whatever work they could find just to be a part of what God was doing. These 32 people answered a call that was so much bigger than me, but as the leader, I carried the pressure. When things got tough, I couldn't just say, *"Hey everybody, I changed my mind. I think I'm going to try something else."*

18

Back in the hotel, we were finishing up our modest attempt at worship. Even as I stood up to inspire these faithful and courageous men and women I wondered, "*What am I doing? Can we actually pull this off? What happens if we don't make it?*" I temporarily quieted the doubts inside my head just long enough to cast the vision of what I thought this new church could be.

The truth was, I needed to motivate myself and stir my own heart as much as any of the others who were listening. This was a safe crowd; it wasn't really even a church service—it was what church planters call a closed meeting where you build with your launch team before you actually go public and invite outsiders to your event.

We needed inspiration, encouragement and vision if this church was going to actually "*launch.*"

> I DIDN'T ALWAYS FEEL
> THIS WAY BUT THE BIBLE
> MAKES IT CLEAR THAT **GOD**
> **BELIEVES IN HIS CHURCH.**

We didn't have a nest egg of resources. There was no cash cow that allowed us to spend ourselves into existence. We didn't have state-of-the-art sound, video, graphics, and artwork. We didn't have an abundance of incredibly talented and gifted church-planters. But we were unified by a shared vision that a church could reach people with the Gospel, and when it did, it would change lives, families, and as a result, the surrounding community.

That's the amazing thing about a group of people who have been changed by God and are desperate to see Him work in their lives. The circumstances don't matter. No matter how big those early obstacles were, we didn't care. We believed that God's Church was worth it.

I didn't always feel this way but the Bible makes it clear that God believes in His Church.

The Who, Then the What

The journey from pastoring a growing church (sure it was dysfunctional, but it was growing) in your early 20s to attending someone else's church, living with your in-laws and working a $10/hour job is a humbling one. But that's where God had me.

My battle with the old church folk left me with some bruises and battle wounds, but I hadn't given up on the church. I still believed it could work. I still wanted to reach people, pastor and preach God's Word in a local church.

I interviewed with seven different churches ranging from Baptist to old school Charismatic in thriving metropolises like Conway, Arkansas, Fargo, North Dakota and Azle, Texas. And at each stop, honestly, they thought they were interviewing me when really I was interviewing them. I was done with maintaining the status quo and towing the denominational lines.

All I could say to God was, "*I can't go there!*"

The process was discouraging, not because I couldn't find a job or a place I felt called. I was discouraged because I thought the church God had in mind was bigger, more dynamic, more engaged with His purpose and His mission to change the world.

I was looking for more than a paycheck or a place to land. I wanted to learn, to grow, to be developed, but in most places the best they could do was say, "*You should go online to the best church staffing website.*"

This experience has stayed with me and motivated me to help others who are trying to discover and develop God's call on their lives.

Brandy was doing some substitute teaching in the meantime and for about six months we wrestled and prayed through what God was asking us to do. This was a painful time, but there was no way we could understand what God was forming through us in this process.

A lot of church planters want to be conveniently or undercover Baptist—they look non-denominational from a distance but they stay in the network to keep their options open. It was a terrible career move, but I couldn't see myself doing it. I'm not saying everybody feels this way—but I knew I would. I didn't want to ignore things I couldn't tolerate to lead a church I didn't want to go to for the sake of job security, retirement funds and faster promotion in an organization.

I was studying the story of Caleb and the spies in the Promised Land. In the passage, nine of the eleven spies were terrified by the giants in the land the people were heading into, and they pleaded to play it safe. The Bible said Caleb had a *different spirit*.[1] I wanted to have that different spirit.

I had enough relational capital to keep climbing the denominational ladder, and there was a chance I could achieve my goal of becoming the president of the denomination. I couldn't do it. It was painful and terrifying, it upset my mom and my mentor, but I knew God had put a different spirit in me.

I wanted our church to have this different spirit too and now people comment every weekend how things at Milestone feel different. I believe what we're experiencing today at Milestone is a result of what I walked through with God at this time.

This was such a defining moment for me. One day when I would have a son, I would name him Caleb so he would have this different spirit too, and

1   Numbers 13:1-33, 14:20-24

God was also showing me a concept that has become one of our most important distinctives at Milestone—your destiny is tied to your relationships. In other words, the *who* is as important as the *what*. While we were working through this we made many of the key relationships that have gone on to form a large part of the core of Milestone's leadership team.

Leadership expert Jim Collins articulates this concept brilliantly: "...*if you begin with 'who' rather than 'what,' you can more easily adapt to a changing world. If people join the bus primarily because of where the bus is going, what happens if you get ten miles down the road and you need to change direction? But if people are on the bus because of who else is on the bus, then it's much easier to change directions.*" [2]

I couldn't have articulated this with the clarity and statistical research behind Collins' statement, but I've seen this pattern demonstrated all throughout our story.

By this point we'd been living with my in-laws for six months. I thought I was a failure. I was ready to give up on the church thing and get a regular job. But God had me right where He wanted me so He could put the right people on the bus.

In this season I met Derrick Wilson who has become one of my greatest partners in ministry. Brandy and I met a young lady named Betsy who would go on to become such an inspiring and integral part of our worship team.

And what happened next was certainly not expected but was another of God's providential steps in our lives that brought us to where we are now.

I set a deadline to take one of the non-ministry jobs I'd been offered. Literally twelve hours before I was going to give in, the phone rang. Through a long, confusing series of relationships a man named Tim Malone had heard about me. He was helping to lead a group of people who didn't know exactly what

2   Collins, p.42.

they wanted in a church but they did know they wanted to love and reach people. They were early in the process of forming an organization—they didn't have clear structure and were looking to develop their identity.

They had set up some lawn chairs in an old furniture store for Sunday morning services in the little town of Chico, Texas. They needed a pastor who could lead them. Who could resist such a compelling offer?

> **HE WIRED US TO DO LIFE TOGETHER. IT'S NOT EASY AND WILL COST YOU A GREAT DEAL, BUT UNTIL YOU EXPERIENCE THESE KINDS OF RELATIONSHIPS YOU'LL ALWAYS FEEL LIKE SOMETHING IS MISSING.**

What I learned in Chico was that people make the church—not the building or your facilities. At the end of the day, life is about relationships and the church is about people. Those other things are important, but not as important as having people with genuine hearts for God who are willing to love and care about somebody else.

All these years later, Tim is like family. He and many other members of the Malone clan have been a part of each of the churches I've led since Chico. I know without a doubt God brought him into my life at just the right moment. It was a gift from God—an encouraging demonstration of His grace and His sovereign hand on our lives.

When you've struggled and fought with people who didn't trust you and share your vision, finding someone God was joining you with is nothing short of a miracle. This truth is so much bigger than Jeff Little or Milestone Church. If you don't get anything else out of this book I want you to understand this is God's design for the local church. He wired us to do life together. It's not easy and will cost you a great deal, but until you experience these kinds of relationships you'll always feel like something is missing.

God moved powerfully in Chico. Lives were transformed and the church started to grow. We moved out the furniture store, raised the money to build a church building and saw God do great things in that community.

While I was serving in Chico I went on a men's retreat and met a man who was leading a church in Abilene. We quickly formed a friendship and he asked if I would come and preach at his church. It went well and after making quite a few trips he told me that he was going to go to Midland to lead a church and he wanted to know if I would take over for him in Abilene.

Brandy and I prayed about it but initially we didn't feel like we should. We loved the people in Chico and we had shaped the culture of the church there from the beginning. Taking over an established church required a different set of leadership skills, but one of our key mentoring relationships felt strongly this was the next place for us. After we prayed about it again, we knew it was what God wanted.

One of the challenges of building authentic community in the local church is that when you love the people, it can be hard to leave when God calls you elsewhere. But you can't have one without the other.

Loving people always leaves you vulnerable to the pain, challenges and adjustments that often come with change. Your amazing small group will end. Your kids you've invested everything in will grow up and go after God's call on their lives. Incredible people you love and depend on will receive new assignments from God they'll need to obey. Life is seasonal.

And just like our season in Chico, Abilene was another amazing experience. It was such a great privilege to lead and pastor that group of believers for the season that God had us there. We gave everything we had to that church and we would have been willing to stay there if God hadn't called us to Keller a few years later.

That's the thing about believing that the body of Christ truly is HIS Church. When it's His, not yours, He can reposition and reassign you as He pleases. While this can be scary (especially in the moment), I've learned that in the end, God knows what He's doing so much better than I do. When He makes a move it's not just in the Kingdom's best interest, it's in mine.

Even when I can't see it yet and I don't understand.

Psalm 119:105 says: *"Your word is a lamp for my feet, a light on my path."*[3] When it's dark, a lamp and a light only let you see a few feet in front of you. You can't see what's ahead down the path and you definitely can't find your ultimate destination.

You've probably felt this way too—like God was calling you to something significant but you had no idea what it meant. I've found God's call is much more like following a trail of breadcrumbs than a well-researched, full-disclosure mission briefing secret agents get in the movies.

You don't get a hi-tech video message from headquarters saying, *"Your mission…should you choose to accept it…"* Instead, God asks you to do something small, something seemingly insignificant. And He doesn't give you the next step until you say yes to the last one. And then every so often you look up and say, *"Wow. How did I get here?"*

For more than a year I had this growing sense God was calling me to start a church that would be not only a blessing to its region but eventually

---

3   NIV. And if you were raised in church you're now singing the Amy Grant song. Don't worry. I won't tell anybody. It was a good song. Much better than "Baby, Baby." Oops. Now you're singing that one.

a sending center for leaders. This vision was burning on the inside of me and I wanted to get after it. An opportunity in Charlotte, North Carolina opened up. It was the best church-planting opportunity I'd ever been given. There were resources—people and finances who were excited for me to come.

In my mind, I was ready.

But I trusted the relationships God brought into my life. Jim Laffoon had become a pastor, a mentor and a spiritual father to me. Steve Robinson was the older brother I never had but always wanted. He was a brilliant strategist, a gifted pastor who believed in the local church the way I did, and the kind of leader I never saw growing up in the church. They both told me to wait—if God was doing something, over time, it would become abundantly clear.[4]

There's a huge difference between jumping out and doing something crazy for God and obeying as you patiently wait for Him to send you. Young leaders often want to run off as fast as they can to do something great—I can certainly relate. It's always been my tendency.

Another one of my mentors, one of the greatest encouragers and the secret sauce in so many great churches, Billy Hornsby, used to say, *"Some were sent…and some just went."* To be sent means you have support—you have people walking with you and carrying weight who are deeply invested in your success.

This makes all the difference.

Coming to Keller to plant Milestone wasn't the first opportunity or the best business decision. But I know in the deepest part of my soul it's what God called me to do.

---

4   The counsel of these two men continues to be vital to the growth and direction of Milestone Church. They're both on our oversight board and give input and wisdom to major decisions we make. I couldn't be more grateful for both of them.

And in those early days…that's all you've got.

A Strategy You'd Never Choose

Which brings us back to the 1970s…err…2002 in the hotel in Keller. Because of the passion, sacrifice, and commitment of those first 32 believers, we didn't stay in the hotel for long. We launched our church in October of that year, and it wasn't long before miraculous things began to happen. It's a good thing too. We didn't have any other options.

At this point, Brandy and I had exhausted our savings and cashed in our home equity. We'd missed two months worth of paychecks. Church planting sounds exciting at a conference or on a banner. In real life it's painful. You're not thinking long-term—you're looking for immediate results.

Everybody loves a miracle, but most of us don't like being in a situation where we need one. It's one of the things I love and hate about planting a church. I love how simple life is—you need God to move supernaturally or it feels like you're going to die. If you hadn't realized it, the constant pressure and feeling of impending death is the hate part.

Once your church grows and gets more established it gets easier to overlook people because you have options. You have whole teams of worship leaders. You have multiple choices to lead small groups, teach Bible studies and coordinate events. But when you're in those early days, you're counting on everyone.

You need warm bodies.

If it had been up to me I wouldn't have put so much stock in a couple of single guys selling multi-level marketing. This is not a strategy a leader would choose—but it's what God chose for us.

Eddie's dream of playing professional baseball had been shattered by injury. He'd recently returned from completing his business degree at Abilene Christian University and was beginning his climb up the multi-level-marketing pyramid. Patrick was a pre-med student who had finished his undergrad but hadn't taken the next step of taking his entrance exams for medical school. He was living on the couch and happened to be the most recently recruited member of Eddie's "*downline.*"

The first time I met Patrick he was eating Fruit Loops out of a plastic cup with water instead of milk. These weren't exactly the kind of pillars you build a dynamic local church on. If I'd had other options, I may not have picked them. And it would have been a huge mistake.

They couldn't have been more different. Eddie was extroverted—he knew everybody, could make friends anywhere and was a natural people person. Patrick was more introverted and thoughtful—he was so hungry to learn, he devoured my old library of teaching tapes.

What God did with these two young men has been one of the defining lessons in leadership for me—so different, so easy to overlook and yet so critically important to what God was doing in our midst.

I'm so grateful He put them on the bus.

We started doing a weekly Bible study at Starbucks—the basics—what it means to be a disciple, what it looks like to follow Jesus, obeying God's plan for our lives and being a part of the local church. In his classic book on discipleship, Robert Coleman describes it perfectly: "*It will be slow, tedious, painful and probably unnoticed by people at first, but the end result will be glorious...*"[5]

Eddie's dad was an alcoholic with nine DUIs whose lawyer had told him he could be facing 40 years in prison. Patrick's dad was a proud, rational oilman and a staunch Catholic who didn't have a relationship with Jesus. But as

---

5   Coleman, p. 35

we kept meeting together and they grew in their faith, each of them played a pivotal role in their fathers receiving Christ. Today Patrick's dad is one of Milestone's elders and Eddie's dad leads small groups and mission trips.

Eddie got out of the prepaid legal business and joined our team. He and his wife came on with our student ministry team, becoming our children's pastors a few years back. In the early days of our church half our visitors were his friends and family.

Patrick went back to school, finished his degree, and is now a doctor working in the ER. He's got a beautiful family and he's as committed to making disciples and building the local church as he was in the early days.

WHAT WE CALLED OUR "PROMISED LAND" MOST PEOPLE CALL A MIDDLE SCHOOL "CAFETORIUM."

From "Quitting" to "Getting It"

God was on the move, and so was Milestone. We left the minor leagues of the funkadelic '70s hotel for the big leagues. We felt like the children of Israel who left the wilderness as we finally entered the Promised Land.

What we called our "*promised land*" most people call a middle school "*cafetorium*."

In case you're unfamiliar with the concept, a cafetorium is a large room that's used as both a cafeteria and an auditorium. It's the place to be if you're looking for a place to get a Sloppy Joe AND see a middle school play. You've got Coke machines humming and if someone gets thirsty during the service everyone gets to enjoy the "duh-duh-duh" of the aluminum can dropping down, followed by the cracking pop of the top being opened.

Not exactly the best atmosphere to plant a church, but when you're just starting out, an easy-to-find location, that's affordable and has room for growth is something you have to be thankful for.

If you're thinking the moment we landed in the cafetorium we hit our stride and became the church we always dreamed of…you'd be wrong. There were more than a few moments where I felt just like I did on that first day at the hotel.

Being a pastor is like being a parent…embarrassing moments are part of the job description.

During our first spring at our glorious new location we had a series of outreaches planned. Like many other churches we developed a special event to coincide with the release of Mel Gibson's movie, "*The Passion of the Christ*." I was preaching a series of sermons on the significance of the story and then as a group we were all going to see the film. On one of the Sunday mornings before the movie came out we wanted to promote this exciting upcoming event. We thought a great way to do this was to show the preview live, in the service.

I realize today everybody watches video clips on their phone, their iPad or their tablet. No big deal. But back then it was a major technological feat. It's always a dice roll when you direct everyone's attention to the screen.

You've been there—the lights go out, the room's dark, and everyone's excited with anticipation. And then…nothing happens. Actually it would have been better if nothing happened. Instead of the preview for "*The Passion of the Christ*" our guests were treated to the bouncing screen saver of the tech guy's family.

You know what happens next. Everyone starts laughing, aspiring stand-up comics are firing off their best one-liners, and you're sure that all the visitors are wondering what kind of a goofball church they've showed up to.

Oh yeah. There's one more thing I didn't tell you. The air conditioning in our facility was controlled at an off-site location and somebody forgot to tell them we were going to be there.

It was so hot and sticky, make-up was melting off some of the ladies' faces.

To try and create some small measure of relief one of our volunteers opened a door in the hopes of catching a breeze or at least some fresh air.

Good idea and I always like it when volunteers take initiative.

Except the wind wasn't the only thing that came through the door—right in the middle of my message, a visitor stumbled past the Coke machines and into the sweaty, humid cafetorium hosting the church with the audio/visual challenges.

We like visitors. No problem. Except this visitor had four legs and was jingling. I thought either somebody was digging in their pocket for change to get a Coke, or they'd decided to pull out a tambourine and do an interpretive dance.

A family pet from the neighborhood had wandered away from home and found shelter in our service. In that moment, he wasn't *man's best friend*.

Trying to ignore the stifling heat and the video challenges was one thing but when that dog busted up in the service it rattled me. What I was hoping to be our big moment had become a disaster.

I was frustrated, angry, upset and for the first time I genuinely thought about throwing in the towel. I wanted to quit.

Have you ever been in one of those moments when you're half-praying and half-complaining to God? If you've walked with Him for a while I know you've been there. I know I'm not the only one—almost half of the psalms in the Bible feature industrial-strength pity parties. I love the fact God didn't take those out. It comforts me.

> # THE CHURCH IS NOT ABOUT BUILDINGS, FACILITIES, THE LATEST TECHNOLOGY OR THE TRENDIEST PROGRAMS. IT'S ALL ABOUT PEOPLE.

After complaining and praying for a while, I sat in my living room staring into the abyss for several hours until Brandy leaned in and said, "*You know… you're going to have to get over it.*"

It hurts when she's right.

Planting a church is incredibly difficult, but when you're in the DFW metroplex and there are churches with petting zoos, retinal eye scans and internationally known super-pastors, every mistake you make feels massive—especially when your facilities are a cafetorium with no air conditioning, sub-par technology and the occasional family dog.

We didn't have state of the art facilities. We didn't have facilities period. Every week we hauled our equipment into a rented school building. But we did have Patrick and Eddie—and many others whose lives were being powerfully changed by the Gospel. Many of them are still with us leading small groups, departments, mission trips and anything else that helps Milestone reach people and build lives.

And that's when I got it. I realized what really mattered. It's so simple.

It's people. The church is not about buildings, facilities, the latest technology or the trendiest programs. It's all about people.

And that's why the church is worth it.

WHAT IF YOU COULD LIVE
EACH DAY WITH A CLEAR
CONVICTION THAT YOUR
LIFE MATTERED?

CHAPTER THREE

THE CHURCH GOD HAS IN MIND

Between your own personal experiences and my comical stories (they weren't so funny then but don't worry, I'm over it) I'm sure you've recognized the reality that there's a big difference between a religious culture with no life and the church that Jesus died for.

That kind of church is irresistible...when you get the opportunity to experience it, no one has to tell you that it's worth it because deep down you already know.

It's that Church that has moved the cause of Christ, God's mission of redeeming the world, through human history. Jesus' Church has toppled empires, stopped slavery and oppression, built schools, orphanages, and hospitals, fed the hungry, healed the sick, cared for widows and prisoners, loved the lost, preached the good news, ministered through God's Spirit and stood strong as the enduring pillar of the community.

Obviously not every local church does all those things, but every great local church preaches the Gospel, makes disciples, inspires the hopeless, comforts the hurting, challenges the proud, and passionately loves and serves their community.

Though you may have never heard of them, there are tens of thousands of these kinds of churches all over the world. God has not given up on the church that His Son died for. And Jesus has not broken His promise to build His Church.

> THAT KIND OF CHURCH
> IS IRRESISTIBLE...WHEN YOU
> GET THE OPPORTUNITY TO
> EXPERIENCE IT, NO ONE HAS
> TO TELL YOU THAT IT'S WORTH
> IT BECAUSE **DEEP DOWN**
> **YOU ALREADY KNOW.**

The church is a beautiful idea and when you see it in action, it's miraculous. I thank God for what He's done through Milestone Church, that He's continuing to mature us as a body, bless us, and give us responsibility, but I believe we've only begun to see what God wants to do in our midst. We're only beginning.

Over the past twenty years everything about the way we share and process information has changed. In the past, colleges and universities were gatekeepers whose admissions departments determined whether or not an individual was worthy of a certain quality of resources. If you didn't go to the right prep schools, if you didn't have high enough test scores, if you lacked an elite educational pedigree, you were cut off. The right degree from the right school resulted in the right job and ultimately, the ideal life.

The world has changed drastically—or I should say, our world *is* changing. Because of these educational changes my children's learning experience will be much different than mine. It already is.

Right now, if you have access to the internet and the tech savvy to load streaming videos, you can watch lectures from the brightest minds around the world and participate in conversations on any subject you can imagine and in some you haven't even heard of.

A similar revolution has been taking place in the church. The old eras of staunch denominationalism are disappearing. There's more collaboration in the body of Christ than ever. It wasn't always this way.

I heard a story about a guy walking across a bridge who saw a man looking over the steep ledge despondently. He was clearly planning to jump. The first man ran over and shouted, "*Stop! Don't do it!*" The second man slowly turned and responded, "*Why shouldn't I?*"

The first man replied, "*Well, there's so much worth living for!*"

"*Oh yeah, like what?*" replied the would-be jumper.

The first man wanted to understand what this troubled stranger was going through. "*Well…are you a believer or an atheist?*"

"*I'm a believer,*" said the man on the ledge.

"*Me too,*" said the new friend. "*Are you a Christian, a Jew, a Muslim, a Buddhist…*"

"*I'm a Christian,*" he replied.

"Me too brother! Are you Catholic or Protestant?"

"Protestant."

"Me too! Are you Baptist, Methodist, Charismatic, Non-Denominational..."

"Baptist."

"Me too! This is amazing. Are you Southern Baptist or American Baptist?"

"Southern Baptist."

"Me too! What a small world. Are you Traditional Southern Baptist or Calvinistic Southern Baptist?"

"Calvinist of course. I'm a five-pointer like Jesus."

"Me too! Are you Complementarian or Egalitarian?"

"Egalitarian."

The first man did a quick double-take, shoved the man off the ledge and shouted, *"Die heretic scum!"*[1]

The story would be hilarious if it wasn't so painfully true. It may be slightly exaggerated but we've come a long way. Shared passion, ministry conferences, open dialogues and a willingness to learn and partner together have allowed the body of Christ to benefit from the unique gifts and insights of different streams.

---

1   This is my adaption of a joke/story that's been passed around but appears to originate with the work of comedian Emo Phillips. Thanks Emo.

I think this is an incredible innovation. Augustine famously said, "*All truth is God's truth.*" If we're wise leaders, we'll study and grow and utilize all the resources at our disposal to develop into who God has called us to be.

I'm not talking about re-inventing yourself with every new ministry model or expecting to replicate the success of others by imitating their pattern. I'm talking about growing into more of who God has called you to be by learning from the insights and wisdom of others so the body of Christ as a whole continues to move the ball down the field and accomplishes God's mission in the earth.

Whether they realize it or not, every church that is making a difference in their community is benefitting from the historic Christian faith. We should expect the Holy Spirit to help us utilize these insights to aid us in our unique mission—the part He's calling us to play.

Here's why this is so vital. The church Jesus is building is not primarily identified by what we're against. The goal isn't to get rid of the skeevy preacher on TV everybody makes fun of, so Christians can be more respected by the culture at large. The goal is bigger than defending the sanctity of marriage, getting prayer back in school or trying to stifle the evolutionary perspective of scientists.

The mission of the church is to demonstrate the life and hope available to all through the person of Jesus. That's why we exist. Not to argue for tradition, but to demonstrate the life-giving presence and power of God to a world that desperately needs it.

I believe the innovation, the shared learning and the partnership across the body of Christ is something God is doing to position the church for massive, exponential growth.

The church God has in mind—the church Jesus is building—will radically transform the world as billions of people, families, communities and even nations give their lives to Christ and live to honor, glorify and obey Him.

The Church as a Family, Function & House

There are so many great churches and leaders that we learn from who have brilliantly described how God feels about His Church. One of these churches that inspire and instruct us is Hillsong Church in Sydney, Australia. You may not have heard the name of this community of believers, but if you've been to a church that has contemporary worship, you've probably sung one of the songs that came out of this amazing church.

Although they've sold millions of albums, sell out concerts in massive arenas and millions around the world sing their songs in worship every weekend, if you think Hillsong is a music empire, you've missed the point.

Hillsong Church is a missional community that is changing their city, their nation, and the world. Their success is not the result of a few super-talented individuals, some catchy hooks and a world-class performance—the values and spirit of the community show the world the heart of God. Bobbie Houston, the wife of Hillsong's Senior Pastor, Brian Houston, wrote a great book that tells Hillsong's story. Listen to the way she describes how God feels about His Church, His bride.

> *Our church (like yours) is God's first love. The Church is the object of His affection, attention, gaze and grace. I sense God's face is towards the Hillsong Church, because the heartbeat and soul of our church is ever towards His face. We have tasted of His favour, we are blessed and we are growing in the revelation of all this wonder.*[2]

This is such personal, relational language. Clearly, Hillsong is not merely following a business plan—they're on a journey with God to build His Kingdom in their city through the church. This is God's pattern for all of us.

---

2   Houston, p. 16.

> YOU CAN'T ORDER IT ONLINE AND IT DOESN'T COME IN A BOX. IT REQUIRES SACRIFICE, PATIENCE, COMMITMENT, AND **MORE THAN ANYTHING ELSE, DESPERATION FOR GOD.**

No matter what you're doing, when you experience incredible success, people come to take a closer look. Pastors and church leaders from around the world have gone in person to see for themselves how they've been able to build the Kingdom. More often than not, people are surprised by what they discover.

Many people are looking for a formula or method for growth, yet let me say that singing our songs as a formula won't do it. Singing great songs will definitely help, but it has to go deeper than mimicking someone else's style. Our songs are actually an expression of our health in God. Copying our programs and events also won't do it. Efforts in this area are merely our tools to let our sphere of influence know that there is a God in Heaven who loves them. Every individual church needs to look intelligently at the needs of her community and act accordingly. Our pattern of teaching also won't do it, because words without revelation, a spirit of love and genuine concern for people are merely words—they carry no fresh breath of the Holy Spirit that in turn yields life.[3]

---

3   Page 17, Ibid.

Many leaders have gone to Australia to visit Hillsong looking for a short-cut or a secret ingredient to their success. They're hoping to find it so they can skip all the painful steps that it took to get there.

The truth is that there's no quick fix, no three bullet points that conveniently start with the letter "p" and no shortcuts to building this kind of church. There's no app you can download in order to experience these incredible results. It's not a franchise like Starbucks or McDonalds, dependent upon identical architecture and quality control. You can't replicate their results by copying their website, Twitter feed or recording your own album. You can't order it online and it doesn't come in a box. It requires sacrifice, patience, commitment, and more than anything else, desperation for God.

You don't build this kind of church to make the leadership famous, sell books or make a name for yourself. You do it so that people would be healed and restored, God would be loved and worshipped, and the Kingdom of Heaven would become a reality on the earth.

This kind of church is living and breathing, and if it's healthy, it's constantly growing. As any parent will tell you, whenever anything grows it requires resources, faces challenges, and ventures out into new areas.

I really like how Bobbie describes the different functions of the church as a family, a body, and a house. It's a family because it offers unconditional love and acceptance to everyone. It's a body because it's designed for effective function as different parts accomplish different tasks that all move toward the same goal. And it's a house because it serves and hosts the community as the means to reach the world.

The Local Church is the Hope of the World

When you encounter this description of what the church can be it fills you with hope. It creates passion and ignites vision. Even when you've had bad experiences with church—and most of us have—when you hear it described this way you can't give up on it. It's too important.

Somewhere deep down on the inside of you a light goes on that allows you to believe that maybe, just maybe, crazy statements like this one could be true.

"The local church is the hope of the world."[4]

Bill Hybels, the Senior Pastor at Willow Creek Community Church, one of the largest and most influential churches in America, made this bold claim. Now maybe if you're still having a hard time believing the church is worth it, you're thinking to yourself, *"Yeah, well that's easy for him to say, he drank the Kool-Aid. He's a pastor. What's he supposed to say?"* I don't blame you for thinking that, but here's a fact you probably don't realize. He didn't make this statement from the friendly confines of his pulpit at one of his many weekend services.

When Bill Hybels and his wife accepted an exclusive invitation to respond to a serious emergency, they stood at Ground Zero on September 21, 2001, just ten days after the awful tragedy that rocked our nation. Amid the rubble, the broken and shattered lives, he fought off tears as he watched people wandering around frantically looking for lost loved ones. Experiencing this firsthand was overwhelming and he found himself wrestling through deep sadness and burning anger. This wasn't a natural disaster—human beings did this to each other. Incredulously he wondered about the capacity for evil in the human heart and how it could be transformed.

In that moment, he heard God clearly say these words to him: *"The local church is the hope of the world."*

Make no mistake, he's right. Think about it: no other organization can meet all the needs a crisis like 9/11 presents. As the body of Christ in the earth, the church provides genuine comfort for hurting hearts. It teaches the sacrifice,

---

4   Hybels, p. 15.

community, and leadership to meet practical needs and move forward into a new tomorrow. It offers a way out of the prisons of bitterness, anger, and vengeance through the miracle of forgiveness. And only the Gospel of Jesus expressed through both word and deed can transform the human heart.

The government can't offer this hope. Neither can Wall Street, Fortune 500 companies or the benevolence of the super rich.

That's why, even in a nation that treasures the separation of church and state, times and locations for church services ran across the bottom of the news in every major city in America. When America really needed hope, it turned to the church. This is our heritage—from the American Revolution to the Civil War, from the Great Depression to Pearl Harbor, in its darkest days and most difficult hours, the United States turns to the church for hope.

The Greatest Force on the Earth

Rick Warren, the Senior Pastor of Saddleback Church and author of the bestselling *The Purpose Driven Life*, believes that the church is the greatest force on earth.

> *The Church is the most magnificent concept ever created. It has survived persistent abuse, horrifying persecution, and widespread neglect. Yet despite its faults (due to our sinfulness), it is still God's chosen instrument of blessing and has been for 2,000 years.*

> *The Church will last for eternity, and because it is God's instrument for ministry here on earth, it is truly the greatest force on the face of the earth. That's why I believe tackling the world's biggest problems—the giants of spiritual lostness, egocentric leadership, poverty, disease, and ignorance—can only be done through the Church.*[5]

---

5   http://www.rickwarren.com/ (accessed 10/27/08)

Warren substantiates his bold declaration with eight distinct advantages the church has over every other organization. The church has the largest participation, the widest distribution, the longest continuation, the fastest expansion, the highest motivation, the strongest authorization, the simplest administration, and the key role in God's conclusion of history.

This is the church, the body of Christ that God has in mind. Since the beginning of mankind, God has been looking for people who will join Him as a community in His mission to redeem the world. He calls that community the church, and He is not giving up on His plan.

No one would argue that at times the church has failed miserably, lost its way, forgotten its story, and lost its identity. But there have been moments when the genuine beauty of the church has shined a light so bright that people have seen a glimpse of what God is like. Once you experience this, you'll never need to be convinced that the church is worth it.

You'll be telling everyone you can find.

A Church Unchurched People Love to Attend

Andy Stanley grew up as a pastor's kid and he watched his dad go through hell. He tells a story about seeing one of the members of his church punch his dad at a business meeting. Andy went off to school intent on doing something else and despite everything he went through he ended up entering the ministry because he believed the church was worth it.

He started serving in his dad's church, gaining influence and reaching people until they realized they had a different vision of who church was for and how it should be conducted.

Charles Stanley was one of the most prominent leaders of their denomination and he understood the importance of tradition and leading in a way people could anticipate. But as a pastor's kid Andy had witnessed firsthand so much church culture he realized many of the things that made people uncomfortable were more about the preferences of church people than the clear mandate of Scripture.

His heart longed for people who had been hurt by church or thought the church had no answers, so he set out to create an environment unchurched people would understand and love to attend—from their very first weekend.

Andy refused to rely on anecdotal data—he didn't want to judge how they were doing based on the reaction of people in the lobby, how many people attended or how big the offering was. He needed a scoreboard, something other than the traditional means by which churches evaluated themselves, because he realized too many other factors could be at play.

He calls this approach, "clarifying the win" and their win for weekend services hasn't changed from the beginning. It's their target.

After describing all the different things they celebrate, appreciate and are grateful for, he clearly defines what they're after.

> But the win—the thing that wakes us up in the morning and keeps us awake at night—is when one of our attendees takes a risk and invites a friend who is far from God, and that friend shows up, is moved, and chooses to return the following weekend. That's the bull's-eye on the target, baby. It don't get no better than that! So we plan our weekend services with our inviters and their invitees in mind. Our service programming teams view themselves as partners in evangelism with our members and regular attendees.[6]

I love this—not because we share the same win, but because of the intentionality, precision and hard work Andy puts into leading his church. The local church is the hope of the world and those who are given the privilege

6   Stanley, p. 197.

of leading it aren't playing games. They've been given an incredible responsibility for which they'll have to answer to God.

The church God has in mind doesn't just show up and hope something happens. They use every gift, talent, resource, energy, idea, and strategy available to them for maximum impact because people matter to God and the church is worth it.

This Isn't A Game

Bobbie & Brian Houston, Bill Hybels, Rick Warren and Andy Stanley are world-class leaders, and they are only a few of the many incredible examples God has used to shape and encourage me. I could list dozens and dozens more.

As I write these words I think back to my days in college when I resisted God's call to ministry because I hadn't seen this caliber of leadership in the local church. I saw it in other places—and the lack of this quality made me question the viability and credibility of the church.

Not anymore. I believe some of the greatest leaders on the planet are using their gifts to build the local church and advance God's Kingdom. And I believe there's no better place to lead.

Recently Rick Warren was asked about the increasing ungodliness of our culture and the perceived waning influence of the church. He said part of the problem was previous generations fell in love with parachurch organizations instead of developing and sending the best leaders to lead the local church. But he sees a renewed commitment to church planting and a growing commitment to raising leaders in the local church which he believes will have a massive, long-term impact.[7]

I couldn't agree more.

That's what God designed the church to do—tell His story to all of creation. Paul described it this way in Ephesians 3:10: "*...so that the manifold wisdom*

---

7   http://www.christianitytoday.com/ct/2013/april/rick-warrens-final-frontier.html?paging=off (accessed 6/12/13)

of God might now be made known through the church to the rulers and authorities in the heavenly places."

The church is not about a building, it's not about a denomination, it's not about people holding on and hiding out trying desperately to protect an old-fashioned way of life. The church is God's only strategy, His one plan to reverse the darkness we see everywhere around us in our culture.

I want you to look at this word Paul uses here, *"manifold."* We don't use the word often—I'm not sure, but I think a manifold is an old part used in classic cars. But that's not what Paul is talking about here. This word means *"multi-faceted"*—like a rainbow. Not the ROY G BIV you learned in kindergarten with seven basic colors, but the amazing, optical miracle you see when light passes through water.

There are an infinite number of colors in the spectrum—as complex as the human eye is, you can't come close to picking out and identifying all of them. Paul is saying God's wisdom, His love, His person is so beautiful you can't even begin to see it all. But the way He shows it to you...is through His Church. When the church lives the way God designed it to function, God's power is demonstrated to all His enemies.

This isn't my idea. A group of the coolest, most successful pastors in America didn't come up with this at a conference. This is God's idea.

He doesn't think His Church is insignificant. He doesn't think it's a crutch for weak-willed, co-dependent people. This isn't a game. The stakes aren't just life and death...they're bigger than that. They're eternal.

Don't ever underestimate the significance of what takes place when God's people come together and live as His Church. Every time you give, you serve, you love someone who's hurting, you pray for the sick, you invest time in the next generation, you forgive, you worship, you connect to others relationally, you're not playing church. You're joining God in His eternal purposes.

The greatest cause of God on planet earth has been entrusted to the church.

When the church becomes the church God created it to be, it declares to every ruler and authority in the earth that there is a higher Kingdom, a greater King, and a Prince of Peace who is on the move to redeem and restore the whole world.

These enemies of God aren't the boogey man, make-believe, or symbols to scare us into begrudgingly obeying God. They are demonic spirits who have been around since the Creation of the earth and they have been terrorizing and intimidating people as long as human beings have walked on this planet.

But they've never seen anything like Jesus. When Jesus sent the twelve out they came back all fired up because these dark forces could no longer walk all over them because Jesus sent them out with His authority.[8]

Every force—systems, behaviors, spiritual forces, governments, and human kingdoms—that stands against the Kingdom of God sits on flimsy lame duck thrones, ruling on borrowed time.

And we're so grateful that King Jesus is bringing His Kingdom in our lives, in our homes, in our neighborhoods, and in our region of North Texas through His Church. Milestone Church is just one part of the larger whole, the body of Christ. We're a community of Christ followers who've been forever changed through the journey of knowing and loving God as a growing family, a healthy body, and a house where everyday people experience heaven.

The church is worth it.

Of course, now you're probably asking, *"Why'd you call it Milestone Church?"*

Good question. Keep reading and I'll tell you.

---

8   You can read this fascinating story for yourself in Luke 10:1-20.

CHAPTER FOUR

WHAT'S IN A NAME?

The Meaning Behind "Milestone"

People often ask us how we came up with the name *Milestone Church*. Sometimes guests and visitors have trouble getting the name right. They'll call it "*Mile-Marker*," or "*Milestones*."

From time to time small groups or people in our church will form teams to play in a variety of the recreational leagues in our community. In the past we've even outfitted our teams with stylish jerseys featuring our church's name and logo on both the front AND the back.

One day after a basketball game a guy on the other team asked me, "*What's the name of your church...Millstone?*"

I started laughing—he didn't know why I was laughing so he played along and gave me a couple of nervous courtesy chuckles. He had no idea I was the pastor and the deciding vote on the name he'd butchered.

I told him it was actually "*Milestone*," before I explained calling the church Millstone would create a whole other atmosphere. I went on to explain how the most famous passage in Scripture featuring millstones was when Jesus said it would be better for a person to tie one of these giant rocks around their neck and be thrown in the ocean than to cause a little one to stumble.

Probably not the most inviting story to build your church around.

I understand it's not the most common name but it means something special to us. I don't really get offended when people butcher it, at least not as much as I used to. By the grace of God I've stopped making fun of people who joke about our name. Mostly.

THIS IS WHAT I BELIEVED GOD WAS ASKING US TO DO—TO **MAKE A MARK, A CLEAR, INDELIBLE IMPRINT IN THE LIVES OF PEOPLE** WHO BECAME A PART OF OUR COMMUNITY.

If you're a parent, you know what it's like to get frustrated when people mess up your kid's name because their name has special significance to you. It reflects who they are and how you feel about them.

Names are important. They convey ideas, they communicate emotions, they help to shape environments and create culture.

The word *"milestone"* is an old English term that dates back to the 1740s. A milestone was a stone that functioned as a milepost marking the distance in miles from a given point. Practically speaking, a milestone defined how far someone had gone in their journey and indicated how far they still had to go.

In time, the word grew to become something deeper, something much more meaningful.

A *"milestone"* is a significant event or turning point in the life, process, development, or journey of a person or a community of people.

Conviction First, Brand Second

Milestone wasn't an obvious choice and it wasn't the result of focus group testing or other clever brand strategies.

When we first came to Keller I was wrestling with God. I'm about as Texas as it gets—born and raised here, went to school here, and nearly all of my significant relationships were here. But I didn't think Texas needed another church.

Dallas/Fort Worth is the giant brass buckle of the Bible belt. It's like the Jerusalem of America. I wanted God to send me someplace with some crazy heathens. I'm talking full-on pagan worshippers that give little old church ladies nightmares. I wanted a change of pace. But God could not have made it any clearer—He wanted me in Keller.

So I started thinking about a church capable of making a difference in a place where most people were religious. In order for this church to be worth it, to be the church God had in mind, it would have to make a genuine impact. It would have to mark the lives of the people in the community in an obvious, measurable way.

The number one question keeping most pastors up at night is, "*Are we making a difference?*" or more precisely, "*If our church disappeared tomorrow, would anyone in our city notice or even care?*" As I thought about this an image popped into my mind.

If you fill a coffee cup a few times, sooner or later some of the coffee will drip down the side of the mug and hit the napkin or the coaster you've put underneath it. You remember to do this because your mom or your wife has told you if you don't, you'll wreck the table. Once you pick up the cup you see a big brown ring, which makes it undeniably clear to anyone who sees it that a cup of coffee had been there.

The napkin, or the coaster has been forever marked. This is what I believed God was asking us to do—to make a mark, a clear, indelible imprint in the lives of people who became a part of our community.

We weren't forming a club of like-minded individuals in order for them to check off the box under spiritual duties. We didn't uproot our families and move to a city we didn't know to play church. We weren't interested in attracting self-righteous crowds to make them feel better about themselves because they weren't like whoever they thought was the problem in our culture.

I remembered seeing a movie where a king or a leader had sent a message to one of his servants. In order to communicate his authority and his personal connection to the marching orders he took some hot wax, poured it on the paper and pressed his seal on top of it.

As our team discussed this idea one day somebody had enough marketing savvy to grab a Thesaurus and start diving through synonyms for "*mark.*" After digging through a list the name "milestone" jumped off the page.

A few days later I was running an errand at the store. On my way to whatever I was looking for I passed the greeting cards section and was stopped in my tracks. There it was on the new Hallmark display—"*Milestones*"—a high-end, classy way to commemorate life's most important events.

Hallmark had recognized something I'd discovered in my experience leading and pastoring people. When you come to the end of your life, when you're there at the bedside of someone who's saying goodbye, no one says, *"Bring me my awards, a summary of my work accomplishments and the latest printout of my investments."*

If they did, it would be incredibly sad.

Hallmark tapped into this human need to mark incredibly significant moments—a wedding, baby's first steps, graduation, your first home or starting your own business.

Life is all about our relationships. They want to see the people they love. They want to say thank you, to mend hurts, to articulate their deepest, unspoken feelings before they're gone.

Surrounded by those they love they want to celebrate and ensure they'll always remember what matters most. That's what a milestone is all about.

Now you might call it an unremarkable coincidence or the over-spiritualized imagination of a young church planter, but I called it confirmation from the Lord.

Right there in the store I was ready to pull the trigger and make it official but I thought it might be wise to pray and see what Scripture had to say about this name I was growing more and more attached to.

Marking Our Past to Move Into Our Future

In several passages of the Old Testament, God tells people who are following Him to mark their journey with large stones as a memorial to what He was doing in their lives for all to consider. This happened during some of the most important moments in the journey of God's people.

Though our circumstances may be different, I think many of us can relate. Maybe we've had moments with God that we marked only to forget.

I don't know about you, but when I was young I made a lot of decisions and commitments I didn't share with anyone else. And usually when things got tough, I lowered my standards. One less set on the bench press, one less hour of studying, one more bowl of ice cream—you know what I'm talking about!

But when you're on a team, when you're in a family, when you're walking in relationships where everyone's future hinges on your willingness to follow through, everything changes. When someone you care about is looking to, encouraging and counting on you, you are willing to go the extra mile.

And then together, you celebrate it. You mark it down. You remember.

If you don't know where you're going, you never know if you have gotten there. There's nothing to celebrate, nothing to mark down. How can you remember what didn't happen? How can you develop passion and invite people into an environment like this?

The truth is…you won't.

Without a clear goal nothing is ever accomplished. It always stays in the tentative limbo of "in progress." One day runs into the next. Vision leaks. Values drift. This is the natural progression of the heart.

Chuck Swindoll commented on this tendency he's seen in churches through-out his long career in ministry. "*We need places in our journey where we force ourselves to pause and evaluate whether or not a drift is taking place. Why? Because a church without milestones will drift.*"

From the very beginning, we wanted Milestone to be a place where a growing community of people could move through life together, marking and remembering the significant moments when the God of the universe transformed their lives.

Not because we're overly sentimental or we like telling the same stories over and over but because we're anticipating that He will take us into something new, something bigger than us, something significant enough to capture the next generation.

For too many people church is a responsibility or a chore, a place where you go and make small talk and use words and phrases that you never speak anywhere else. They can't remember what happened there last week, much less last year.

We believe that's not how God intended it. We believe that each of our relationships with God should be marked by change—transformation. God is taking us somewhere. As we serve Him and walk through life together, our lives will be marked, just like these giant stones, by His undeniable presence and power at work in our lives.

When this happens, it's not just a big deal for us. It doesn't just make a difference in our lives. Our children will ask us, *"What did God do in your life back then?"* and when we tell them, it marks both their story and our own. God's plan for your life is so much bigger than you. It should mark every significant relationship in your life…even the ones you don't have yet.

These memorial stones, or milestones, remind us of what God has done in our lives and they tell a story to our children and everyone else in our lives that we've been transformed by His powerful hand. You see, when God really moves in your life, you don't need a clever reason to convince someone to come to church with you. They'll see the change for themselves and they'll ask you what's going on.

It might sound crazy, but we believe this should be normal. A healthy church should be filled with constant stories of lives that are being marked by powerful stories of transformation.

Released To Your Inheritance

Joshua is one of my favorite leaders in the Bible. His job wasn't easy—he followed in the footsteps of one of the most influential leaders in history. He walked with Moses, listened to him, learned from him and took on responsibility from him, but he wasn't Moses.

He was wired differently.

But the same God who was with Moses was with him. When Joshua takes over, God tells him over and over: *Don't be afraid, be strong and courageous, I'll be with you.* This encouragement filled Joshua's soul—it became the fuel that allowed him to run the race God had for him, to fulfill his purpose and to finish strong.

By the grace of God, that's the kind of leader I want to be. I want to run my race, but I want to finish strong. The best way I can do this is by setting up others to succeed. That's what a leader does.

Joshua's story comes to a close in Joshua chapter 24. No other passage of Scripture had a greater impact on the name of our church. In this little story I heard God communicate the kind of place He wanted Milestone Church to become.

The generation that God rescued from Egypt wandered and complained with Moses in the wilderness for 40 years but in their place emerged a new generation. They believed God would go before them, they followed Joshua, and supernaturally the Lord drove out all the enemies from the Promised Land. The majority of the second half of the book of Joshua is devoted to dividing the inheritance in this new land for God's people. He challenges the leaders to remember what God had done for them and to be faithful to live according to His Word.

> **THE STONE WAS A REMINDER OF THE COMMITMENT THEY'D ALL MADE TOGETHER TO THE LORD.**

By the time we get to Joshua 24, he's old and well advanced in years—he's giving his final appeal and blessing. He gathers all the people of God together and he reminds them of their story[1]—the hundreds of years, the ups and downs, the incredible faithfulness of God that had brought them to this moment.

He challenges all the people to fear the Lord, to serve Him with sincerity and in faithfulness by putting away the gods their fathers served before they crossed the river. He gives a famous command—*choose this day whom you will serve...but as for me and my house, we will serve the Lord.*

The people immediately respond—they want to serve the Lord.

Then Joshua does something really interesting. He tries to talk them out of it but the people won't change their mind. They've come too far. They've seen too much of God's goodness.

So like the pattern we described, Joshua takes a large stone and sets it up under a tree, which was next to the place where the priests met with God. The stone was a reminder of the commitment they'd all made together to the Lord. Once the entire community had come together, each tribe and every family was released into their inheritance.

---

1   Joshua 24:2-13

And once again…the phrase jumped off the page at me. Just like when I first saw the name "*milestone*," this phrase pulled it all together.

The inheritance—the piece of land and resources that God was giving them—had been set aside long before this. But Joshua didn't release any of them until all of them had come together as a people.

It may seem like a small detail, but the significance of this is huge. This is a markedly different attitude than the previous generation Moses led out of Egypt. That group complained about everything. Like many of us, that group viewed the world through a simple filter: "*What's in it for me?*"

This new generation was more concerned with what God was doing through them for the sake of others. They didn't want what God was giving to them until they knew the rest of their family was provided for.

These two attitudes, these two ways of relating to God and evaluating life still exist today. A Moses generation wants to know when they're going to get what they've been promised. A Joshua generation gives of themselves out of their love for God to see others receive the promises and blessings of God. And as a result, they're blessed in the process.

A Moses generation relies on the faith and obedience of their leader—when he succeeds, they succeed. They can't go to God on their own; he goes for them. He hears the voice of the Lord and relays it to them. When he fails or asks them to do something, they complain and go worship their own idols.

A Joshua generation goes together. Their focus is not on themselves but on the community they're serving. Receiving the promises of God was not something an individual did on their own—it was a process the entire community walked in together, like when all the people marched around Jericho[2] or when all the people suffered because of the disobedience of Achan[3].

---

2   You'll find this story in Joshua 6.
3   This fascinating story follows in Joshua 7.

I believe this principle hasn't changed. We're trying our best to build it into the fabric of Milestone Church.

The church isn't a place where you go to become more spiritual, to do "*the God thing*," or to inspire you to do enough good that God will be obligated to let you into heaven. You don't go to church as a spectator to watch "the man of God" exercise his gift. It's not about who has the style of worship you enjoy or the best vocalists, as if our worship was a talent competition more centered on us than glorifying to God.

The purpose of church is not a networking center designed to help you find the spouse, the job or the home of your dreams. The church doesn't exist to promote your personal brand, to get you Twitter followers and a speaking career so you can launch your ministry.

I've seen countless people, in all kinds of churches in all sorts of places, who put these expectations on the church only to be disappointed. When it doesn't happen for them they get mad at people, at God and ultimately at themselves. This process is devastating for the soul.

But it doesn't have to be this way. We can be like the Joshua generation who believed God always blesses us to be a blessing.

It wasn't about creating their best and most fulfilled lives to bring them glory. It was about serving God's purpose in their generation and impacting those who would come after them. The reality is, there's no more fulfilling, no more significant way to live life.

The incredible paradox is when you stop making your life about you and what you get, then and only then, can you begin to experience the life you've been looking for all along.

The only thing better than being released into your own inheritance is to help someone else receive theirs.

CHAPTER FIVE

A MONUMENT
OR A MARK

One of the most tragic figures in the entire Bible is David's son Absalom. He was gifted, handsome and charming. He was Jerusalem's most likely to succeed, the golden child, the one everybody knew was going places.

But when his sister was brutally violated by his older brother, Absalom went nuts. Not in a screaming, ranting, I'll-take-on-you-and-your-army kind of crazy—but the cold, black-eyed serial killer kind of crazy.

He carefully and deliberately plotted the murder of his older brother. He patiently waited two years for the exact moment to execute his plan. He manipulated the circumstances to the degree that allowed his servants to murder his brother.

Then he took off into hiding.

David mourned the loss of both his sons—the murdered Amnon and the fugitive Absalom. Eventually when one of the king's advisers brought him back, Absalom married a young woman, fathered three sons and a daughter and then years later was finally reunited with his father.

The damage had been done in Absalom's soul—he was so embittered and angry with his father he was determined to destroy him and steal his kingdom.

Because of his incredible influence and abilities, Absalom was able to win over the people to such a degree, that King David fled Jerusalem. He was the king. He had an army and soldiers at his command, but the combination of his own guilt and shame and Absalom's guile convinced him his best move was to run.

One of the most fascinating parts of this story is the fact that he actually accomplished his plan…for a brief moment. But the Lord prevented his plans from succeeding—as he was fleeing a devastating loss in battle on his donkey, his head got stuck in a tree, and some of David's soldiers found him and they killed him.

As dark, horrific and painful as this story is, I haven't even told you the worst part. At the end of this story there is one little verse you could easily miss; every time I think about it, it gives me chills.

> *During his lifetime Absalom had taken a pillar and erected it in the King's Valley as a monument to himself, for he thought, 'I have no son to carry on the memory of my name.' He named the pillar after himself, and it is called Absalom's Monument to this day.*[1]

Absalom was so consumed by his pain, his pride and his own plans he lost everything. The story tells us he had three sons. It doesn't tell us whether they died, or he forgot or what happened to them. The unmistakable takeaway is Absalom was so consumed with himself, that he literally built his own monument because he was afraid it was the only way he would ever be remembered.

---

1   2 Samuel 18:18 (NIV)

If you don't raise your sons, you're left to either hire some away from some-body else or lose the ones you already have. In both cases, your preoccupation with yourself sabotages your soul and hurts others in the process. We're all hard-wired for relationship and when we lose sight of this, we leave a path of broken lives. The first place we can see it is in our own lives, and yet un-fortunately, many of us don't find out until we are deep into a major crisis.

In our culture of celebrity, materialism and entitlement, we hear everyday over-and-over about what we deserve. As kids we're told if we work hard enough, if we really want it, we can be and have anything we want. And then we wonder why it's never enough, why it seems impossible to genuinely be content.

We're trained to step over whomever we need to in order to take what we want. But it's a lie—an empty promise without any power to deliver on its claims.

Our region is filled with people who are killing themselves trying to build monuments to themselves. They're trying to undo the pain of their past by proving their parents, their sibling, their coach, their friends or anybody else who told them they weren't good enough, wrong.

It's never enough. You get the dream job, the dream spouse and the dream house, yet before it's even done you're already thinking about what's next. You can build giant, beautiful skyscrapers and put your name on them. It won't satisfy the deepest longings of your soul.[2]

You can become the most accomplished, most celebrated, most respected figure in your industry. It can't quiet the voices on the inside.[3]

You can even turn your kids into a monument to yourself, but I wouldn't recommend it. You've seen this guy…he's vicariously living through his kids

---

2   Ask Donald Trump.

3   Ask Michael Jordan. Better yet, ask his kids and his wife. Or his 8th grade coach he's still bitter enough about to call out during his Hall of Fame acceptance speech. Read that again. That sentence is absolutely ridiculous and yet it happened.

all-star season and getting him ready for a college scholarship, a professional career, and a long list of lucrative endorsements.

The kid is five years old.

Or maybe you've seen his wife who drives their daughter all over the country for beauty pageants or acting gigs because they're sure she's the next Carrie Underwood or Gwyneth Paltrow. Anyone who doubts them immediately becomes their sworn enemy and gets added to the list of haters who'll ultimately be proven wrong.

None of these things can satisfy the soul because we weren't created for them.

Theologians use this beautiful phrase, "*imago dei*"—from the Latin, which is a dead language, but the concept is brimming with life. It means "*the image of God.*"

You were created to reflect God's love, glory and beauty to everyone. To be an image, a reflection, a mirror that bears an image of the One who designed you for His glory.

The problem is, on your best day, you will never be good enough to accurately portray the depth, holiness and beauty of God.

Being more spiritual won't solve it.

Having a dad or a grandfather as a pastor or a ministry leader won't get the job done.

Neither will faithfully attending every church service for a year...or ten years.

Selling everything you own and giving it to the poor wouldn't even be enough.

You could even become a missionary and travel around the world and still fail to be the image God created you to be.[4]

You see, our problem can't be fixed by trying harder or doing more. We can't fix what's broken on the inside of us by avoiding our deepest character flaws. Our mirror is cracked, it's shattered by our sinful nature.

Even at our best, we can only portray a fractured image of God. The only way we can solve this dilemma is to get a new mirror...a new nature.

That's why Jesus said we have to be born again.

The Ultimate Milestone Moment

I believe the church is worth it. I believe the local church is the hope of the world. I'm blown away by all the incredible things God has done at Milestone Church. I'd love for you to become a part of our community.

But if you made me choose, I would much rather have you join Jesus than Milestone Church.

Maybe you grew up in church. I've met so many people who've been around church or been around Christians who look at their own lives and think, *"I've been here for a while, I like this atmosphere, we're all on the same team."* But you don't become a child of God, you don't get a new nature, you can't be born again by osmosis.

Or maybe you've never been to church, you've never really liked Christians, and you simply couldn't see yourself associating with these types of people

---

4   I can say this confidently because the founder of the Methodist faith, John Wesley, lived this experience. He was traveling on a missionary voyage and his ship was about to go down when he realized he didn't truly know God. There was a group of missionaries who were singing and worshipping even as they were preparing to die and when he saw them he realized his experience had been religious instead of a relational. History remembers him as a fiery evangelist and the Methodist symbol is a cross on fire. [The Moravians and John Wesley, Christianity Today/Christian History magazine, 1982]

or being welcomed in these environments. But entering into a relationship with Jesus isn't about becoming culturally Christian.

I don't want to go any further without giving you the opportunity to enter into a genuine relationship with Jesus. The hope of being even a small part of this gets me out of bed in the morning. There's nothing like it.

I met Alex and his wife Stacey when my wife and I agreed to carpool our kids to school together several years ago. Alex is an Emergency Room physician and at the time Stacey was practicing internal medicine in our area. They'd met in medical school, began dating and within a few years started a wonderful family and very successful careers here in the metroplex. From every appearance, they were living the American Dream.

> **ALEX GAVE HIS LIFE TO JESUS— IT WAS A MOMENT THAT HAD BEEN BUILDING FOR SOME TIME.**

Alex had been a high achiever his whole life. He came from a home with loving parents and he excelled at everything he participated in—a three-sport letterman, class valedictorian, even class president.

Yet somehow, his long list of accomplishments—the love and support of his family, the respect of his loved ones and peers, financial security—wasn't enough. Something was missing.

It made ethical and rational sense for him to attend church at Stacey's insistence, but he didn't get much out of it. He was indifferent about God and didn't place any interest in pursuing what he felt was missing from what he viewed as being more religious.

As our families started to spend more time together, he began to become more interested in the idea of faith. I invited him to ask questions without rushing him to answers. He was really struggling with the idea of taking a step of faith. We'd go to coffee and he would wrestle with what he perceived as unresolved dilemmas. Like so many of us, he felt like he had a lot of questions and not many answers. It was clear he was worried about starting a relationship with God only to fall out of it later. I assured him Jesus wasn't intimidated or put off by this. In fact, He invites us to come to Him with our doubts, our questions and our pain.

After a series of meetings I felt like we'd reached a key moment in the journey so I called and asked if the four of us could sit down and talk. We gathered around their kitchen table and as we began to talk one of the most powerful storms any of us had seen blew through our city. In the early evening the sky took on an ominous color as rain and golf-ball sized hail pelted roofs, windows and cars. Throughout the region, reports of tornadoes touching down kept coming through TV reports, text messages and phone calls. When the storm passed through the city there was this incredible sense of calm.

And in that peace, Alex said he experienced this surreal feeling that God was real and the Holy Spirit had been with them. In the light of God's presence, his questions no longer mattered.

Alex gave his life to Jesus—it was a moment that had been building for some time.

Within a few weeks Alex took his decision public and was baptized. Looking back he realized how patiently God had been revealing Himself to Him— through a grandmother faithfully reading her Bible and praying for him, a phone call from his brother years earlier when he'd given his life to Christ, a conversation with his brother-in-law about Jesus as they worked in the garden, watching me pray with his father to receive Christ on his deathbed in the hospital, and even an answered prayer he'd prayed when his dear friends' son nearly drowned.

The whole time Alex had been wrestling with questions, God had been demonstrating His goodness in his life.

In Luke 15 Jesus tells three stories of loss—a lost sheep, a lost coin and a lost son. In the first two stories, once it's been discovered something of value has been lost, they're searched for with urgency and passion until they're found. But each of these stories is a set up for the story Jesus really wants to tell.

You've probably heard this story. Mark Twain called it "*the greatest story ever written.*"[5] At the center of this story is a father with two sons.

The younger son demands his inheritance—in the ancient world this was the equivalent of saying, "*I wish you were dead.*" Despite this insult, the father acquiesces and gives the younger son the money he would have received when his father passed away. He leaves and quickly spends all he was given to indulge every pleasure he could chase. This leaves the son destitute and ultimately fighting with pigs to eat some of the garbage and slop they were given.

In his brokenness, he remembers the kindness of his father and decides to return home because even if his father is ashamed and relegates him to life as a servant, it would be better than his present circumstances. When he arrives at the road leading to his home, his father comes running out to him, throws his arms around his son and calls for a celebration. In the ancient world, men didn't run—their robes made it difficult and awkward so it was an undignified act. But the father didn't care—his son, who he had lost, was finally home.

The older son watches this scene play out and is disgusted. He's bitter at his younger brother for taking his money (a larger portion of the inheritance always went to the older son and they saw the estate as their own) and he's astonished by his father's response. He feels slighted, taken for granted and insulted by their behavior. He refuses to participate in the celebration—he's

5   Majernik, p. 85.

throwing himself a major pity party. His father leaves the feast to look for him and challenges him for not being there with the rest of the family.

Jesus cuts off the story at this point. The younger son who acted so shamefully is reconciled, while the older son's story ends unresolved. The primary audience Jesus was telling the story to would have certainly vilified the younger son while identifying with the older brother. This isn't sweet, gentle Jesus rocking Birkenstock sandals, the blue sash and feathered, seventies classic-rock hair.

The religious leaders in the crowd wanted to *kill* him because of what he was saying.

Whether we're like the young son who selfishly wastes our life pursuing pleasures or the older son who dutifully obeys while growing increasingly self-righteous, either attitude breaks our relationship with the father.

In my years of ministry I've realized most people relate to being either the black sheep or the good child. Sometimes we're both. But the bottom line is whether we're consumed by pleasure and bad choices or self-righteous pride; we're not in a right relationship with God.

The great news is the Father looks for us when we're lost. He waited for the younger son to come home and he went after the older brother when he protested the celebration.

Wherever you're at, the Father is pursuing you. He's calling you into relationship with Him—not on the basis of your righteousness—your mirror is cracked. The only way you can enter into a relationship with God is through receiving a new mirror, a new nature.

You have to trade the life you're living for the life you were created to live. You can't relate to God on the basis of what you've done. It will never be good enough. The only way you can find peace with God is to live a perfect life. I don't know about you, but I blew that one a long time ago.

It's like when you go through security at the airport. You get out your boarding pass and your ID and you shuffle towards the first checkpoint. The guy checks to make sure it's you and then points you on to the bins and the conveyor belt. You put your laptop, your belt and your shoes into the bin, put your bag on the belt and then step over towards the scanner.

Now the old machines would beep if you forgot your belt or had change in your pocket. If you were lucky enough to have that happen twice, they'd bring out a guy with a wand to check you. We don't need the wand anymore because the new technology is the 360-degree camera that spins completely around you. It sees everything. Whatever is with you (literally) is visible to the guy watching the monitor.

Imagine stepping into that machine not with a little change in your pockets or a belt you left on, but with a handgun or a bomb. You'd be freaking out because you knew you were about to get busted. There's nowhere left to hide at that point.

God's ability to see our sin, our failures and our brokenness is a lot better than our best technology. He sees it all. If we had to pass through a sin detector, we'd all be terrified because deep down every one of us knows we've blown it.

But this is where Jesus comes in. He lived the life you should have lived but couldn't. He died the death your sin demanded before a holy God. This is why He's so amazing. This is why He's worth it. He did all this out of obedience to the Father, but now He invites you into the same peace, love and joy they share. It would be like, at the last moment, Jesus jumped in the detector for you. When God scans Jesus it always comes back perfectly holy.

2 Corinthians 5:21 summarizes this amazing idea beautifully: *"God made Him who had no sin to be sin for us, so that in Him we might become the righteousness of God."* [6]

Righteousness is a legal word that means "right standing." God knew in your own strength you could never be good enough so He sent His Son to be the righteousness you needed but were powerless to produce. Now He invites you into this peace, this right standing with God through Him. He took the scan in your place and invites you into perfect peace with God.

The hope we have in Jesus is not about what we do—it's about putting our complete trust in what's already been done for us. It's not a way for bad people to become good—it's the only way for dead people to come back to life.

THIS IS WHY

HE'S WORTH IT.

Romans 10:9 tells us, *"If you declare with your mouth, 'Jesus is Lord,' and believe in your heart that God raised him from the dead, you will be saved."* [7]

It's really that simple. You've got to repent—a biblical word that means *"to change your mind."* It's a military term that meant you were marching one way but you do an about face, and head in the other direction. You repent from your sin, from trusting in your own good works, from the idea you can please God on the basis of your own ability and you turn to Jesus, put all your trust in Him and commit to love and follow Him. When you do that He gives you a new nature, a new life and the ability to be the image bearer God created you to be.

---

6   NIV

7   NIV

We call this *"the Gospel"*—the good news. And it is good news. Not just for us personally, but for this broken world filled with all kinds of evil, death and hopelessness. The incredible good news of the Gospel is Lord Jesus, the One True King of the universe, came to redeem and restore everything in this world that's broken. This is so personal that it includes you and me, but it's also so massive it includes every group of people, every nation and all of creation.

In Acts 2, Peter preaches the first sermon in the history of the church. It wasn't a seeker sensitive message. He was preaching to the people who were there when Jesus was brutally beaten and crucified. They had witnessed these events with their own eyes…and he called them on it. Weaving the words of the prophet Joel with several of David's psalms, Peter finishes by saying, *"Therefore let all the house of Israel know for certain that God has made Him both Lord and Christ—this Jesus whom you crucified."*

But instead of being offended or defensive, the Bible says the words pierced or cut to the heart, and all they could say was, *"What shall we do?"* Like the coffee mug on the table or the sealed message from a king, these men had been marked. Peter answers them by calling them to repent and be baptized—in other words, when you recognize Jesus as Lord, you're recognizing Him as the final authority in your life.

Repentance is both a *turning from*—your old life, your choices, your feelings, your pattern of sin, and a *turning to*—you embrace His life, His Word, His commands and His righteousness.

You commit to love and obey Him regardless of how you feel about it. It's not about joining a religion or trying harder to become a good person. You trade the life you're currently living for the life you were created to live.

If you've never done this I want to invite you to bow your head and pray this with me—it's not about the words, it's about the decision you're making to put your trust in Jesus: *"Jesus, thank you for living the life I should have but couldn't and dying in my place to make me right with God. I repent of my sin and trust in your righteousness. I want you to be my Lord and I commit to walk with you for the rest of my days. I receive all you have for me and I thank you for all that you've done. In Jesus' name, Amen."*

This is a massive moment. Jesus said all of heaven rejoices when one who is lost comes home. You don't gradually drift into this. Every story is unique and I want you to take the time you need to process, but make no mistake… this is a milestone moment worth celebrating.

The enemy will do whatever he can to prevent this. He wants one day to turn into the next; he wants you to find any of a million reasons to put this off. C.S. Lewis said, *"Indeed the safest road to hell is the gradual one—the gentle slope, soft underfoot, without sudden turnings, without milestones, without signposts."*[8]

If God is speaking to you, let this be your moment. Make it a milestone in your life and a reason for all of heaven to celebrate.

I want to celebrate with you too and help you take your next steps. If you prayed with me, I have some resources I'd like to get in your hands—all you have to do is email me at itsworthit@milestonechurch.com. Tell me your name and address and we'll get them right out to you.

---

8   Lewis, p. 61.

WHAT IF YOU COULD
HAVE THE KIND OF
AUTHENTIC RELATIONSHIPS
YOU'VE ALWAYS WANTED?

CHAPTER SIX

LESSONS IN LEADERSHIP

You might be surprised to discover that despite my rugged exterior and many years spent growing up as an offensive lineman[1], I love to learn. Believe it or not, by the grace of God I've earned both a bachelor's and a master's degree.[2]

It's amazing how, now that I'm done with school, I think I enjoy studying and learning more than ever before. Maybe it's the lack of midterms and finals. Whatever it is, I find myself constantly drawn to reading and research.

There's nothing I find more interesting and fascinating to study than leadership.

While most guys read to check the latest sports or business news[3], I could literally read about leadership every day. I'm absolutely fascinated by this

---

1   FYI—my illustrious football career went no further than high school. I did play club rugby at Baylor.
2   I received a Bachelor's degree in Pastoral Ministry from Baylor University and a Master's in Theological Studies from Southwestern Seminary. And remember, this was before the days when you could get your term papers off the Internet so it's legit!
3   I'm definitely one of "these guys" too.

subject. But I don't just study to acquire knowledge or information—I'm committed to growing into the best leader I can be.

I like leading—in my home, in my community and in our church environment. I enjoy the process of building a team as they develop and implement strategy in order to execute the vision. There's a process of calculating the risks and the rewards and then actually stepping out and then evaluating what worked and what didn't.

I appreciate what happens as we face challenges and as a result learn to work together to accomplish our goals and influence real change—not just in a classroom but in the lives of real people.

Let me explain why I find it so significant.

Leadership affects all of us—even though for many it feels complicated, confusing and completely outside of their control. But the truth is you don't have to be a leader to be impacted by leadership…you just have to be alive.

In every healthy environment you've ever experienced—a loving home, an encouraging classroom, a rewarding athletic team or an inspiring workplace—whether you noticed it or not, quality leadership created and sustained that culture.

In the same way, I believe that all of the problems in the homes, neighborhoods, churches, communities, organizations, cities, states and nations in our world can be traced back to failures in leadership. These failures usually come back to one of two basic issues: the leaders in place made repeated, critical mistakes or no one was willing to embrace the challenge to lead.

Leadership is the difference between success and failure, between healthy environments and dysfunction, between life-giving atmospheres and toxic cultures. Every problem that exists in the world today is a leadership problem. It's not the only factor, but it is the most important one.

We see this pattern repeated over and over throughout Scripture. From the very beginning, God has been looking for the man or woman who would answer His call to lead. I believe God has called all of us to lead at some level.

As we'll discover, this doesn't always look the way we imagine it.

What is Leadership?

As I've studied leadership and spent the last decade working with people from a leadership position, I've heard all kinds of excuses and misguided opinions.

I've heard that leadership is a rare skill that only a select few have. I've heard that leadership only exists at the top of an organization. I've heard that all leaders are exceptionally gifted people. And I've even heard that leaders are just people willing to manipulate others to get them to do what they want.

Unfortunately, we've all suffered under bad leadership. We don't have to read about it to understand it. We know what it feels like to be blamed for things beyond our control, to be used as a pawn, to be disrespected and to be underdeveloped but leadership is all about valuing people.

Yet through all of my own experiences and my study of this subject, I keep coming back to one all-important, life-altering bottom line.

As much damage as bad leadership can do (and it's a lot), it can't compare to the amazing difference that one, godly, Christ-centered leader can make when they stand up and lead.

That's why I spend so much time working on this issue. I trust whole-heartedly in God's sovereignty, but when it comes to man's role, there's no issue more critical than leadership.

Leadership 101

Leadership isn't about having an impressive title, a fancy job, or a powerful role that comes complete with a shiny badge.

Leadership isn't about who is the most talented, who knows the most, who's been around the longest, who's got the most money or power, who's come from the right family or has the perfect resume and pedigree. At the end of the day, it's really simple. As John Maxwell says, *"Leadership is influence— nothing more, nothing less."*[4]

If you have influence in someone's life (including your own) then you're a leader—it's as simple as that.

LEADERS EMBRACE

RESPONSIBILITY.

All of us have experienced the pain that comes from poor positional leadership. This approach leans on hierarchy, organizational levels & food chains. Poor positional leaders don't care about people; they only care about what people can do for them.

People will tolerate this type of leadership if the incentives (usually a good paycheck with job security) are valuable enough, but they will only give the bare minimum effort. You will get accomplished tasks but you'll never capture their passion or their imagination.

---

4   Maxwell says this all the time, but you can find it both in *The 21 Irrefutable Laws of Leadership* and *Developing the Leader Within You.*

Parents can lead small children this way—but it doesn't work once they grow up and move out. Bosses or managers can lead employees who don't have other options this way—but a quality employee who's demonstrated their value to clients will leave to work for another company and become your competition.

Pastors and church leaders can't lead this way—especially in our community. We don't have positional leverage. A Christian in the DFW area has lots of options—if your "*leadership*" consists of positional manipulation, eventually people move on.

Spiritual leadership is not about what people can do for you, but how you can add value and create godly influence in the lives of those He's placed in your life.

Willing To Carry Weight

Leaders embrace responsibility. They carry weight. Authentic leadership isn't about getting credit or being on a platform others look up to. The majority of the leader's daily life takes place apart from an audience. Nobody else sees what you're doing. Nobody is there to encourage you and tell you when you're doing a great job.

A leader is someone willing to carry a weight others aren't willing to haul to help people who often don't know they need it.

The most basic form of leadership is self-leadership. All of us are responsible to lead ourselves. Often, we're the most difficult person to lead. Some people are incredibly hard on themselves. Nothing they do is good enough and so they come to the point where they're paralyzed to move forward because they are convinced they're just going to mess things up.

Some go the other direction. It's never their fault. They have a reason why they missed their deadline, why they didn't follow through or why it was really somebody else who dropped the ball. This attitude of entitlement is running wild in our culture. People don't want to carry the weight of responsibility but they want to receive all the benefits of what a great leader accomplishes.

Because we're all called to lead ourselves, every one of us is created to be a leader. We're not all given the same amount of natural leadership ability—in the same way we're not all given the same intelligence, emotional intelligence, athletic ability or musical talent. I don't think any of us would try to argue this point.

We're all responsible to develop the measure of leadership we've been given. Jesus demonstrated this principle in two similar stories, the parable of the talents[5] and the parable of the ten servants.[6]

In both stories, Jesus tells about a king or a ruler who gives resources to an individual under their authority before leaving for an extended period of time. In both stories, the resources the ruler gives are different for each servant but the expectation and standard of measurement is the same. Everyone who was given resources was evaluated by what they did with what they were given. If they used their resources well, they were given much, much more.

This leadership principle is as relevant today as when Jesus first spoke it. God is looking for leaders He can trust—this first shows up in the individual's commitment to God and their desire to grow closer to Him.

Are you closer to God today than you were six months ago? I've often heard it said that most Christians' have been educated beyond their obedience—if they just did what they already knew to do, they'd be completely different people...better followers of Christ and more trustworthy leaders.

---

5   You'll find it in Matthew 25:14-30
6   Read it for yourself in Luke 19:10-27

If you want to grow as a leader, the place to start is the same for you and me as it was for the servants in these two parables: show yourself faithful in what you've already been given.

Leaders don't wait for someone else to change; they go *first*.

The first place this shows up is in the leader's own character. Your character is the first place where the quality of your leadership becomes evident. If you are married, the health of your relationship with your spouse would be the next indicator. If you have children, your family dynamic demonstrates how well you're carrying the weight God has given you.

This is the pattern for leadership Paul sets out in 1 Timothy 3[7]—if you want to lead in God's house that's a good thing—but you demonstrate your capacity by first leading in your own home.

This isn't a contest to see who's the biggest leader. We need every gift. God gives everyone unique talents and gifts and every one of us is entrusted with these for the sake of the body. He doesn't give us these gifts to make us happy and individually successful—He empowers us to bless and enrich the lives of others.

You may not be a "10" in the area you would have chosen for yourself, you may not be a "10" in more than one area, but I believe you can be a "10" in something. I believe that's how God sees you. But no one rolls out of bed a "10"—it takes development, time, experience, and a willingness to grow.

Let's Get Honest

Two of the things that I've learned about all great leaders—no matter what area they're leading in or who they are, is that they all place tremendous value on honesty and humility.

---

7   1 Timothy 3:1-5

They're not constantly spouting hyperbole and overpromising like a hype machine, they're not ignoring the realities they're facing or their own weakness, they're not blaming everything on others. They place a high priority on what Jim Collins describes as "*Confronting the brutal facts.*"[8]

Great leaders don't surround themselves with "*yes people*" who only tell them what they want to hear—they create environments where others feel empowered to be open and honest. They invite response and feedback and genuinely listen when they get it; not because they lack vision or ideas, but because they are confident in who they are.

Having humility is not becoming a doormat or having a disproportionately low view of oneself, it is the ability to see and meet the needs of the larger picture. It's the capacity to take yourself out of the equation and to stop viewing everything through the lens of how it affects you.

If I were sitting with you having a cup of coffee this is the point where I'd lean and ask you directly: What kind of a leader are you? Do you create an environment where others feel empowered to be honest? Are you humble enough to see beyond your own immediate needs? If I asked the people you're doing life with, how would they describe your leadership?

Is the Holy Spirit producing this kind of fruit in your life—love, joy, peace, patience, kindness, goodness, faithfulness, gentleness, and self-control?[9] This shows up in how you're treating the people in your life, especially those closest to you.

Leadership always comes back to the difficult and exhausting reality of cultivating relationships and loving people. You can't do this without asking some hard questions:

---

8   Collins, p. 65.

9   You'll find this challenging and inspiring list in Galatians 5:22-23.

- Do my words encourage others and build them up or do I manipulate others to my own outcomes?
- Do I invest in others to help them succeed and celebrate with them or do I minimize, resent or discredit their accomplishments?
- Do I have a genuine passion for the cause I'm leading in or am I only interested in the privileges that go with the position?
- Am I willing to embrace healthy conflict or do I avoid the difficult but necessary conversation?
- Am I developing my character and integrity in areas where most people don't see or do I primarily do things to be noticed?

If these questions are foreign, if you're not regularly thinking this way, it's probably a clear indication that there's room for growth in your abilities. I'm not asking you this to make you feel bad or to guilt you into more religious duties. That's not what this is about. I am trying to hold up a picture of what the Bible describes as a leader because I believe that is what God wants you to become.

God is not looking for perfect leaders—He already found the One and only perfect leader—His Son. He's not after perfection...but He is looking for progress. He's looking for leaders who have embraced the process. I love what Paul told Timothy: "*Give your complete attention to these matters. Throw yourself into your tasks so that everyone will see your progress.*"[10]

Any time I'm around someone who is passionately in love with God and who wants to follow Christ with all their heart it makes an impact on me. It doesn't matter if it's one of my children, someone I just met, a man, a woman, young or old, someone who just gave their life to Christ, or a pastor who's served Him for years, that example always *influences* me—and leadership is all about influence.

---

10   1 Timothy 4:15 (NIV)

That's why you don't need permission to lead, you don't need a title, and you don't need to be charismatic enough to capture the attention of the entire room. You don't need all the answers and the greatest ideas.

All you need is a willingness to serve and create an atmosphere where others can thrive—in your home, in your workplace, in your school or in your church.

A Leader God Chooses

Leadership isn't about being famous. It isn't about being the biggest or the strongest or the most accomplished. But there's something in our broken human nature that wants to be famous, that craves recognition and praise, and this is an area that often attracts that desire.

In his classic book "*Spiritual Leadership*," J. Oswald Sanders describes so clearly the kind of leadership that God is looking for. "*True greatness, true leadership, is found in giving yourself in service to others, not in coaxing or inducing others to serve you. True service is never without cost.*"[11]

Some people shy away from leadership not because they lack ambition, but because they're unwilling to pay the cost leadership demands. Make no mistake—it always costs you something to lead because it forces you to serve others. Leadership can be lonely. Never forget that hours and hours of unseen preparation always go into the moments that others see whether you're describing a parent, a coach, a businessman, a pastor or a politician.

Of course you pay a price to shirk leadership too—you won't live the life God created you to live if you're unwilling to embrace the responsibility and die to yourself.

In Matthew 20:20-28 James and John roll up to Jesus…with their mom. And believe it or not, their mom is the one who asks Jesus for a big favor. Think

11   Sanders, p. 15.

about that—you know a story is off to a bad start when two grown men go with their mom to Jesus. This is the kind of thing you expect to see at a little league game, a dance recital or at a school play…not with the Savior of the Universe and two of His closest followers.

But that's how it went down.

Mom wants Jesus to give her two baby boys the places of honor next to Him. After warning these three that they don't know what they are really asking for, He answers their question with a question. I imagine Jesus found this whole scenario to be pretty hilarious—or a little sad and pathetic.

Jesus asks them if they can drink "the cup I am going to drink?" and it's the boys, not the mom, who enthusiastically answer "We can."[12]

Like so many of us, James and John saw Jesus' crowds, the love and honor He received, the growing notoriety and recognition and they thought, "*We can handle that.*" What they didn't see was the price Jesus paid daily of dying to Himself. He knew they had all the wrong ideas and He also knew where their journey was going to take them—to a similar place of suffering and dying to self, not to the glory and fame they imagined.

When the other disciples heard about this little episode, as you might imagine, they weren't too thrilled. They wanted to lay hands on their brothers and not in the spiritual sense, if you know what I mean.

Jesus cut through the drama and spoke directly to the real issue. "*You know that the rulers in this world lord it over their people, and officials flaunt their authority over those under them. But among you it will be different. Whoever wants to be a leader among you must be your servant, and whoever wants to be first among you must become your slave. For even the Son of Man came not to be served but to serve others and to give His life as a ransom for many.*" (Matthew 20:25-28 NLT)

12   Matthew 20:22 (NIV)

If we're following Christ and not our own agenda, the ways of the world, or poor leadership models, then being a leader will always begin with service. In the big picture, it will always put the needs of others ahead of our own.

Positional leadership looks down the food chain at people who exist to help them accomplish their goals. In this approach, it's not about motives or relationships—it's only about results. If you've experienced this you know how frustrating it can be. At one point or another, we've all been guilty of wrong motives and bad choices.

The good news is God's not done with you or me. Not only can we become *better* leaders, I believe we can become *good,* and even *great* leaders as we study and apply God's Word to our lives.

Some of the greatest leaders in Scripture were the most unlikely candidates. They weren't in the popular crowd, they weren't the first ones picked at recess and they weren't the obvious choice. They doubted, complained, made mistakes and did the kinds of things that make you wonder if God had second thoughts about choosing them.

They all paid a price to lead. They suffered hardship, they endured challenges to their influence and they were forced to press deeper into God. In the end, the world was changed because they answered God's call on their lives. Not because they were perfect but because they cooperated with the work He was doing through their lives.

Joseph was an imprisoned slave who'd been sold by his brothers and accused of sexual harassment. He ended up becoming the second most powerful man in the world.

Moses was an 80-year-old has-been sheep farmer with a speech impediment. God chose him to lead millions of his people out of slavery from the world's global superpower as he experienced first-hand the most fantastic miracles in the whole Bible.

Rahab was a prostitute whose only righteous contribution we know of was lying to the leaders of Jericho when they asked about the Jews. Yet her influence on the spies and the officials was enough for God to place her in Jesus' lineage and list her in Hebrews 11's "Hall of Faith".

Gideon was the weakest guy from a family everyone else thought was weird. He went from hiding in a cellar to freeing the Israelites from a vicious army that outnumbered him one thousand to one without ever picking up a weapon.

David was the youngest of ten brothers and nobody even remembered to call him when the prophet showed up.

I could keep doing this all day. Or I could list all the guys in Scripture who led through their position instead of their influence.

It's All About the Team

I just listed a series of memorable leaders from Scripture, and while most Christians recognize their names and know a little of their stories, the truth is not a single one of them succeeded on their own.

At times leadership can be lonely, but we never lead alone. We don't all carry an equal measure of responsibility, but you can't lead well all by yourself. Just as all of us were made for relationships, every leader finds their greatest contribution in the context of a team.

Teams require work; they require sacrifice, commitment and communication. Each of these taxes our energies in different ways: mental, physical and emotional. But there's nothing like being on a great team. On a great team every member is valued, they understand and embrace their role, and they willingly give themselves fully, not for their own end, but for the larger mission of the whole.

When you get these factors working together, two incredible things happen. The first is synergy—the product of the whole is greater than the sum of the individual parts. The second is a contagious attitude of empowerment—people begin to look for ways to ensure the success of others. When these two factors are operating together, you begin to find extraordinary results—no matter what kind of team you're talking about. This kind of company, department, band, design firm or sports squad will consistently outperform their peers—even those with more talent and resources.

You may have heard me say that I'm definitely not the smartest; I'm not the most talented; I'm not that cool or innovative—but one thing I've always been able to do is rally gifted and creative people.[13] I do my best to inspire, encourage and empower talented people to leverage their gifts for maximum impact in the Kingdom of God. I listen to people who push back against the conventional ways of thinking and the status quo. I value the perspectives and the voices different from my own.

Milestone Church has never been built around a one-man team or a superstar gift. It never will be. We're a community of pastors who each bring different gifts, strengths and perspectives to the table. And we're better for it.

In the course of an average week, nearly everything I do is done in the context of teams: an elder team, an executive team, a pastoral team, a teaching team and a creative team. This isn't easy. It's not always efficient. It can be challenging and time-consuming, but our entire church family benefits from this approach.

---

13   This is another one of those things I say in every Discovery 101 gathering.

Leadership is Vision

Leadership is influence. It's service. It requires character and integrity. It's costly and it always comes back to people. It's done best in the context of teams. And leadership is about vision.

If you're not going somewhere you can't lead. In order to be intentional and to have direction, you need to have a clear, pre-determined picture of the ideal future. We call that *vision*.

There are groups that have good chemistry, healthy relationships, and who enjoy being together, but if they're not working together towards a common goal, eventually their commitment to each other will waver.

Vision inspires, it unifies, it motivates, and it gives meaning to life. A clear vision will allow you to overcome struggles and challenges because you know why you're paying the cost.

MILESTONE CHURCH HAS NEVER BEEN BUILT AROUND A ONE-MAN TEAM OR A SUPERSTAR GIFT. IT NEVER WILL BE. WE'RE A COMMUNITY OF PASTORS WHO **EACH BRING DIFFERENT GIFTS, STRENGTHS AND PERSPECTIVES TO THE TABLE.** AND WE'RE BETTER FOR IT.

Hebrews 12:1 tells us that Jesus never wavered from the road that led to the Cross because He could clearly see the joy and the eternal value of what His suffering at Calvary would accomplish.

If you're going to follow Christ as an individual you're going to need an understanding of what that looks like. If your family is going to follow Christ, you need a picture of what you're aspiring to.

And if a church is going to become the kind of Church God had in mind from eternity, it can't get there without a vision.

Several thousand years ago, King Solomon, one of the wisest men who ever lived wrote under the inspiration of the Holy Spirit: "*Where there is no vision, the people are unrestrained.*" The Message says it this way: "*If people can't see what God is doing, they stumble all over themselves.*"

Without vision, it doesn't matter where you're going. It's impossible to be lost. Where you're going is where you are. Life becomes frustrating and meaningless without vision. And in that environment, anybody is going to end up stumbling all over themselves.

As a leadership team at Milestone, we believe God has given us a clear picture of who He wants us to be as a church family. It's not measured by numbers, buildings or how well known we become.

It's measured by the values He's given us.

CHAPTER SEVEN

THE VALUE OF VALUES

In the United States, there are roughly 350,000 churches—there are tens of thousands in Texas, and in our city alone, there are several hundred Christian churches.[1]

If you visited on a Sunday morning and asked, *"How do you do church?"* or *"What do you value as a church?"* nearly all of them would give you similar responses.

You'd hear a lot of comments like, *"We're just doing what the Bible says,"* and *"We're doing our best to follow Christ as a community."*

Those are good answers—sincere and certainly consistent with Scripture and sound theology, but they don't exactly clear things up. Does doing what the Bible says mean you're following Levitical law, dietary restrictions and selling all your possessions and giving the money to the poor? Those are all in the Bible.

---

1   http://www.asarb.org/ (accessed 7/23/14)

And what about following Christ—does that mean you have no place to lay your head like the Son of Man, hate your mother and father, and give everything but your underwear to someone who's stolen from you? After all, Jesus did describe each of these things as *"following"* Him.[2]

Part of the answer depends on how you read, interpret and apply the Bible, but the bottom line is, how you answer those questions really shows what is most important to you.

Every church, every local body of believers has priorities—principles, causes and issues that they believe are more important than anything else. We call these values.

Values shape culture. They form decisions, guide strategy, create the grid for discipline and conflict management, attract certain types of people and repel others. This is true in any environment—a business, a school, a family and certainly a church.

Values are one of the most important ingredients in any church because what a church values, it will become.

The truth is, a church will *only* become what it values.

Most churches' names, bulletins, websites, promotions and statements of belief sound very similar—sometimes they share names, mottos, teaching series titles, buzzwords, sing the same songs and use the same terminology.

But if you spend enough time with the people, the leadership and the programs at the church, sooner or later what the church really values will become exceedingly clear.

Values aren't what you put on your website, what you paint onto the walls of your foyer, or what you frame in decorative artwork. Values are what you

2 Luke 9:58, 14:26, 6:29

are investing your resources in—your time, your manpower, your creative energy and your finances.

The reality is, many times, organizations have well-crafted, inspiring values on all of their materials and publications, but there's a significant gap between who they think they are and what they're modeling.

Unfortunately in these cases, the organization and its leaders are caught in the uncomfortable and awkward position of seeing themselves differently than the way everyone else views them. Often they're the last to know. And many times, they're unwilling to believe what is painfully obvious to everyone else.

Remember the first time you heard your voice played back on a recording? Most people are caught off guard and respond in shock—*"No way! I don't sound like that...do I?!?"*

Two Sets of Values

This difference between the values an organization hopes they have and the values they're actually modeling is common—they represent two sets of values—*aspirational* and *actual.*

Aspirational values are the values an organization hopes they have; the ones they put on their website and communicate in their promotional materials. They're idealistic. They're the best-case-scenario. They're the ones they talk about when they're trying to inspire their members.

The problem is, when you're actually interacting with the organization, you don't see the aspirational values. This is the culture they're aspiring to...not the values they're living with every day.

Have you ever needed help from a company that you purchased something from? I don't even have to know what company it is to be certain that somewhere on their website they claim to care deeply about customer service. You won't find out if that's really a value until you contact them.

If you can't get in touch with a real person, if no one has the authority to help you, or if you can't understand the person on the phone and you never get any real help, that company may say they value customer service, but what they really value is cutting costs.

Their behavior seems normal until you find a company like Nordstrom or Costco—places that don't just say they value customer service—it's an indispensable part of their culture. Service isn't something they talk about in their promotional materials or annual meetings, they invest in it on a daily basis—through training, re-training, regular evaluation, and a unwavering commitment to do what it takes to make it a reality in their culture. They don't take their own word for it—they ask the customer.

It's not an aspirational value…it's an actual value. No matter which store location you go into, you know you'll find it in their culture. And if you don't, they immediately take the steps they need to re-shape their culture.

They value letting the customer know how important they are more than they value the profit on an individual purchase. And they value building and maintaining that reputation among their customers. That's why both companies have created fierce loyalty among a good portion of their customer base.

Every organization has a culture that is built over time. Cultures aren't developed through random events, one-time accidents or unique circumstances. Organizational culture is the result of intentional language, behavioral patterns, and expressed values modeled by leadership and implemented at every level of the organization.

When a visitor interacts with any department of your organization, their experience reveals what you value. Your environments, your programs, your language, your priorities all communicate your values. Put whatever you want on your website or on your walls, but once we interact with you we'll discover what you really value.

Your values are so deeply imbedded in your culture it goes far beyond the behavior of your staff and your volunteers. One of the comments we get repeatedly from visitors is how people go out of their way to welcome and include them. They expect the greeter or the guy in the parking lot to be nice and chat with them—but they don't expect it from the person sitting next to them in the sanctuary. That's another way you can spot the difference between actual and aspirational.

As a leader I live with this reality on a daily basis. You never outgrow the need to re-focus and clarify the values. It helps me to think of it this way: if I'm not sick of talking about our values, then our staff and our volunteers don't know them yet. And these are some of our most committed people in our environment.

In his book, *The Advantage*, leadership expert and consultant Patrick Lencioni argues that the most important ingredient in any organization is the health of its culture. In his experience many leaders overlook this because they think this approach is overly simplistic, available to everyone and fiscally free. It costs time and emotional energy, not money. Here's how he describes organizational health: *"An organization has integrity—is healthy—when it is whole, consistent, and complete, that is, when its management, operations, strategy and culture fit together and make sense."*[3]

If this is true, and I strongly believe that it is, then we have a responsibility to ensure that our values are consistently expressed in every area of our church.

You might be saying, *"Jeff, why are you making such a big deal out of this?"* Great question. Here's why this is so important: remember, our world is filled with people who've given up on the church. They don't think it works. They don't think it's the hope of the world. And one of the main reasons is

3   Lencioni, p. 5.

because churches have been mismanaged or misled—nobody was asking these questions.

Don't hear what I'm not saying. The church is not a business. It's not a company. We don't have customers. But God entrusts us with people, and one day I'm going to stand before Jesus and He's going to ask me what I did with the people He entrusted to me. I take this very seriously. I want to be able to say I did everything I could to create the healthiest environments possible.

Values help you set priorities. They help you say no. They're the vitally necessary tool which allows you to keep the main things the main things.

Our Motto: Reaching People, Building Lives

I don't have a tattoo, and I'm not going to get one, but I make my kids laugh sometimes when I tell them I'm thinking about getting a giant spider web on the top of my bald head. They think it's funny.

But what makes them roll around on the floor laughing hysterically is when I suggest I'm going to put a big Elmer Fudd on my stomach peeking into my belly button saying, *"Come on out of there…you wascally wabbit!"*

If I passed on the biker tat and the Elmer, I'd want to permanently ink onto my body Milestone's motto: *"Reaching People, Building Lives."*[4]

I don't have to get a tattoo to remember this. I live it everyday. It's why Milestone Church exists. One day if we look up and say, *"We're doing so many cool things!"* but we're not reaching people and building lives, we've lost our way.

Reaching people may sound nebulous and esoteric, but it's not to us. It couldn't be more clear. Reaching people means men, women and children

---

4   This phrase comes from my great friend and big brother Steve Robinson. He gets all the credit. I saw how it was modeled at Church of the King so we made it a part of Milestone from the beginning.

are giving their lives to Christ—entering into a life-changing relationship with Jesus and committing to follow Him all of their days.

Building lives is equally measurable—it represents the personal growth of Christ followers to serve and lead others. We believe it's our responsibility to do everything we can to develop every person into who God created them to be. The specifics of this are incredibly broad and diverse—moms, students, businessmen, pastors, entrepreneurs, grandparents, kids, doctors, lawyers, carpenters, small business owners—but the values are shared.

At every point in our journey, from the early days in the hotel, the cafetorium and the building in the shadow of the Catholic Church, to our current locations in Keller and McKinney and everything beyond, our focus has been and will always be, reaching people and building lives.

It's that simple. It has to be. Anything that's healthy grows. And everything that grows needs guidance, direction and training. Growth without guidance gets crazy.

Every weekend I'm in the foyer visiting with people—it is part of how I live out our values. Every weekend someone comes up to me with a new idea, a new opportunity, a new program they are convinced Milestone should embrace. This isn't a bad thing—it encourages me to know people are filled with passion and ideas. In the early days I was tempted to accommodate everyone and do everything, but by God's grace we were able to keep our focus and continue to clarify values.

If we try to be everything to everyone we create expectations we can't meet. It's not loving. It sets people up for hurt and disappointment.

We can't say yes to everything and maintain a clear, healthy culture. It's like the difference between Chick-fil-A and Jack In the Box. One makes one thing and they make it really well. The other makes burgers, tacos, chicken sandwiches and all kinds of other things but none of them are outstanding. Chick-fil-A is always busy. Ever waited in a long line at Jack in the Box?

Most churches emphasize either reaching new people by constantly reinventing themselves or building lives by keeping an "us four and no more" approach to life.

Twenty years ago the church realized so much of what they were doing was confusing to people who'd never been to church. The length of the service, how people talked, the way Scripture was presented, expectations and assumptions were all built for "church people." Several key church leaders realized how problematic this was and began to rethink how to create environments un-churched or de-churched people wanted to attend.

This "*attractional approach*" was often described as "*seeker sensitive*" and became the subject of significant discussion and occasional controversy. I love the idea behind it because it's all about reaching people. Like anything, it can be taken to an unhealthy extreme where you compromise the message, telling people whatever they want to hear to get as many people as possible to show up.

In reaction to this some churches become all about going deep and they say things like, "*We're going past the surface to get into the meat of the Word.*" They want every believer to be strong, a student of God's Word, uncompromising in their faith and free from the distractions of the world. All of those are good desires we share, but taken to an extreme, it can get weird really fast.

I don't believe you have to pick one or the other. You don't have to sacrifice depth to reach people and you don't have to micro-manage people to develop them into powerful, godly leaders.

I'm not saying we've solved this. We don't have it all figured out. There is no killer app or perfect system. But we're okay with this divine tension. I've found God has designed most things this way—we find the healthy place God wants us to live in once we've identified the unhealthy extremes.

When I was twelve years old I served on a church committee in my small town. In a small church when a family or a new person stops coming around you feel it. It's not hard to notice. This bothered me.

So I had asked, "*What happened to* _____?" and the response I got was often: "*Yeah, it's too bad. They fell through the cracks.*" This made no sense to me at 12…and it still doesn't today. If there were big cracks in your house or your business, you'd do something to fill them…long before people started falling through them and disappearing.

The same should be true for the church.

I don't expect to please everyone, and I don't expect everyone to stay, but I want to know we've done everything on our end to close up the cracks. We evaluate everything we do—is it working, is it helping people love Jesus more, are we meeting needs, impacting our city and developing leaders? If we're not doing these things, we have cracks—and we don't stop until they're filled in.

We're not perfect and we're one small piece of a big body, but we realize how serious God is about His Church. He has no Plan B.

We'll never sacrifice reaching people to build lives, and we'll never stop doing everything we can to build everyone who God reaches through Milestone Church.

The one thing I can promise you—everything we do must help us accomplish this mission of reaching people and building lives.

The Problem with Programs

Churches love programs. A program can be an event—like an annual men's retreat, a discipleship weekend, a leaders' gathering, a mission trip, a community service project—anything a church does to help accomplish its mission. A program can also become a ministry—for example, at Milestone we have a wide variety of ministry environments specifically designed for different demographics, circumstances and seasons of life.

Programs allow you to specialize, to create subcultures, and to develop new leaders. But most programs have a shelf-life. Unfortunately, you realize this the same way you figure out the milk's gone bad—you take a drink without looking at the expiration date and you get a mouthful of nasty chunks.

Just because something was successful at one point doesn't mean it's supposed to continue until Jesus returns. Change is hard for most people, which is a problem because so much of life is seasonal. Have you ever asked why a certain activity took place and the response you got back was, "*It's tradition. This is the way we've always done it.*"

As soon as I hear this response I think to myself, "*Uh oh. This could be a problem.*"

When we first started Milestone we used to pray on Friday nights at 11pm. We were young and didn't have too many kids. These were passionate and inspiring times of prayer for our community. We were starting from nothing and so we had to pray our church into existence.

For the few and the proud, spiritual enough to start late Friday and go early into Saturday morning, these were some incredible times. Every so often I think back on those days and miss them. And believe it or not, occasionally I'm tempted to bring them back.

The reason I don't do it—aside from the fact I'm older and can't stay up as late—is because we don't do programs for the sake of doing them. Programs are tools that exist to help you live out your values.

Once a program is no longer the best way to live out your values and accomplish your mission, you need to take it out back and shoot it. If this offends you remember two things: 1) I'm from Texas and that's how we roll and 2) I want to make sure I get your attention.

Stale programs that have exceeded their expiration date are an energy drain on everybody. They kill momentum in your organization. They frustrate the people who lead them because they feel like nobody else cares about their program. They don't. Which is the other reason they're a drain—nobody wants to go but often they care about the people leading it and they don't want to let them down.

This is why it's so important for us to know our values and constantly evaluate how we're living them out. We want our values to be *actual*—easy to experience and clear to all, not *aspirational*—only existing in our minds or on our website.

As the lead pastor, this attitude has to begin with me. And it's not easy or comfortable. Every year our leadership team gathers for several days and we put all our programs and initiatives on the table. We ask the hard questions:

What do we need to stop doing?

Are these bearing fruit or have they become an empty tradition?

Healthy relationships have enough trust and relational capital to get this honest, even when it means we don't agree and we have to work through conflict. Our values are too important not to go there. There's too much at stake.

I don't stop with the programs, I take it another step further. I ask, "*What do you want me to stop doing?*" When you empower people to be honest, they will. And sometimes the truth hurts.

They've told me, "*We want you to get off your phone when you come into a meeting. You prowl around like a panther and get all fired up.*"

Okay…that's true…I'll work on it.

"*You need to trust us to do our job and stop micro-managing.*"

Tell me how you really feel.

"*No more emotional outbursts. It freaks us out.*"

Living this way makes you vulnerable, but it also creates a culture of openness and trust. I live this way not because it's easy or it's comfortable but because I don't want there to be a gap between the me I think I am and the me everybody else lives with. I want my values to be actual, lived out in each of my relationships. That won't happen without constant evaluation.

Over these next few chapters I'll describe our values in detail, why they're so important to who God's called us to be and how we live them out on a daily basis in all our environments.

CHAPTER EIGHT

THE BIBLE IS WORTH IT

Core Value #1: Bible

We value the Bible as God's revealed truth and the catalyst for life, transformation and change.

The Word of God is one of the greatest gifts He has given us. It's so many things—divinely inspired, relevant, applicable, perfect, supernatural, simple, complex, comforting and challenging. It literally is the last word—nothing will be added to it and it has the final say in the questions of how we live our lives, lead our families, and function as a church.

So many great stories have a twist—an unexpected plot development that completely changes your perspective. You don't see it coming and then all of a sudden…BAM! Everything you thought you knew gets turned upside down.

This is not that twist.

Nope. This is an official announcement from the department of redundancy. This one comes straight from Captain Obvious.

Grass is green. The sky is blue. Milestone Church loves and values the Bible.

I'll give you a minute to recover.

I realize this makes me sound like a second-grade Sunday school teacher. I understand you saw this one coming. I'm aware that for many people this makes me sound old-fashioned, unrefined and out of touch. Now I may be some or all of those things, but it's not because of God's Word.

You may be thinking, *"Jeff, you have to say that…you're the pastor. You sit around all day reading the Bible with a candle saying, 'Helloooo brooo-thherrr."*

I get it. I know how most people imagine the life of ministry. They think it's all Bible reading and golf.

But I don't love and value the Bible because I'm a pastor. It's not for my job security or to stay on good terms with *"The Man Upstairs."*

I'm not trying to solve the Bible Code, discover the secret identity of the antichrist or prepare for the final exam we have to pass in order to get into heaven.

I value God's Word because I desperately need it.

The Bible is the primary means by which we relate to God, we grow closer to Him, we understand who He is, what He cares about and how He's called us to live.

I don't have to read it…I *get* to.

Two Very Different Things

Not only is the Bible the best-selling book of all-time, but the desire to replicate it was the driving force behind the invention of the printing press, which has resulted in the printing of books as we know it today. Gutenberg invented his machine with the goal of creating his masterpiece—the Gutenberg Bible, manufactured sometime in the 1450s.[1]

This makes sense when you consider the name "Bible" literally means "*the books.*"

To this day it's still the most widely owned and most read book in the United States. 88 percent of the population owns a Bible and 20 percent of all Americans have read it from beginning to end at some point in their lives. 8 out of 10 people believe the Bible is sacred or holy and 61 percent wish they read it more often.[2]

Even young people see the value in the wisdom of Scripture and are twice as interested as the general population in what the Bible has to say about family conflict, parenting, sexuality and dating.

The statistical evidence is overwhelming. Americans value the Bible, but here's the problem: this is clearly an aspirational value, not an actual one.

After years of research and analysis George Barna and Jim Castelli said, "*Americans revere the Bible—but, by and large, they don't read it. And because they don't read it, they have become a nation of biblical illiterates.*"[3]

Americans like the idea of reading the Bible much more than they actually like to read it. They want it to sit on their bookshelves or nightstands as

1   Incredibly, 48 of these are still around today including one on display at the New York Public library.
2   These statistics come from a fascinating study conducted in a partnership between the American Bible Society & the Barna Group. https://www.barna.org/barna-update/culture/605-what-do-americans-really-think-about-the-bible (accessed 6/24/2013)
3   http://www.albertmohler.com/2004/06/29/the-scandal-of-biblical-illiteracy-its-our-problem-2/ (accessed 6/24/2013)

a spiritual prop, but they're generally unwilling to turn off the TV, their phone or their computer to focus on the Scripture.

It's one thing to say you value the Bible—it's something very different to have your life shaped and transformed by God's Word.

The gap between these things can be pretty funny. Some of this same research shows 12 percent of those polled identified Joan of Ark as Noah's wife. More than 50 percent of high school seniors thought Sodom and Gomorrah were husband and wife, and more than 80 percent were certain the Bible says, *"God helps those who help themselves."*

This list could go on and on. Biblical literacy in our culture continues to plummet. Recently The New York Times, long considered the bastion of journalistic integrity, in an editorial mourning the declining influence of the positive values religion provides, mistakenly described Saul, David and Esther as characters from the Torah (*the first five books of the Old Testament*) before quoting Jesus' words to the Corinthians.[4]

Great, right? The liberal media finally gives Jesus a favorable shout-out. Except it wasn't Jesus…it was *Paul's* letter to the Corinthians.

The fact that The Times had to print an embarrassing retraction meant it wasn't only the best-selling and award-winning author who didn't know the details of Scripture…none of the editors did either.

Unfortunately, we can't blame the media, young people, or the average American. Like most things, the problem starts with the church. Lifeway, the publications division of the Southern Baptists did a massive study in 2012 and learned only 19 percent of Christians read their Bible on a daily basis. [5]

---

4   http://www.nytimes.com/2013/06/14/opinion/brooks-religion-and-inequality.html (accessed 6/24/2013)
5   http://blog.christianitytoday.com/ctliveblog/archives/2012/09/lifeway-research-ed-stetzer-most-churchgoers-do-not-read-bible-daily.html (accessed 6/24/2013)

The survey wasn't looking for "*an hour of power.*" They didn't set a standard of a solid 30 minutes of study. They didn't read it at all.

Before you start feeling judgmental, consider this wasn't a group of lukewarm attenders. 90 percent of them said they "*desire to please and honor Jesus in all that I do,*" and yet 8 out of 10 of them don't read the Bible on a daily basis.

Clearly, there's a gap between saying we value God's Word and living in a way that supports this belief. If you talked with enough people and did significant research you would probably find a variety of reasons why this is the case. But in my experience there are two reasons far more common than the rest.

The Two Main Reasons People Don't Read the Bible

The first reason people struggle to actually read God's Word is because they find it difficult to understand. If you've ever opened the "*Good Book,*" you know it's not really a book—it's a collection of books. It's more like a library than a book. Over a span of nearly 1,500 years, forty men used three different languages to write the sixty-six different books included in the official canon (collection) of Scripture.

Occasionally when someone realizes this it leaves them a little puzzled or intimidated and they want to ask:

- Where should I start—in Genesis or somewhere in the New Testament?
- Are the Old Testament and the New Testament part one and part two?
- Why does it have all those complex instructions about what to wear and eat?
- What do all those ancient, cultural customs have to do with us today?

Then this person they work with had a friend who read *The Da Vinci Code*... or saw a documentary...or read this blog on the internet...or knew this skeptic who said the Bible was written by the church to oppress people.

By themselves, any of these objections are goofy, but combined with the complexity of Scripture it leaves the Bible unread on the shelf or the nightstand. It may impress your friends and make you feel more spiritual but it won't impact you if you've never read it.

Objections and critiques like these are never enough to keep someone who's hungry from diving into God's Word, but like the guy who loves donuts and pizza more than he loves his diet, if you're already looking for a reason to give yourself an out, you'll find one.

The trustworthiness of Scripture has been ridiculed and attacked for centuries by some of mankind's most gifted thinkers. The problem is, the facts are overwhelmingly in favor of the Bible.

Usually the critic is only left with personal vendettas and arrogant bluster—like the guy who confidently declares, "*The Bible is filled with contradictions!*" When you ask him to show you, he flips and flips but for some reason can't seem to find one. Another favorite notion of skeptics is this idea that the Bible is a tool used to oppress people and to promote the church's agenda—which sounds compelling until you actually read either Scripture or history.

In the context of its culture the Bible was miles beyond anything the world had ever seen in its dignity for servants, women and children, the poor, the sick and even enemies. The origin of hospitals, colleges and universities, music and the arts, and the end of the European slave trade can all be traced back to the body of Christ in the earth. The writers of the Bible also included all kinds of embarrassing details about themselves that I would have left out if I was telling the story to make myself look good.

As for manipulating people by twisting Jesus' words, it turns out lots of people wanted to make a name for themselves by writing their own version of a gospel—portions of more than 28 of them have been discovered. The early church dismissed them because they were fabricated, riddled with crazy thoughts and weren't inspired by the Holy Spirit.

And what about the guys who actually wrote what we consider the New Testament? Nearly all of them were murdered because of what they believed. If they had fabricated or manipulated Jesus' words they probably wouldn't have been willing to die to protect their secret.

Charles Colson, one of President Richard Nixon's advisors went to prison for his role in the Watergate scandal. He was not a follower of Christ but while he was serving his time he came to the conclusion that if his peers—brilliant, cunning, Ivy League-educated advisors to the most powerful man in the free world—couldn't keep their secret when facing prison and public scrutiny, then a bunch of uneducated fisherman and tax collectors wouldn't have been able to keep their secret from mankind.

Tens of thousands of ancient manuscripts of the Bible have been discovered and their consistency is remarkable. This demonstrates the authenticity of God's Word—they don't just agree in concepts and big ideas, they line up in phrases, words and in most cases, each letter. History is filled with critics and skeptics who set out to disprove Scripture...only to end up discovering and worshipping the God of the Bible in the process.[6]

If you genuinely want to learn, not understanding the Bible isn't a quality excuse not to read it—if anything, it should be motivation for further and more committed study. To their credit I've met many people who had genuine questions about the Bible, Jesus and the Christian faith who studied Scripture, engaged in open dialogue and processed through their issues.

---

6   Two noteworthy examples are Lee Strobel (journalist and author of "The Case for Christ") and Simon Greenleaf (Professor Emeritus of Law at Harvard who wrote the basis by which all jury testimony is administered in court to this day).

I love this approach and welcome anyone, with any doubts, to walk along this journey with us.

What I have a difficult time respecting is someone who makes up their mind without committing to this process. I've found when you feel obligated to do something—doing high school math homework, or eating more broccoli and less ice cream—you may give it a shot for a little while, but you're looking for any reason to give up.

But when you're passionate about something, you throw yourself into it, you lose track of time, you stay up way too late and put off other things even when you don't totally grasp all the intricacies. I've seen dozens of guys do this with golf, hunting, the stock market, and twenty other time-consuming hobbies.

Nobody has to nag or inspire them to spend hour after hour reading up on the best swing techniques for their driver, future trends to build the best portfolio or countless hours in their garage fine-tuning their new bow.

Okay, you probably figured out that one may apply to me but I'm even more excited to read Scripture.

And yes, ladies do this too—I may not relate or know what consumes their time (or I don't want to guess and get myself into trouble), but it happens constantly.

In a moment, I'll give you a few practical tips to help anyone who really wants to understand and benefit from reading the Bible and who has the courage to actually do what it says.

Which is the biggest reason why people stop reading Scripture—it's not because we don't understand. That's not the deal breaker. The real problem is we don't like what it says.

Jesus' Love Language

If you grew up in America, you probably read Mark Twain in school—remember Tom Sawyer and Huckleberry Finn? Twain was an outspoken critic of religion but from time to time he said some incredibly insightful things. I love what he said about this issue.

> It ain't the parts of the Bible that I can't understand that bother me, it's the parts that I do understand.[7]

If you only read The Sermon on the Mount[8] for the rest of your life, you'd have enough to challenge you every single day. This is especially true for Christians. Anyone who's spent considerable time with the Bible will tell you—you don't read it…it reads you.

[GOD'S WORD] ABSOLUTELY JUDGES THE THOUGHTS AND INTENTIONS OF OUR HEARTS.

Hebrews 4:12 says it this way: *"The word of God is living and active and sharper than any two-edged sword, and piercing as far as the division of soul and spirit, of both joints and marrow, and able to judge the thoughts and intentions of the heart."*

It's sharp. It cuts deep. It was written thousands of years ago by forty different men who lived in ancient, agricultural cultures in languages we can't speak and yet it jumps off the page and slaps us in the face.

---

7   Mark Twain quoted from http://www.goodreads.com/quotes/tag/bible?page=2 (accessed 6/24/2013)
8   The greatest sermon ever preached and the single longest teaching Jesus gives in Scripture can be found in Matthew 5-7.

It absolutely judges the thoughts and intentions of our hearts.

The brilliant philosopher Søren Kierkegaard observed this tendency and captured this truth so clearly.

> *The Bible is very easy to understand. But we Christians are a bunch of scheming swindlers. We pretend to be unable to understand it because we know very well that the minute we understand, we are obligated to act accordingly.* [9]

Ouch. That's gonna leave a mark. At least he included himself and said "*we.*"

Some of you at this point are thinking, "*Jeff…come on…the guy's name (it is a guy, right?) is Søren. Who cares what he thinks.*" Okay. I hear you but you're not getting off this easy. He's not the only one who feels this way.

Jesus isn't freaking out over these survey results. He's not the least bit surprised. Better than anyone, He understands the challenges of the human heart. This problem is not new to our generation.

One day as He was walking along teaching and ministering to people He asked a simple question. "*Why do you call me 'Lord, Lord,' and do not do what I say?*"[10]

The Bible doesn't tell us how the large crowd gathered around Him responds. He's speaking to the disciples and I imagine most of them were looking down at their sandals, off into the distance or pretending to wave at somebody they recognized in the crowd.

---

9   Søren Kierkegaard, "Provocations: Spiritual Writings of Søren Kierkegaard" http://www.goodreads.com/quotes/tag/bible (accessed 6/24/2013)

10 Appropriately, this passage actually comes from Luke's abbreviated version of the Sermon on the Mount. You can find it in chapter 6:46-49.

Any option other than looking back at Jesus would have been more comfortable.

Jesus isn't trying to condemn them, to guilt them into obedience, or to get them to be more religious like the Pharisees. He's trying to redefine their relationship with God's commands.

He doesn't want them to follow rules—He wants their hearts to be connected to His.

Before they have a chance to answer, He goes on to give the parable of the wise builder who builds his house on the rock, not the sand. God's Word, His commandments and His laws weren't given arbitrarily. They're not random or insignificant. They're designed to give us life and to help us overcome the pounding storms life will continue to throw at us. But they're not purely pragmatic either.

By the time we get to the fourteenth chapter of John, things have kicked up several notches. Within days Jesus will be betrayed, arrested, tried, beaten and ultimately crucified. In anticipation of these events, He shares some of His most insightful and emotionally charged words with His disciples. In this context He returns to this idea from Luke 6, but this time His language isn't pragmatic—it's deeply relational.

Jesus never read Gary Chapman's book on love languages, but He makes it really clear how He receives love. Several times He tells them the one who loves Him is the one who "*keeps my commands.*" But this time the reward for this obedience is not a house that endures storms—it's far more relational.

The first time Jesus defines what it means to love Him, He promises the Father will send anyone who lives this way an Advocate, the Spirit of truth who will never leave them.[11] He also promises not to leave them as orphans but to return to them and to show who He is. One of the disciples

---

11   This is the Holy Spirit and Jesus elaborates more fully on their coming relationship with the third person of the Trinity in chapters 15 and 16. We'll talk about the Holy Spirit more explicitly in Chapter 13.

doesn't get this—we're not sure if he doesn't think it's fair or if he wants to know how he got invited to this "in crowd."

This is the third time Jesus connects loving Him with keeping His commands. He is intentionally as definitive as He can be so that His disciples are crystal clear on the issue.

> Jesus replied, 'Anyone who loves me will obey my teaching. My Father will love them, and we will come to them and make our home with them. Anyone who does not love me will not obey my teaching. These words you hear are not my own; they belong to the Father who sent me.'

This may not sound like a big deal for you and me but for the disciples this was mind-blowing. The Father's home was the Holy of Holies and only the High Priest could enter there once a year after a series of elaborate sacrifices.

Jesus was suggesting the God who created the universe, who appeared to Abraham, who met with Moses in the burning bush and on the mountain, who parted the Red Sea, who brought His people into the Promised Land, who thundered from the heavens when His Son was baptized…this God would make His home…IN them.

That's kind of a big deal.

Once we see it this way it changes everything in how we approach spending time with God in His Word. Reading the Bible isn't a spiritual chore like flossing or going to the gym. It's not a box we're supposed to check off and get out of the way so we can enjoy the things we really like doing.

Too many of us think of it this way.

It's not something we have to do—it's an incredible privilege we're invited into that literally millions of men and women who loved God with their whole being were never afforded. For the overwhelming majority of Christian history, the idea of having multiple copies of the Bible sitting around our house, our work or our car that we never actually read is unimaginable.

Jesus felt so strongly about this He repeated Himself multiple times and attached promises to how the Trinity responds to the one who knows and keeps God's Word.

Remember the research Lifeway did? Ninety percent of Christians want to please and honor Jesus in all they do. Jesus appreciates this so much He makes it unmistakably clear.

You can get a T-Shirt, a bumper sticker, go to church every day and shout how much you love Jesus from the rooftops and completely miss the point.

You say you love Jesus? Great. He said you show it by keeping His commands.

Good intentions can't get this done. Willpower alone, even from the most disciplined among us, doesn't work. The only way this is possible is by spending time with God in His Word. Psalm 119:11 echoes this idea, "*Your word I have treasured in my heart, that I may not sin against you.*"[12] Some versions say "hidden" instead, but I like "treasured" better.

Whatever we treasure most, fills our heart.

Whatever our minds focus on will dominate our thoughts. Paul explains it this way: "*So letting your sinful nature control your mind leads to death. But letting the Spirit control your mind leads to life and peace. For the sinful nature is always hostile to God. It never did obey God's laws, and it never will.*"[13]

We don't read the Bible to make God love us; we do it to demonstrate our love for Him. Of course, as we do, we quickly realize we only love Him

---

12   This is the NASB. The ESV says "stored" while the NIV, the NLT and NKJV all use a version of hid/hidden.

13   Romans 8:6-7 (NLT)

because He first loved us. When we were hostile in our minds, disobedient in our hearts, broken in our nature and evil in our intentions, He loved us perfectly and completely. We don't realize this on our own—we need God's Word to transform us so we can see this clearly.

Religion is powerless to lead you here. It nags, torments, compares and ridicules you into doing more to show yourself righteous. A genuine relationship with Jesus says that on your own you can never be righteous enough, but it won't leave you there.

Like Jesus said in John 14, your Advocate, the Spirit of truth, comes along side to lead and guide you into truth and to show you who Jesus is as God makes His home in you. This is why we read the Bible—in order to know and love God.

When you see God for who He is you discover His presence is irresistible. You don't ever want to go back to living without Him. Save your to-do list for your errands. Reading your Bible is much more about who you're with than what you're doing.

So How Do I Get Started?

It wouldn't be right for me to challenge you so hard without giving you some practical ways to live this out.

The first thing you need to do is to commit to study the Word in church. Listen, pay attention, take notes, talk about it in small group and reflect on it during the week. I can't overstate the importance of this.

Most people don't realize the idea of individual quiet time is at best a couple hundred years old. I believe in it and I want to help you do it, but the primary way throughout history Christians have studied God's Word has been in community, not isolation. As Americans we believe fiercely in independence; we're quick to pull the "*Me & Jesus*" card as if it were more spiritual.

You can quickly get yourself into trouble when you break out on your own and start saying things like, *"God showed me this,"* or *"This is what this means to me..."*

I've never met anyone who said, *"Someday I'd love to become a heretic. I want to read all kinds of crazy ideas into the Bible that aren't there,"* but I've met a lot of people this statement accurately describes.

The Bible is for everyone—it's not reserved for scholars, theologians and a select few. But that doesn't mean we shouldn't use every wisdom and resource we can to seek the clearest possible meaning.

In our weekend services and in all of our ministry environments, we always try our best to model a coherent, accessible approach to studying, interpreting and applying Scripture. This is highly intentional—our goal is to model what this looks like together so you will have the confidence and the ability to do it on your own.

> # THE BIBLE IS NOT RESERVED FOR SCHOLARS, THEOLOGIANS AND A SELECT FEW.

To do this we spend a great deal of thought and energy describing the context of a passage. Context leads us to ask all kinds of questions: who wrote it, who were they writing to, what kind of literary genre is being used, how does it relate to the rest of Scripture, how does it point to Jesus and how can it best be applied to us today?

This is the most common mistake people make. They treat the Bible as a disconnected series of stories, commands and promises—like a box filled with fortune cookies, an encyclopedia or one of those magic 8-balls you played with as a kid. They shake it up, pull out a sentence and take it as an isolated direct line from God.

Although it spans sixty-six books penned by forty men over the span of approximately 1,500 years, the Bible is one big story. And you're not the main character. Neither am I. All of Scripture points us to Jesus in order that we might know and love Him more. That's why it exists.

One of my favorite Bibles is for children, but I've seen it help many adults understand and appreciate Scripture in a whole new way. *The Jesus Storybook Bible* connects the dots for you as it tells the stories through a lens that always points back to Jesus. It's almost like training wheels—after you've seen it modeled it becomes much easier to do it on your own.

The Bible is not an instruction manual. It's not the original self-help/how-to book. It's not a mysterious series of code filled with the directions to a treasure or the identity of the second shooter on the grassy knoll.

This isn't something unique to Milestone and I'm certainly not breaking new ground here. The healthy, vibrant church has always related to Scripture this way.

Martin Luther wrote, "*It is beyond question that all the Scriptures point to Christ alone. The whole Bible is about Him.*" His fellow reformer John Calvin said it this way: "*We ought to read the Scriptures with the express design of finding Christ in them.*"

If God created an all-time ranking of preachers or communicators, I'm guessing Charles Spurgeon would be in the Top 10. History remembers him as the "*Prince of Preachers.*" He stated, "*Preach Christ, always and everywhere. He is the whole gospel. His person, offices and work must be our one great, all-comprehending theme.*"

Here's how you can live this out practically. When you sit down to read the Bible, or put it on in your car, or read it on your phone, your computer or your laptop, before you begin simply say, "*Jesus, I'm reading your Word because I want to know and love you more. Help me to find you in all your power, your glory, your love and your goodness and give me the ability to obey you with my whole heart.*"

This is also the reason why I encourage first-time readers to start with the Gospel of John. While the whole Bible points to Christ, in John He practically jumps off the page. As you become more familiar with Him, you'll find it easier to understand.

The guiding principle for basic Bible interpretation is to always read and understand Scripture from the whole to the part. This means when you read any single verse, you always do so in light of the larger message of Scripture.

For example, in John 6:53-54 Jesus tells the disciples unless they eat His flesh and drink His blood they have no life, but all those who do so will have eternal life and be raised up on the last day. Taken out of context you might assume Jesus imagined cannibal or vampire training to be part of the discipleship process.

But when you consider the rest of the story, how the crowd and the disciples responded, Jesus' understanding of the dietary laws of the Old Testament and His desire to please the Father in everything He did, it becomes clear that this is not His intended meaning.

In Philippians 4:13 Paul writes, "*For I can do everything through Christ who gives me strength.*" At first glance it sounds like a blank check from Jesus— make a wish, any wish, and magically it will be yours. But in context Paul is talking about trusting God to meet his needs, and that whether he has everything or he has nothing, he's learned to be content in whatever God provides.

A great way to practice this is to utilize one of the principles Howard Hendricks suggests: zoom in/zoom out. Healthy, balanced study of the Bible includes zooming in—on one passage, verse, sentence or even a single word—and then zooming out—to the chapter, the series of chapters, the book as a whole, the New or Old Testament and finally all of Scripture.

Consider the verse we just discussed. Encouragement and insight can be found focusing on the phrase, "in Christ" or the word "everything." But to really grasp the passage we should also think about chapter four as a whole—in verse six Paul encourages us not to be anxious or worry about anything but to pray.

If we do this, verse seven promises the peace of God will guard our hearts and our minds. We can zoom out further and discover all the ways God provided for Paul and the incredible love and goodness God showed him.

Viewing the World the Way God Does

Another phenomenal benefit of reading and applying God's Word is, over time, you'll begin to value what He values, love what He loves and develop a biblical approach to every area of your life.

The Bible has so much to say about the things we deal with on a daily basis—how we handle our money, how we develop a loving environment in our homes, how we conduct ourselves at work, how we study and learn, how we treat our neighbors and care for our community, and so much more.

God cares deeply about all of these basic assumptions we make everyday about how the world works, what we value and how we live our lives. Look at the book of Proverbs—it's divided into 31 chapters (one for each day), covers every one of these subjects, and is broken down into bite-sized pieces.

As a young boy my dad challenged me to read the book of Proverbs every day. Growing up in church people would say, "That boy has wisdom beyond his years." It didn't fall out of the sky—it came from reading Proverbs every morning.

Scholars call the result of these unchallenged assumptions a "*worldview*." It sounds so intelligent and impressive—but the truth is we all have one. If you have the sudden urge to stop reading so you can text a friend and tell them you're developing your worldview…go ahead. I understand.

I'll be here when you get back.

While all of us have a worldview, most of us don't put much effort into it. We fall into what feels right, what we heard somewhere, or what lets us do what we want in the moment. These are unchallenged assumptions—nobody carries around a printed copy of their comprehensive worldview, but when somebody asks you, "*What's the most important thing in your life?*" your worldview determines your answer.

And while you may have a fish on the back of your car, a pack of Testamints and the latest update of YouVersion on all your gadgets, there's no guarantee you have a biblical worldview.

ONE OF THE BEST WAYS TO FIND OUT MORE ABOUT WHO WE ARE IS TO ATTEND A MONTHLY GATHERING WE CALL *DISCOVERY 101.*

Lots of people who call themselves Christians believe that while the Bible may be true for them, that doesn't necessarily mean it's true for everyone.

Others suggest there are many equal and culturally defined paths to God. Still more suggest the traditional understanding of marriage and family is outdated and in need of new and more progressive definitions.

Each of these answers is directly determined by a worldview.

When someone is new to Milestone one of the best ways for them to find out more about who we are is to attend a monthly gathering we call "*Discovery 101.*" If you're a part of the Milestone family you probably remember when you attended—it's an opportunity for me to share our values and for you to kick the tires, ask questions and see what we're all about.

Somewhere along the way I started this habit of taking a Bible and lifting it over my head. And every time at least one person tells me how much it helped them understand what I was talking about. I've done it ever since.

My intention is not to generate some much-needed comic relief—I seem to do alright in this area. The gesture demonstrates our commitment to the authority of Scripture. The Bible has the last word, the final say in how we view life. It doesn't matter how we feel in the moment. It's not up for a vote. The Bible—not our own whims, thoughts or desires—ultimately decides what's true.

Our culture is filled with narratives—carefully crafted stories that attempt to explain why the world is the way it is. Many of these narratives are incredibly compelling—they appear to have definitive, concrete answers that help us make sense of the world. If we don't continually evaluate our worldview on the basis of God's Word, we can easily be deceived by half-truths, faulty assumptions and flat-out lies.

This danger is compounded by the reality that each of us are lied to constantly, every day of our lives. We lie to ourselves, we read intention into statements that is not there, we're manipulated by clever marketing and the values of this fallen world. The primary way the enemy attacks us is through lies.

In John 8 Jesus describes the devil as *"a murderer from the beginning, not holding to the truth, for there is no truth in him. When he lies, he speaks his native language, for he is a liar and the father of lies."* The only way you can discover a lie is if you know the truth. The Bible doesn't view truth as a series of propositional truths to be remembered, but a person to be known. Jesus didn't say, "I know the truth." He said, "I am...the Truth."[14]

If you tell me you want to know the difference between the truth and a lie, according to Scripture what you're really saying is you want to be able to recognize Jesus' voice above the enemy's[15]. The Word is the tool He gives you to help you do this. He modeled this for us when He went into the desert to be tempted by the devil in Luke 4. Every time the enemy lied to Him, Jesus used the Word to drive him away.

> # THE ONLY WAY YOU CAN DISCOVER A LIE IS IF YOU KNOW THE TRUTH.

You didn't get to choose whether or not you wanted the devil to lie to you— he's hated your guts since before you were born. But you do get to decide what you're going to do about it.

I get so sick of watching Christians get kicked around by this toothless bully—but I see it all the time. A few years back, the Barna Group found more than 41 percent of people who called themselves Christians didn't believe the devil was real—he was a symbol of evil, not an actual, supernatural being.

---

14   John 14:6

15   This is what John says in 1 John 3:10. He says the children of God and the children of the devil are obvious to everyone because God's children do what is right.

It's hard to fight back against someone you don't believe in.

Have you put the Word above your feelings, what our culture says, what seems right to you or what the majority has decided is true? If not, you've got a worldview...but even if you love God, it's not biblical.

Even if you have embraced the Bible as the ultimate authority in your life, in order to make this an actual value and not an aspirational one, I want to give you two more practical tools to help you live this every day.

"To Chew" & "Say the Same Word"

For the past 19 months, I've had the same small card on the dash of my car. It's not directions. It's not a grocery list I keep forgetting to throw away. It's not a dry-cleaning stub.

On this little card I've written out Ephesians 3:20, Leviticus 25:23 and Psalm 24:1. Every time I drive somewhere I look at them, I say them out loud and I think about them. I chose these Scriptures because they remind me of God's character and His Word, not of my circumstances or my feelings. I've got an active mind. If I don't keep it reigned in, it bounces all over the place and before I know it I'm a nervous wreck.

What I've been doing is...meditating.

Hang on. Don't freak out. Don't chuck this book across the room. I didn't sit in the lotus position. No crystals were involved. I didn't do hot yoga. I never said, "*Ohm.*"

I know people get scared when they hear this word—it brings an image of a weird, Eastern mystic contorting himself. But that's not what the Bible means when it uses this word—and it uses this word a bunch.

When God called Joshua into the Promised Land, over and over He told him to be strong and courageous. But then He told him how to do it. He said, *"Keep this Book of the Law always on your lips; meditate on it day and night, so that you may be careful to do everything written in it."*[16]

The word meditate means *"to chew."* One of the reasons some of us are put off by meditation is because the Eastern version focuses on staring off into space as you empty your mind. But biblical meditation isn't about emptying your mind—it's about filling it with God's Word.

I'm not trying to be gross (or make you hungry) but when you chew on something, you turn it over and over again until it breaks down to a point where you can digest it. That's what it means to meditate on God's Word. When I put those verses on the dash, every time I drove somewhere it turned over and over in my mind until I digested it and embraced it as truth.

When I didn't do this, my mind raced all over the place, I thought about everything that could go wrong and what I would have to do in those circumstances. I'm a naturally gifted worrier. I could have easily gone pro.

If you can worry, you can meditate. The first uses lies and fear to break you down emotionally before anything has even happened. The second takes the timeless truth of God's Word, fills you with perspective and gratitude and builds you up not because of your circumstances but because of the goodness of God.

Which one would you choose?

Before God tells Joshua to meditate, He instructs him to keep the law on his lips. It's not enough for Joshua to read silently to himself. He won't get the full benefit from thinking about these things. He had to say it out loud. The same is true when it comes to reading the Word. We call this "confession."

---

16   Joshua 1:8 (NIV)

Confession means *"to say the same word."* It's an agreement. You're going to agree with something. Intentionally leaning in to God's Word through confession is making the choice to agree with God, not because you understand everything, you have no problems or you have the overwhelming feeling to do it.

At first, you may even feel like a crazy person. You're talking to yourself. You're wondering if the person in the car next to you can see you. But when everything around you starts shaking, you may find yourself desperate enough to try it. And once you see how it changes you, you'll never go back.

Confessing God's Word keeps you sane and off the emotional rollercoaster all of us find ourselves on from time to time. I'm passionate but I'm not emotional. I think about feelings more than I feel them. And yet I'm convinced something powerful happens when we say out of our mouths what God has declared in His Word. It calibrates our hearts and our minds.

Some people are a little skittish about this because they've seen or heard somebody abuse this—the old *"name it and claim it."* Confession isn't manipulating God to force Him to do something He doesn't want to do. It's not digging through spiritual fine print to find some sort of loophole. God's not a cosmic bellhop who responds to *"magic words."*

The primary reason we confess God's Word is because we want to align our hearts with His Word and like the old hymn says, our hearts are *"prone to wander."*

When everything in the world starts to shake the one thing you can count on is the Word of God. People anchor their lives to all kinds of things —their ability, their success, their favorable circumstances. But the only thing you can count on, the only thing you can be certain of is the truth of God's Word.

This isn't only for pastors, theologians or Bible scholars. You're never too young, or too old, to get started.

CONFESSING GOD'S WORD
KEEPS YOU SANE AND OFF
THE EMOTIONAL ROLLERCOASTER
ALL OF US FIND OURSELVES ON
FROM TIME TO TIME.

BIBLE

Key Points

- I value God's Word because I desperately need it. The Bible is the primary means by which we relate to God, we grow closer to Him, we understand who He is, what He cares about and how He has called us to live.
- Americans like the idea of reading the Bible much more than they actually like to read it. They want it to sit on their bookshelf or nightstand as a spiritual prop, but they're generally unwilling to turn off the TV, their phone or their computer to focus on Scripture.
- It's sharp. It cuts deep. It was written thousands of years ago by forty different men who lived in ancient, agricultural cultures in languages we can't speak and yet it jumps off the page and slaps us in the face. It absolutely judges the thoughts and intentions of our hearts.
- God's Word, His commandments and His laws weren't given arbitrarily. They're not random or insignificant. They're designed to give us life and to help us overcome the pounding storms life will continue to throw at us.
- It's not something we have to do. It's an incredible privilege we're invited into that literally millions of men and women who loved God with their whole being were never afforded.
- We don't read the Bible to make God love us; we do it to demonstrate our love for Him. Of course as we do, we quickly realize we only love Him because He first loved us.
- The guiding principle for basic Bible interpretation is to always read and understand Scripture from the whole to the part. This means

when you read any single verse, you always do so in light of the larger message of Scripture.

- The Bible has the last word, the final say in how we view life. It doesn't matter how we feel in the moment. It's not up for vote. The Bible, not our own whims, thoughts, or desires ultimately decides what is true.
- The primary reason we want to confess God's Word is because we want to align our hearts with His Word and like the old hymn says, our hearts are "prone to wander." When everything in the world starts to shake, the one thing you can count on is the Word of God.

Discussion Questions

- What do you find to be the biggest barriers to reading Scripture on a daily basis?
- What are some key tools you can use to help you study while reading and interpreting Scripture?
- What is the value in meditating on and confessing Scripture?

Practical Steps

- Study the Scriptures in church, take notes, reflect on them during the week, and talk about them in your small group.
- Remember the Bible is one big story. You're not the main character— it's not about you. All Scripture points to Jesus. Start by reading the Gospel of John.
- Context matters. Always read and interpret any passage or verse in light of the Bible as a whole. Zooming in and zooming out will help you do this.
- Develop a biblical worldview. Reading one chapter of the book of Proverbs each day will help.
- Meditate on and confess God's Word.

CHAPTER NINE

THE MISSION IS WORTH IT

Value #2: Mission

We value the mission of God to reach and redeem individuals, families, neighborhoods, and beyond.

From the Garden of Eden to the Red Sea, from the wilderness to the Promised Land, from Nazareth to Calvary, and throughout all of history, God has been at work to love, save and restore people. Now that story continues in each of our lives.

As a loving Father, God initiates this process—He loves us, calls us, and pursues us long before we look for Him. His greatest desire is for all of us to turn from lives lived for ourselves to receive the life God has created us to live. When we do, He invites all of us to join Him in His mission in our own unique way. Though our

contributions are different, God values them all as we give and
contribute to what He's doing in the lives of people.

The world was a different place when I was a kid.

I'm not waxing nostalgic and I'm not about to launch into a tirade on all the ways our culture has eroded and how we need to work hard to bring back the *"good old days."* Some things are worse, some are better—but either way, spending your time and energy trying to bring back the good old days will leave you frustrated and exhausted.

When I was a kid I spent a lot of time playing outside. After school or during the summer, if I wasn't working on a project with my dad, my mom would send us outside to play. We didn't spend hours playing video games or surfing the internet—and not just because they hadn't been invented. For my generation, Mom sent you outside to play and you weren't coming back until it was time for dinner.

Between my active imagination and strong competitive instinct, I always found a way to keep busy. Back then you didn't specialize year round in one sport—you played them all. Football, baseball, basketball, golf—if the game had a ball and you kept score, I played it. I also roamed around my neighborhood with my BB gun, keeping my family safe from the dangerous threat of predators like squirrels and songbirds.

For every young man in a small town or rural area, your one constant companion is your BMX bike. A bike to a kid is like the Batmobile to Batman or Silver to the Lone Ranger. It's more than your primary source of independent transportation; it is your ticket to adventure.

For those unfamiliar, the purpose of a dirt bike is to ride through mud, rocks, fields, and of course, off homemade jumps. Through the eyes of a kid, the thin padding on the handle bar and the neck of the bike makes you virtually indestructible. If you could find a log, a rock, or just about anything with a little size and strength to it, along with a flat piece of wood…you were ready to fly like Evel Knievel.

We didn't watch the *X Games* on TV; we lived it on the dirt roads and muddy trails all over our community. Nobody wore bike helmets back then either—it's a good thing I've got a thick skull.

One of my friends who lived down the street was a kid named Chris Jones. We rode our dirt bikes everywhere, constantly challenging each other to jump higher and ride faster in our pursuit of adrenaline.

My StrengthsFinder test results tell me my number one theme is *"maximizer."* What this means is God wired the neural pathways in my brain to constantly ask the question, *"How can we do this bigger?"* or *"This is good, but we need to take it up several levels."*

If you know me, this doesn't surprise you.

Bigger and next level for 13-year-old-Jeff meant higher dirt bike jumps with bigger thrills. I've told you I'm a worrier, but my dad also taught me to think strategically. I'd walk around the jump adjusting it slightly, inspect the landing area, nod in approval once everything checked out and confidently make my way back to the take off zone. No way I was going to chicken out.

In those moments before I charged off on my bike pedaling as fast as I could, my thoughts often settled on, *"Okay, if I don't make it, I may break my arm, my leg or even die…but I feel so alive!"*

The truth was, death or serious danger was never in play. The jumps only seemed big—but in my mind I seriously thought I was risking my life. Before I took off I'd shout out, "If I die, tell my mom I love her!" as I raced towards the 18-inch ramp at the end of our makeshift runway.

A Baptist kid who spends his afternoon thinking about dying in a horrific bike accident naturally wants to make sure he's going to heaven when he dies. It's a no-brainer. More than a few times in church I'd heard, *"If you were to die tonight, do you know for certain you would escape the fires of hell?"*

I was convinced Chris and I had cheated death more than a few times and so I thought the good, Christian thing to do was to make sure he was going to escape those fires too. At church they'd encouraged me to tell other people about Jesus so I thought I'd give it a shot.

I asked Chris if he had a relationship with Jesus and he said he wasn't sure, so I told him about everything I knew about the gospel. When Chris heard Jesus loved him and died in His place so he could trade his sin for peace and eternal life with God, he said yes. He gave his life to Christ right there in my front yard as we prayed, leaning over the handlebars on our BMX bikes. We went to church on Wednesday night and he went public with his faith by celebrating in the waters of baptism.

It was the first time I'd led someone to Christ and in that moment something profound happened to me. Everything changed.

The thrill of partnering with God in His mission to reach the world was better than anything I had ever done on my dirt bike. I'd participated in making an eternal difference in the life of someone I cared about. It's a moment I'll never forget.

Almost 30 years later, I've never been more passionate about the incredible opportunity God gives us to join Him in what He's doing.

The Mystery of the Gospel

It's one thing for God to love us and to make a way for us to know and love Him in return, but to entrust us with this responsibility of demonstrating

His love to the world is hard for us to grasp. That's been God's plan from the beginning.

When sin, death and darkness covered the earth, God's mission to redeem and restore His creation wasn't simply done for mankind. God has always invited them to participate in the process. In Genesis 6 the earth is filled with so much wickedness God wants to press the reset button and start over. But he reaches out to Noah and his family and invites them to join Him.

In Genesis 12 God comes to a man named Abram and promises to bless him to such an incredible degree that all the nations of the earth would be blessed through his family. Six chapters later, God again comes to visit this man, whose name has been changed to Abraham. The Lord tells him He's on His way to destroy Sodom, but Abraham asks Him to spare them...and God agrees.

Scripture makes it abundantly clear God is sovereign (in total control) and all-sufficient (lacking nothing). He doesn't need our help to accomplish His purposes and yet because of His love for us and His desire to make us like Him, He invites us to participate with Him in His mission to redeem and restore the world.

From Abraham's children—both his natural and spiritual descendants—God has chosen to give His children a place in His mission. Although He made His covenant with one man and one family, God's purpose and His heart has always been to reach every family on the planet with the message of the Gospel. When Scripture talks about the end of history, God's Word is unmistakably clear this won't happen until every ethnos (group of people) on earth has heard the message of the hope and life available through faith in Jesus.

The principle is clear—whenever God moves in your life, whenever He blesses you, whenever His grace and peace transform you—it's always bigger than you.

He never intends His goodness to stop with you.

All those years back when I gave my life to Christ around my dining room table…God wasn't only thinking about me. He was thinking about Chris Jones, Eddie and Patrick, my own children, Alex Hatcher and very possibly…you.

He doesn't see me this way because I'm a pastor—He sees me this way because I'm His son. And if you're His child, He sees you the same way too. He's inviting you into His mission.

God's purpose for Abraham was bigger than him—it was for Isaac, Jacob and his twelve children. Those 12 children would form a nation, and through them the whole world would come to know and love the God of Abraham.

> # HE NEVER INTENDS
> ## HIS GOODNESS TO STOP
> ## WITH YOU.

God's purpose for Jesus was bigger than His Son—it was about 12 unknown, easy-to-overlook men who would follow Him, establish His Church and take the Gospel to the world.

It can be easy to overlook this pattern. For many years of his life, when he was known as Saul of Tarsus, the Apostle Paul completely missed it. He came to refer to it as "*the mystery of the Gospel*" throughout the New Testament.[1] God didn't change His mind or make it up as He went along—it had always been His plan from the foundation of the world.

---

1   Romans 16:25, 1 Corinthians 2:7, Ephesians 1:9, 3:3-9, 6:19, Colossians 1:26-27, 2:2, 4:3 and 1 Timothy 3:16.

That's what made it a mystery; once your eyes had been opened to it, you could see it written on every page.

The Great Commission…Who's Supposed To Do It?

God wanted to reach the whole world and He planned on using His children to do it. People who were far from God weren't to be treated as enemies, rivals, or objects but long-lost children waiting to come home.

The word *"mission"* comes from the Latin word meaning *"to send."* Before Jesus went to be with the Father, He made one of the defining statements in all of Scripture. It has come to be known as *"The Great Commission."*

And Jesus came and said to them: *"All authority in heaven and on earth has been given to me. Go therefore and make disciples of all nations, baptizing them in the name of the Father and of the Son and of the Holy Spirit, teaching them to observe all that I have commanded you. And behold, I am with you always, to the end of the age."*[2]

As a kid I remember holding up a handheld mirror to one of the big bathroom mirrors and freaking out. As I looked in the large mirror, inside the little mirror was an infinite image of another mirror. There were no broken links—it was open-ended.

That's what Jesus is saying here—*"You go make disciples. And you can tell they're disciples because they obeyed what I commanded you to do; which includes making disciples."*

This was the expectation of all of Jesus' followers in the early church. I love how Paul describes the mindset of someone who wants to share the Gospel and make disciples:

---

2   Matthew 28:18-20 ESV

So we have stopped evaluating others from a human point of view. At one time we thought of Christ merely from a human point of view. How differently we know Him now! This means that anyone who belongs to Christ has become a new person. The old life is gone; a new life has begun!

And all of this is a gift from God, who brought us back to Himself through Christ. And God has given us this task of reconciling people to Him. For God was in Christ, reconciling the world to Himself, no longer counting people's sins against them. And He gave us this wonderful message of reconciliation. So we are Christ's ambassadors; God is making His appeal through us. We speak for Christ when we plead, 'Come back to God!'[3]

I've read this passage hundreds of times. I've preached from it. I've memorized it...and still the words crackle and spark with life and power.

We've stopped evaluating others from a human point of view...anyone in Christ is a new creation...we've been given this wonderful message of reconciliation...we are Christ's ambassadors...God makes His appeal through us...we speak for Christ.

I don't know how anyone can take these words seriously and think God's pleased when people "play" church. This is not a game—God has given us a great deal of responsibility in His mission.

Notice what this passage doesn't say. It doesn't qualify "*we*" or "*us*" as pastors, missionaries, theologians or Bible teachers. Remember...this was one of Paul's letters to the Corinthians—a church so filled with drama and problems most American Christians would've left and started writing blogs about it. Yet Paul challenges them to embrace this mission to give everyone a chance to come home to God!

---

3   2 Corinthians 5:16-20 (NLT)

From God's perspective, all of His children, no matter if they've been with Him for five decades or five minutes, are His ambassadors. In fact, the role of the pastors and leaders is not to do ministry while the people watch. Ephesians 4:11-12 tells us it is the opposite.

> *So Christ Himself gave the apostles, the prophets, the evangelists,*
> *the pastors and teachers, to equip His people for works of service,*
> *so that the body of Christ may be built up...*[4]

The role of pastors and leaders isn't to accomplish the mission of God while everyone else works their job and lives their lives. It's to equip His people to serve and build the body of Christ.

As a Christian, my responsibility is to be equipped and do works of service—to love my neighbors, to tell people about Jesus, pray for those who are discouraged and sick and to make disciples. As the lead pastor of Milestone Church, my responsibility is to equip God's people to do the work of the ministry.

This distinction is massive.

So many people come to church to watch the pastor lead, preach and teach. They assume their role is to attend, observe and try to remember at least a little bit about what the pastor said. While this is a common cultural idea, it's not biblical.

The job of a pastor isn't to do ministry—it's to train and develop the people to join God in His mission to reach the world through the church.

Which brings up the question—what is God's mission? We know it includes individuals repenting of their sins and giving their lives to Christ, which then leads to telling others about Jesus...but could there be more?

---

4   NIV

God's Mission Is His Kingdom

From a distance, Jesus' life doesn't make a lot of sense.

For starters, the Bible makes it clear He's both fully God and fully man. Hebrews 1 tells us the universe was made through Him and He is the exact representation of the Father[5] and yet He humbled Himself and took on the form of a baby in order to come and live with us. He created the universe so He could have surrounded Himself with the fanfare and prestige fitting a king, but instead He chose to become the firstborn child of an older man and his teenage fiancée.

Most Bible scholars agree Jesus knew who He was by the time He was twelve years old, but He didn't leave His role as a carpenter until He was thirty. His public ministry consisted largely of walking around with twelve seemingly insignificant, average guys with the occasional miracle and dustup with religious leaders. Three short years and it was over.

The world has never been the same.

If Jesus' mission was to start a religion, reclaim the Holy Land and rebuild the temple or even to found a new nation with a mighty army to drive out all of His enemies, His strategy was terrible.

This is what the people in His day wanted from a Messiah. In some ways, it's still what most people want from one. Because His mission was not what they expected, a great number of them missed it completely.

I don't want this to happen to us.

After waiting 18 years, Jesus laid down his carpentry tools, left the shop and began to preach God's Word. Mark 1:14-15 records this historic event. *"Now after John was arrested, Jesus came into Galilee, proclaiming the gospel*

5   Hebrews 1:2-3 (NIV)

of God, and saying, 'The time is fulfilled, and the kingdom of God is at hand; repent and believe in the gospel.'"

These words are surprising. He doesn't mention heaven or hell. He doesn't say, *"Join my new group and you'll become a good, thoughtful, spiritual person."* He doesn't promise to make anyone's dreams come true. He's not accepting shout outs for platinum records or sports trophies like so many in our world today think He's after.

According to Jesus, God's gospel—His Good News—is that the kingdom of God is at hand. Other versions substitute *"come near,"* but the idea is clear: in the middle of human kingdoms, empires and nations, the time has come for a new Kingdom to break through. It's unlike any kingdom the world has ever seen—it's not ruled by a man, it wasn't seized by plotting or scheming, and it is governed by a set of values completely foreign to mankind.

This is Jesus' message—God's Kingdom has come. When He sends out His 12 disciples, this is what He instructs them to say to all those they meet. When He sends out seventy of His followers, this is what He commands them to communicate. And when He teaches how we should pray, among the first things to lead with is this desire for the Kingdom to rule on the earth as it rules in the heavens.

In this first century world, the announcement of the arrival of a new reigning kingdom was equivalent to a declaration of war. Jesus could have chosen to frame His message in any number of ways, but He chose this announcement of a kingdom and His identification with the Son of Man from Daniel 7.

> *In my vision at night I looked, and there before me was one like a son of man, coming with the clouds of heaven. He approached the Ancient of Days and was led into His presence. He was given authority, glory and sovereign power; all nations and peoples of every language worshipped Him. His dominion is an everlasting*

dominion that will not pass away, and His kingdom is one that will never be destroyed.

This isn't *"hippie Jesus"* hugging sheep and kissing babies with flowing brown locks encouraging people to find love and peace in whatever way felt right to them. It's a radical message—terrifying enough to make rivals want to kill Him and disprove His claims.

From the very beginning Jesus' point was clear—*"I'm not just a dude from Nazareth with messianic delusions. I'm following the will of my Father. He set this plan in motion and there's no stopping Him. In me, His Kingdom has finally come."*[6]

Right before Jesus starts announcing this, He's baptized, and something incredible happens. The Father booms from heaven in an audible voice (think about that!), *"This is my Son whom I love; with Him I am well pleased."*[7]

The Creator of the Universe, the Architect of Eden, the Grand Designer, the Author of Life has finally initiated His plan to redeem and restore this world. Freedom for the captive. Healing for the sick. A family for the orphan. Forgiveness for the guilty and rescue for the refugee. The kingdom Daniel saw while in exile in a foreign land. The kingdom the great prophets promised had finally come.

This wasn't a new way of thinking or a new ideology—this was a whole new way to be human.

Real Hope for A Broken World & Broken Lives

As I'm writing these words, Twitter is filled with reports of a government coup in Egypt. Protesters have been filling the streets demanding the current

---

6   This is my paraphrase—not an actual passage of Scripture but I'm guessing you already knew that. But hey, good job reading the footnotes!

7   Matthew 3:17, Mark 1:11, Luke 3:22

President (*an Islamist who was "elected" under dubious conditions a year ago after another similar removal from power*) relinquish his power and surrender his position. The nation is in turmoil and the people are filled with the sense that the world is broken.

We may not have military coups in our nation, but every election year our groups trot out their would-be messiahs who attempt to explain in detail how they've uniquely identified our real problems and how they alone hold the answers and the solutions necessary to ensure all of our dreams will come true. Power is exchanged, newly elected officials get their chance to make things right and the cycle goes on.

I'm not belittling the political process—I'm thankful for our nation and I believe we experience great freedom and opportunity here. I'm grateful for the men and women who serve our nation in any capacity—civil servants, law enforcement, and the military. I know many people (especially young leaders) feel a call to these roles and God makes it clear He works through every government in every nation.[8]

While our hope for change includes government and politics—it's much bigger than that. Our hope doesn't lie in laws or nations or rulers…our hope is in God. With the passing of each failed promise for change, our cynicism grows. Like many of the psalmists we wonder what God's up to and when He will make the wrong things in our world right. We feel tempted to doubt whether or not this perfect kingdom we're longing for will ever come.

Deep down we all know this world is broken. The earth is in decay—at a far more critical level than polar ice caps and disappearing rain forests. War, cruelty, famine, disease, murder, hatred, slavery, greed, and injustice continue to thrive all around us. Unless we choose to bury ourselves in a bubble of our own selfishness, we all have this undeniable sense that this world we live in desperately needs to be rescued.

---

8   Romans 13—a really interesting passage about God's sovereignty, especially when you consider the cruel and hostile way Paul was treated by his ruling authorities.

When we're honest with ourselves, we realize that the flaws are so great, even on our on best day, the best and brightest this world has to offer will not be enough.

Mankind is in desperate need of rescue.

A billion people live on less than a dollar a day. The leading cause of death in the world results from the fact that more than a billion people don't have access to clean water. There are more slaves today than at any other point in human history—including more than 2 million children trapped in sex slavery.

Educated and talented young people walk into schools and movie theaters on suicide missions. Religious zealots throw bombs at unsuspecting racers. Doctors who promise to "first do no harm" perform late-term abortions on babies. Cancer ravages the young and the old across demographic lines. Natural disasters rip through neighborhoods leaving physical and emotional damage that will be felt for decades.

It's not only the danger on the outside—the darkness on the inside of each human heart seems insurmountable. Even the most privileged, the most successful and famous are often the most miserable, overcome by selfishness and greed, guilt and shame, depression and anxiety, phobias and insecurity, despite enjoying every benefit the world has to offer.

These problems are so massive it's difficult to figure out where to begin. That's why we lean on our values—God's Word makes it clear—our hope comes from Jesus, working through His Church, redeeming and restoring everything that's broken. This darkness shouldn't make us run and hide. We should see it as the incredible opportunity it is.

When you buy a diamond, there's a reason they pull out a big black piece of felt—the light always shines the brightest against the deepest darkness.

God's mission is to destroy the effects of sin—both at a personal and a cosmic level. At a personal level, when we put our faith in Jesus, He takes our disobedience and gives us His righteousness. We're set free, washed clean and born again into this living hope—as citizens of His Kingdom and beloved children in the family of God. He doesn't just take our sin away—He puts His righteousness in us through a new nature—created to love what He loves and live like He lives.

At a cosmic level, the rival deities, idols, false hopes, and destructive forces of darkness are being driven out of this earth as the borders of this Kingdom expand into new hearts, homes, neighborhoods, businesses, schools, nations and ultimately into the world. History is the story of the progression of this Kingdom through the ages—those who receive Him are welcomed—those who oppose Him eventually discover and acknowledge He is who He claims to be.

Colossians 1 tells us the world was created for Him and through Him and He holds all things together by the power of His word. Like the most famous verse in the Bible tells us—He loves this world a lot.

Abraham Kuyper captures this idea perfectly: *"There is not a square inch in the whole domain of our human existence over which Christ, who is Sovereign over all, does not cry, 'Mine!'"*[9]

Another Divine Tension

The way this process unfolds has been the subject of much debate throughout church history. Some have argued the church's role is to primarily focus on these broken aspects of our world by building hospitals, orphanages, schools, food banks, homeless shelters and other practical expressions of God's love.

Others have said the greatest needs are always spiritual and choose to bypass expensive and administratively demanding projects in favor of crusades and

9   Abraham Kuyper, http://www.goodreads.com/author/quotes/385896.Abraham_Kuyper accessed 7/9/13

extensive preaching campaigns designed to allow as many as possible to pray and receive Christ and the eternal security of a future in heaven.

This ongoing struggle between these different approaches has often divided the body of Christ, splintered denominations, and resulted in division in local churches. And it seems each new generation revisits the discussion and comes to its own conclusions.

But as I read Scripture, the distinction between these two is arbitrary—this is another one of those divine tensions we've looked at. It's reaching people and building lives. The Kingdom of God advances throughout the earth toppling rival kingdoms, systems of injustice, abuse, poverty, violence, greed and every other form of wickedness.

God has no interest in planting churches where people gather once a week, make an individual commitment to Him, then return to a wicked, dying world growing increasingly worse, that His Church is incapable of impacting.

At the same time, the mission of God is not to simply ensure every child has all of their basic needs, a loving home in a safe community, a good education, quality health care, plenty of recreational activities and the life of their dreams, but destined to die selfish and separated from God.

If what we're preaching fails to transform marriages, homes, neighborhoods, communities, regions and the culture at large…it's not really the Gospel.

If our message is incapable of leading men and women to genuine repentance, lasting transformation and a lifestyle of sanctification and fruitful discipleship…it's not the Gospel of the Kingdom.

It's *the Great Commission*—go therefore and make disciples and it's *the Great Commandment*—love the Lord your God with all your heart, soul, mind and strength and love your neighbor as yourself. We don't separate them. They're two powerful truths existing in divine tension.

It's reaching people (*personal evangelism*) *and* building lives (*transforming culture*).

Our Part In God's Mission

The unfortunate reality is many of God's children aren't joining Him in His mission. A recent study of professing Christians who regularly attend church found eighty percent believe they should share their faith with others. I'm not sure what the other twenty percent were thinking, but at least most of them get it.

However, less than four out of ten had actually done so in the previous six months. Sharing their faith isn't even the issue—forty-eight percent hadn't even invited someone to church during that same time span.[10]

Even those who have shared their faith have rarely reached the ultimate goal. Another study shows only five percent of Christians have led someone into a relationship with Jesus.[11]

The sad truth is this: God has given us a part and we're not doing it. There are all kinds of reasons and attitudes to explain this.

I don't know enough.

I'll wait until I'm more mature as a Christian.

What if someone has a question I don't know the answer to?

There are others far more qualified than me to tell my friends about Jesus.

---

10   http://www.lifeway.com/ArticleView?storeId=10054&catalogId=10001&langId=-1&article=research-survey-sharing-christ-2012 (accessed 11/20/14)

11   www.barna.org (accessed 11/20/14)

These kinds of excuses make sense if we're talking about basic acts of kindness like donating blood or providing canned goods for a food pantry. If you're a follower of Christ, the eternal destiny of your family, your neighbors, your co-workers or your friends is slightly more important.

I don't mean *"eternal"* as in *"when they die"*—I mean eternal as in their lives now. When the Bible talks about eternal life it has more to do with the *quality* of life than the *quantity* of it. Why would you want anyone to spend one day separated from God?

Even the magician and outspoken atheist Penn Jillette understands this.

> *If you believe there's a heaven and a hell, and people could be going to hell or not getting eternal life, and you think that it's not really worth telling them this because it would make it socially awkward...how much do you have to hate somebody to believe everlasting life is possible and not tell them that?*
>
> *I mean, if I believed, beyond the shadow of a doubt, that a truck was coming at you, and you didn't believe the truck was bearing down on you, there is a certain point where I tackle you. And this is more important than that.*[12]

What a powerful perspective. Mission isn't easy. It's not convenient. It costs us something. It's messy. People have challenges and problems. If you genuinely make yourself available and begin to listen to them, talk with them, pray for them and invest in their lives, it will cost you. But it's how the Kingdom has been advancing in the earth since the days Jesus announced its arrival. You give your time, your energy, and yourself and God determines the results.

Sometimes this is glorious...and other times it's heartbreaking.

---

12   http://www.thegospelcoalition.org/blogs/justintaylor/2009/11/17/how-much-do-you-have-to-hate-somebody-to-not-proselytize/

Chris Jones was the first person I ever prayed with to receive Christ but his story didn't end the night he was baptized at church. As we grew older our journeys took different directions. I went on to Baylor and he didn't have the best influences in his life. He started using drugs and when his girlfriend dumped him, he ended up taking his own life.

When I heard the news, it hit me like a ton of bricks. I immediately went back to the moment on my front yard. This isn't a game. It's not a contest like selling raffle tickets or seeing how many people we can get to sign an email list.

God gives us incredibly significant moments. In a movie, you can always tell when something important is about to happen because of the music. It builds dramatically to get you to pay attention. Life doesn't work this way. We never know how important a few words in one moment can be. That's why we always need to be ready and stop evaluating people from a human point of view.

We need to see these moments and each person the way God sees them.

It's Not "What We Know," It's "Who We Know" That Matters

When we first planted Milestone Church, mission wasn't an option—it was our only hope of survival. My kids weren't old enough to play sports but I started coaching. Brandy started serving in different groups and clubs in the community. As our relationships grew, so did our influence and opportunity to join God in what He was doing. He guided us into relationships with people He was pursuing and we began to love them and model His heart the best way we knew how.

Some of them received Christ, became disciples and joined Him in His mission. Others wanted someone to listen to their problems, complain about their spouse/boss/kids, and to feel validated for why everything wrong in their lives was somebody else's fault.

We did our best to love them all the same—we couldn't determine how they'd respond. That wasn't our choice. But we could keep loving people out of our deep love for God.

That's what evangelism and mission are all about. It's not what you know, it's who you know that matters. If you love Jesus, stay close to His heart, and choose to value what He values, living any other way will seem weird. But if you have a distant, functional relationship with Jesus where you do your thing and see Him on Sunday for an hour, not much will change.

We love because He first loved us.

This is the heart of Milestone Church, and I pray by the grace of God we never lose it. I'm not used to this idea. It doesn't bore me. It still blows me away.

On my worst day, after my biggest mistake, in spite of my pride…Jesus loves me. He knows me. He tells me I've got nothing to prove and nobody to impress. He invites me into His purpose to seek and save those who were lost.

How else can you respond to this kind of love?

You can't stop talking about it. You want everyone you meet to experience it. You can't rest knowing there are those out there missing out.

That's what it means to be a part of God's mission.

You don't have to be me. Your role isn't my role—but we can't be the church God wants us to be if each of us doesn't do our part. God gives each of us gifts for His mission we leverage to the best of our ability so others can experience His love.

Jesus told us when He was lifted up that He would draw all people to Himself. He was talking about His atoning death on the cross, but there's also a critical principle here. When you make Jesus the focus, when you make His name, His character, His mission the highest priority, it captures hearts and transforms lives. We do everything short of sinning to create the absolute best ministry environments we can, but we leave the heavy lifting to Him.

It's not your building, your message series, your video, your coffee, your parking lot or your choice of music style that matters most. It's whether or not people can see Jesus.

> # WE LOVE BECAUSE
> # HE FIRST LOVED US.

A gifted evangelist can preach a great message that may powerfully persuade many people and help them see Jesus. But an entire community, committed to the mission of God can give a much bigger, more nuanced and multi-faceted image of God than any one individual, no matter how gifted they are.

This is why He leans on His Church—it's filled with an abundance of diverse gifts, personalities and callings—and they're all invited into this mission.

What Milestone Is Doing

I told you initially I didn't want to plant another church in the metroplex, the brass buckle of the Bible Belt, American Christianity's Jerusalem. I wanted to go to some place radically un-churched, even aggressively anti-God. I like a good fight. A city that immediately made everyone think, "*Yeah…that place could seriously use a great church.*"

It seems so stupid to think that way now.

Not just because of all the lives changed in the history of Milestone but because of how quickly our region is changing. It's one of the fastest growing areas in the country with un-churched, professional people streaming into North Texas from both coasts. For several years now they've outnumbered the native Texans in our Discovery 101 events. When people make a major life change like a cross-country move, they're far more open to change, and as a result, more open to the Gospel.

Here's a shocker—God knew what He was doing all along. Research shows the overwhelming majority (as high as ninety-five percent) of people who give their lives to Christ do so before the age of twenty-five. And with every passing year of age, the numbers shrink exponentially.[13]

When a man in his forties gives his life to Christ, it's a genuine, biblical miracle. It happens dozens of times every year and we're blown away by it but we're not satisfied. There's so much more work to be done.

Here's the bottom line: In our region there are literally millions of people who are far from God. Some realize it, others don't, but we're not okay with this. This responsibility doesn't fall solely on Milestone—there are many, many phenomenal churches in our region—but we're determined to do our share to bring in the greatest harvest and establish as much of the kingdom as we possibly can.

Practically what this means is every time Milestone Church comes together we expect people to give their lives to Christ. Not on special outreach weekends—every weekend. Obviously it's not uniform—some weeks there are a few and some weeks it's many—but if there aren't any we ask, "*What can we do differently to help people who are far from God begin a relationship with Him?*"

---

13   https://www.barna.org/barna-update/article/5-barna-update/196-evangelism-is-most-effective-among-kids#.VG4R2UtFuus

This starts with our weekend service but it doesn't end there. In our wide variety of small groups [and ministry environments], Restore (our freedom ministry), Elevate (our student ministry), Annex (young adults), Flourish (ladies), and in the daily lives of the people in our communities, we see lives changed every week.

We believe the local church should be diverse and we all benefit from walking together, but there's also a place for demographically-based ministry environments that help people come to know and love Jesus as well. When we identify one of these, we don't immediately start a program or an event to reach them. Before we jump into it, we wait until we have the right leader who is willing to pay the cost and carry the weight of the responsibility of leadership.

One of the areas we're still learning is our work with single moms. The Bible says in the first chapter of James[14] that God sees loving and caring for the fatherless and the widows as pure love and devotion to Him. These groups struggled because of the absence of responsible loving fathers, and in our suburban culture of young families, we think caring for single moms (no matter how they ended up this way) is a great way to live this out.

Originally it seemed like a good ministry idea. My dad was raised by an incredible single mom. (My grandfather passed away in a car accident when my dad was nine.) She never remarried, never changed her name, never took off her ring and raised two boys by herself. She could do anything—fix the car, give her friend a perm, mow the lawn, teach the boys to fish and play baseball and cook the kind of food that sticks to your ribs.

Whenever Brandy leaves me with the kids for a couple of hours, my mind drifts to the idea of trying to lead and care for your family by yourself—it feels impossible, and yet, this is where so many in our community live every day. I thought it would be a great way for us to love and care for our community.

---

14   James 1:27 (NIV)

What started as a good idea has now become a massive burden from God. Every year we give away more than $100,000 to families led by single moms to help meet their needs and show them how much God loves and cares about them. Anybody in our church family who participates in these events can never find enough Kleenex. We gave one family a car and it was so powerful we're thinking of ways to do even more. We're creating mentoring programs, and outings with our dads & families, helping with job assessment and support groups for moms and we're only getting started. We haven't even scratched the surface of what God wants us to do in this area.

Perhaps the biggest thing we realized in the process was once again how critically important Dad is to the family unit. We love single moms and we're going to give them everything we have to help them succeed, but the best solution is to build godly men who love and serve their families.

In the early days we did a few events for men but what we quickly realized was men don't want to get up early to act religious and eat pancakes. They want to be developed. Their lives are filled with pressure—to produce in the office, to connect at home, to find a place where they feel strong and valuable.

When a man's identity isn't rooted in Christ, he goes on a never-ending search to find it elsewhere—the money, promotion and power from working 80-100 hours every week, the attention and affection of the young lady at the front desk or at the gym, in his toys (cars, lake houses, boats, gadgets), or in the endless pursuit of another rec league championship or the perfect hunt.

This is what men do—all men—they just do it in different ways. Whatever you find your identity in is what you worship. What you worship controls you and remakes you in its image.

Apart from Jesus, this process is always damaging to a man's soul and usually in the end, to everyone else who depends on him.

We started development groups—not accountability groups. Sitting in a circle admitting what's in your browser history isn't a long-term solution either. You've got to paint a picture of what it looks like to lead in your home, to lead at your office, and to lead in your own soul as you become a stronger disciple of Jesus.

If you can help a man do this, you'll capture his heart and he'll be with you—not because he likes your music, your coffee or your preaching—but because God has planted him in the house and he knows what it means to be a man.

Reaching and developing men is one of our best strategies to establish God's Kingdom in our region, but we're committed to do everything we can to transform the culture. We regularly serve in our senior center and partner with organizations with a proven track record for serving the poor and disadvantaged in our community, and we expect these commitments to grow and develop into new life-giving ways to communicate God's love to our region.

Ringing the Dinner Bell

From the very beginning, as a church, we've given ten percent of our budget to advance God's mission in the earth though we've only recently formalized a missions department. We didn't need a department to be engaged in global missions—it's part of who we are.

Globally, the mission of Christ in the earth goes back to the church. God doesn't have a plan B—His purpose and His mission comes back to what Jesus promised to build—His Church. At the same time, throughout Scripture we see the clear mandate to help the poor.

Due to these factors, Milestone has always looked for two things when investing in missions—helping the poor and building the church. Bringing immediate relief to the poor is the short-term solution, planting churches is the one, true, long-term solution.

When your most basic and immediate needs aren't being met, you're thoughts and attention will be consumed with survival. But if you can meet these needs, your compassion brings hope and joy that create extraordinary openness. Drilling water wells, feeding the hungry, providing medical care or freedom from captivity all ring the dinner bell to come and taste the goodness of God.

This was Jesus' pattern. When He sent out His disciples He told them to heal the sick and to cast out oppressive or tormenting spirits. He multiplied one kid's sack lunch and fed thousands of people after telling the disciples to feed the masses.

In order to do this effectively you need great administration and an established presence in the community. This takes time and resources and it is one of the reasons we always look to partner with other organizations when we're working globally. If we built offices in other countries we could build better PR and get credit for what we're doing, but it wouldn't be nearly as cost-effective and we wouldn't get the return on our investment we get now.

Some of these relationships begin because we're familiar with and respect the work of an organization. Other times we're introduced through a mutual friend and in some cases, God supernaturally creates a unique relationship with a ministry and your partnership becomes so close you feel like family. A close friend and a pastor to me, Jacob Aranza, calls this approach *"fans, friends and family"* and we've adopted it as we determine where and how we're going to be involved.

As a church family, we don't just give—we go. We send multiple teams across the globe every year with people of all ages. Over the past few years our student ministry has raised money to build two children's homes and several churches in India and participated in the largest mission trip in history. More than 80 students, parents, young adults, empty nesters, doctors, nurses, dentists and business people went to Honduras to love and serve the people there. They demonstrated the love of Christ and preached the Gospel—and they saw thousands respond.

When you experience God move like this you can't get enough of it. We've built this into the culture of our church. Every year, as more people in our community participate in God's mission, we'll see more lives changed and more volunteer to be a part of what He's doing.

What You Can Do

We've spent all this time talking about God's mission, His plan to establish His Kingdom and redeem the world. I know what you're thinking—"*Okay Jeff...we get it. But what can I do?*"

Great question. It's fairly simple. Not easy, but simple. There are four things you can start doing today and each of them will help you answer God's invitation to join His mission and change the world.

1) LOVE

You don't have to raise any money or get on a plane and fly around the world to do this. Some people do, without first loving their neighbor or their co-worker they see every day. It doesn't make any sense. Jesus told the disciples to start in Jerusalem, then move to Judea and Samaria and then to the ends of the earth[15]. Basically He was telling them to start in their city, then their region, and then keep going until they covered the globe.

Don't feel like you need to preach a sermon. Take a genuine interest in people. Love them the way God loves you. Listen to what they're saying... and what they're not saying. Pray for them, care about them, and tell them about what Jesus has done in your life. To do this part, you'll probably want to spend some time with Him, talk with Him about them, ask Him the best way to love them and do what He says.

This is the biggest one. If you'll live this, all the rest will follow. It sounds simple, but it's really difficult. It will inconvenience you. It will force you to

---

15   Acts 1:8

get off the couch, to cancel your plans, to have people all up in your personal space, to go places you don't want to go, to wait, to be disappointed and to make yourself vulnerable. If you're doing this to get credit or look spiritual, I have bad news for you. But if you're doing this because God's love is so incredible you can't think of living any other way, you'll find His love is so much greater and beautiful than you know.

2) PRAY

I have a prayer card in my Bible I had when we first planted Milestone. It's filled with all kinds of requests, but on the side, there are lists of names, and many of them are crossed off. I cross off a name when the person I've been praying for gives their lives to Christ. Most of the time it's not instant gratification and we don't know what our part in the process will be.

Sometimes we get the conversation started (plant the seed), sometimes we help move it along (water), and sometimes we're the ones who lead them to the moment they give their lives to Christ (harvest). Each role is crucial and each requires us to pray.

Prayer sometimes feels like flossing or going to bed an hour early—something we plan to get around to, but have a hard time making a priority. But if we're in an emergency, we'll stop everything and pray.

I don't think it's possible to genuinely pray for someone without caring about them more, thinking about them more regularly and seeing them from a different perspective. For that reason alone it's worth doing.

Unlike talking with people about Jesus or speaking in public, you don't have to be bold to pray but you do have to care.

Remember when Jesus taught the disciples to pray, He led with bringing the Kingdom on earth. God cares about all your needs but your prayer list shouldn't look like a grocery or wish list with only your requests. Regularly pray for God's Kingdom to break into your heart, your home, your neighborhood and your community.

I would also encourage you to put a list of names of people who are far from God in the front of your Bible or someplace where you can see them as a reminder to continue to pray for them. As you do, your ability to love and speak truth to them will grow as well.

3) SERVE

Meeting needs is like ringing the dinner bell for the Gospel. Think about someone in your life who loves you, makes you a priority and goes out of their way to put your interests ahead of their own. When they talk honestly with you, how do you respond? You listen and really take it to heart, right? Me too.

Serving reminds us it's not about us. In this kingdom, we're not the King. This doesn't go over too well in America, but it's at the heart of many of our most fundamental problems as a culture.

If you're a part of the Milestone family or if you're thinking about it, there are so many different ways for you to serve with us. We'll even give you an assessment to help you get to the right place.

4) GIVE

There's a saying among detectives and investigators (at least the ones in TV and movies): *Follow the money*. It's true. If I really want to know what matters to you, I won't ask you, I'll look at your bank statement. Whatever dominates your resources is what matters most to you.

Jesus said where your treasure is, your heart will be also.[16] It was true then and it's even more accurate today in our hyper-materialistic culture. There's

16   Matthew 6:21

no way you can say you want to join God in His mission without giving… and giving generously.

You can start these today. I've lived this way for years and I'll never stop trying to improve and mature in each of these areas. Not in order for God to love me, but because He already does. I'm convinced there's no better way to live.

There's a reason you're here. You can have as much purpose and meaning in life as you're willing to embrace. You'll find it as you join God by throwing your unique gifts and resources into His mission.

It's scary and wild at first, but once you've experienced it, living any other way is boring.

MISSION

Key Points

- Scripture makes it abundantly clear God is sovereign (in total control) and all-sufficient (lacking nothing). He doesn't need our help to accomplish His purposes—and yet because of His love for us and His desire to make us like Him, He invites us to participate with Him in His mission to redeem and restore the world.

- The principle is clear—whenever God moves in your life, whenever He blesses you, whenever His grace and peace transform you—it's always bigger than you. He never intends His goodness to stop with you.

- God wanted to reach the whole world and He planned on using His children to do it. People who were far from God weren't to be treated as enemies, rivals, or objects but long-lost children waiting to come home.

- So many people come to church to watch the pastor lead, preach and teach. They assume their role is to attend, observe and try to remember at least a little bit about what the pastor said. While this is a common cultural idea, it's not biblical. The job of a pastor isn't to do ministry—it's to train and develop the people to join God in His mission to reach the world through the church.

- This is Jesus' message—God's Kingdom has come. When He sends out His 12 disciples, this is what He instructs them to say to all those they meet. When He sends out 70 of His followers, this is what He commands them to communicate. And when He teaches how we should pray, among the first things to lead with is this desire for the Kingdom to rule on the earth as it rules in the heavens.

- When we're honest with ourselves, we realize the flaws are so great, even on our their best day, the best and brightest this world has to offer will not be enough. Mankind is in desperate need of rescue.

- These problems are so massive it's difficult to figure out where to begin. That's why we lean on our values—God's Word makes it clear—our hope comes from Jesus, working through His Church, redeeming and restoring everything that's broken.

- If what we're preaching fails to transform marriages, homes, neighborhoods, communities, regions and the culture at large…it's not really the Gospel. And if our message is incapable of leading men and women to genuine repentance, lasting transformation and a lifestyle of sanctification and fruitful discipleship…it's not the Gospel of the Kingdom.

- It's *the Great Commission*—go therefore and make disciples and it's *the Great Commandment*—love the Lord your God with all your heart, soul, mind and strength and love your neighbor as yourself. We don't separate them. They're two powerful truths existing in divine tension.

- If you genuinely make yourself available and begin to listen to them, talk with them, pray for them and invest in their lives, it will cost you. But it's how the Kingdom has been advancing in the earth since the days Jesus announced its arrival. You give your time, your energy and yourself and God determines the results.

- That's what evangelism and mission are all about. It's not what you know, it's who you know that matters.

- On my worst day, after my biggest mistake, in spite of my pride… Jesus loves me. He knows me. He tells me I've got nothing to prove and nobody to impress. He invites me into His purpose to seek and save those who were lost.

- When you make Jesus the focus, when you make His name, His character, His mission the highest priority, it captures hearts and transforms lives.

- A gifted evangelist can preach a great message that may powerfully persuade many people and help them see Jesus. But an entire community, committed to the mission of God can give a much bigger, more nuanced and multi-faceted image of God than any one individual, no matter how gifted they are. This is why He leans on His Church—it's filled with an abundance of diverse gifts, personalities and callings—and they're all invited into this mission.

Discussion Questions

- Have you shared your faith with someone else in the last 6 months?
- Have you ever led anyone into a personal relationship with Jesus Christ?
- What makes it difficult to share your faith with others?
- What are four things you can do to join God in His mission to change the world?

Practical Steps

- Make a prayer card with a list of names of people who are far from God. Place it in your Bible or somewhere you will see it every day and pray over the names.
- Make a plan to bless someone this week with no expectation in return. (Send an encouraging note, bring donuts to your workplace to share, pay for someone's groceries or gas etc...)
- Include in your budget funds to donate to missions through your local church.

WHAT IF YOU COULD GO BEYOND SIMPLY CHANGING YOUR BEHAVIORS TO BECOME THE BEST VERSION OF WHO YOU WERE CREATED TO BE?

CHAPTER TEN

SPIRITUAL FAMILY IS WORTH IT

Core Value #3: Spiritual Family

We value developing genuine community through authentic relationships that come from loving God, sacrificially giving, and serving each other.

Spiritual family doesn't just happen—you have to work at it. Jesus said that the world would know we love Him by the way that we love each other. Yet, so many people feel alone, they feel unloved, they feel insignificant, and what they really want is to feel like they belong. This is where we come in.

We believe the church should be a safe place where people can be honest, where they can share their challenges, where they can wrestle with truth and where they can look for help in a time of need. People matter to God and He wants all of us to experience His love through genuine community and authentic relationships.

This doesn't happen through coming together for a few hours a week—it's what happens when people do life together. We believe you don't join a church based on personal preference—we believe God adds you to His body and places you where He wants you.

If you've ever been to a Costco on a Saturday morning, there's no disputing the fact that people absolutely love it. The parking lot is packed and inside the store it's bumper-to-bumper traffic with over-sized shopping carts. Costco has all kinds of things Americans love—massive quantities, good deals and free food.

When you time it just right, you can push your cart down the aisles at the exact moment they put out fresh samples. I'm talking chicken wings, pizza, shrimp, grilled salmon, chili, fruit smoothies and maybe even a chocolate pastry for dessert. It's like a bite-sized buffet of happiness that makes waiting in line to buy 60 rolls of toilet paper seem like fun.

Costco figured out a strategy compelling enough to change the way most people buy their groceries. They had to—the marketplace and the competition for business is tough.

Traditional stores like Kroger used to have it easy, but now they have to create a different atmosphere than the big warehouse stores can offer. Target and Wal-Mart attempt to combine the best features of each environment and specialty stores like Whole Foods, Central Market and Sprouts appeal to the farm-fresh/organic-only healthy crowd.

Each of these stores is fighting over consumers by trying to create more incentives and more values to lure away the market share. They realize, for most people, their loyalty is as strong as the most convenient way to get the best deal. They want to get the absolute maximum while paying the least possible price.

It's the way capitalism works, but it's not how God designed His Church.

Yet in our current culture, many people approach their local church with the same level of commitment with which they purchase their groceries: I'm going with whoever gives me the best deal.

- Who has the best play area for my kids with the shortest lines and state-of-the-art retinal eye scans for my children? And don't forget…the Goldfish snacks must be organic AND gluten-free.
- How many weeks do I have to wait before I can sing on the platform?
- I want a message on the seven keys to making all my dreams come true—and I want them all to start with the same letter. When are you going to give that message?
- Do they have a petting zoo with live animals because I heard another church in the area has that?
- How long will it take me to get a parking spot, a cup of coffee and a seat close enough for me to see everything yet near enough to an exit so I can sneak out early and beat the traffic?

I'm not trying to be harsh. I didn't pull these out of thin air—they're all based on real stories. This is where so many people live.

Environments matter. We do everything we can to give every person who visits Milestone Church the opportunity to hear from God and experience His presence while they feel loved and welcomed in our community.

But we're not Costco—the customer isn't always right. We'll never make everyone happy. And our primary goal is not to please people—it's to honor God.

Don't hear what I'm not saying—these two things are not mutually exclusive.

The most common response we receive at our events for people who are new to Milestone is, "*We felt so welcomed—everyone here is so friendly.*" By the grace of God, this isn't a coincidence.

It's not because our greeters are more outgoing than the ones at Wal-Mart or because they try to be more charming than a TV weatherman. It's not because we have amazing, fair-trade coffee, state-of-the-art screens or swanky interior design. We know we're not that cool.

I believe the reason people experience this is because we believe and attempt to live out what the Bible teaches about the church—it's not a business, it's not a social club, it's not a non-profit organization.

More than anything else, it's a family.

God's Basic Building Block

Whenever God wants to do something significant, He always starts with a family. There was always going to be an Eve for Adam, which would lead to Cain, Abel, Seth and all their other children. God didn't look at Adam wandering around with the animals and decide human beings needed a love connection too.

Later when He pushed the reset button in Genesis 6, He didn't simply choose Noah—He picked his whole family. And when He comes to make a covenant with Abraham in Genesis 12, it's as much about Isaac and Jacob (and all their descendants) as it is about their father.

When God thinks about people, He always frames those thoughts in the context of relationships, and the primary context for every relationship is family. Jesus is fully God, uncreated, without a beginning or an end, and yet the Bible intentionally uses phrases like *"the Son of God," "the Son of Man,"* and *"the firstborn among many brothers"* to describe Him.

There are many words we could use to describe family, but convenient and inexpensive don't show up anywhere on the list. Family is costly—it requires all of our resources—time, mental, spiritual & emotional energy, talents and of course as every parent realizes…lots of money.

In God's economy, few things are more valuable than family. In fact, all throughout Scripture He makes it abundantly clear we are all designed for family. He has a plan for every family—a picture of a preferable future filled with life and hope.

No matter how dysfunctional, screwed up and toxic the family has become, God always has a plan. Ephesians 3 tells us every family in heaven and earth was given their name by Him. Not a single one, anywhere on the planet, has escaped His notice because it's how He's designed the world to function.

None of us are meant to be alone. And when we are alone, His greatest desire for us is to come home. All throughout Scripture God describes His great care for the orphan and the widow—those who've been separated or cut off from family.

Family isn't easy. It's difficult and challenging. But it's worth the effort. When you find the kind of family God created you for, you realize its incredible value. You won't trade it for anything. It's a treasure buried in a field.

This is the culture of God's family—to go and look for those without family and to bring them home to be welcomed into His.

The Bible describes it this way in Psalm 68:6: *"Father to the fatherless, defender of widows—this is God, whose dwelling is holy. God places the lonely in families…"* God places us in His family. This is a critical concept. I don't know about you, but I didn't choose my family. It wasn't an option. I was placed into it.

The same is true of God's family—His Church. A child who developed a big file filled with pros/cons of all the characteristics he was looking for as a guide to interview potential families doesn't sound normal—it sounds like the plot of a movie.

It's crazy enough to grab our attention. But it's a fairly accurate description of how many people choose their church.

Do I like the worship? Are my needs going to be met? Am I going to get some stage time? Are they going to challenge me or will they give me my personal space? If they don't give me what I want...I'll have no choice but to find a new church.

It doesn't surprise me when people feel this way—it's how our culture trains us to think. Which is why so many people have a low view of the church. This attitude creates disposable relationships, hypocrisy, selfish ambition and unmet expectations in the church the same way it does in a family.

But when you believe God placed you in a body of believers, to serve and love Him as you serve and love others, not because it's easy or you always feel like it, it has a massive impact upon the culture of the church. You don't see the church as an organization, a religious gathering, a business, or a network. You see it as a family. This changes everything.

Although they don't realize it, I believe this conviction is what people are responding to when they comment on how friendly and loving people are at Milestone. One of our small group leaders used this metaphor to describe how this happens: "*Everybody loves the apple pie, they just don't know the recipe.*"

To keep the illustration going, this conviction is the secret ingredient.

When you believe you don't choose a church the way you choose a place to shop, you won't leave the first time you get offended. And you will get offended. Your feelings will get hurt. This isn't unique to the church—the same is true at work, in your marriage, in your family, or in any relationship with any other imperfect person.

There's only one person who's perfect—and He's the One who created you, who lived the life you should have lived but couldn't, who died the death you deserve, who promised to never leave you or forsake you, who has given you everything you need for life and godliness and who has a purpose and a plan for your life.

> **"EVERYBODY LOVES THE APPLE PIE, THEY JUST DON'T KNOW THE RECIPE."**

When you see Him this way, don't you think we should trust Him when it comes to where He places us in His family? Read that sentence again.

This conviction begins with realizing it's about Him, not you.

Americans Love Independence

As an American, I'm not sure you could find a more countercultural idea. Our forefathers came to this new land to flee the authority of the king. You don't have to listen to someone else—no one can tell you what to do or who to be. You are your own king. This is the land of the free and the home of the brave where all our greatest dreams come true and anything is possible.

We call the celebration of our history, "*Independence Day*," and it's one of our most cherished values. Now don't hear what I'm not saying. I love this country and I'm proud to be an American. There are some wonderful things to celebrate in our history.

It is no coincidence that as a nation we value independence and individualism as life's most important values and wonder why the condition of our marriages and families are crumbling. If your primary goal is your own comfort and happiness, sooner or later you'll drift from your spouse and disengage from your children.

When it comes to church, the majority of our earliest settlers came here for religious freedom. They disagreed with the bureaucracy and the politics of the church and they wanted the ability to break off and form their own group. Again, I'm not discounting the reality of the abuses of the church. The Reformation was a genuine and necessary move of God that corrected terrible theology and an abuse of leadership.

It's one thing to honestly and genuinely work through challenges in the church and something totally different to doubt or mistrust the idea of church altogether. If you think the church is man's idea and you're responsible to them, it's easy to get upset and leave the first time your will gets crossed. It may make you feel better, but you'll never experience true spiritual family.

You'll never taste the apple pie. You may even argue whether or not apple pie even exists.

However, if you believe the church really belongs to God, that it's the hope of the world, that it's God's Plan A (and He has no Plan B), and it's the one thing Jesus promised to build, then you'll look for ways to serve and invest in others instead of having your own needs met.

It's His Church. He calls the shots. He places me in it. My job is to obey Him.

"But in fact God has placed the parts in the body, every one of them, just as He wanted them to be."[1] Paul didn't write these words to the healthiest, most peaceful and prototypical church in the Bible. He wrote it to the Corinthians—they were a total and complete mess. Any savvy, church-shopper probably wouldn't have heard these words from Paul because they would have left the church a long time before.

This conviction is so much bigger than Milestone Church. I don't believe this because I'm a pastor—I believe it because I'm a follower of Christ.

Trusting God to place you in a family of believers means you have to hear God's voice and obey. Living this way is costly. It's inconvenient. It keeps you up at night. Spiritual family greatly increases your personal, emotional and spiritual investment in others. When people struggle or turn from God, watching them deal with the consequences is painful.

You know *"the love chapter"* in the Bible that always shows up at weddings? Guess where that passage comes from in Scripture? It's not in a section on marriage counseling. It's the next chapter in Paul's first letter to the Corinthians. It's a description of how the church is supposed to function.

Here's why this is so important. Maybe more than any other value I've listed, the people of Milestone love this one. They experience God's love through loving each other. They long for it in the deepest parts of their soul, and when they experience it they have to share it with their friends and loved ones.

No Family Is Beyond Redemption

I understand some of you cringe when you hear the word *"family."* For you, this word doesn't produce cherished memories. Instead, it brings to mind pain and drama you're trying to get as far away from as possible. Trust me...I get it.

---

1   1 Corinthians 12:18 (NIV)

Working with people over the years I've heard so many shocking stories of dysfunction and abuse I feel like nothing could surprise me. So many times the ones who should protect us and love us end up becoming the greatest menace in our lives. I wish this wasn't the case and I'm truly sorry if this was your experience.

Most people who share this background react in one of two ways. The first group tries as quickly as possible to build their own family, with their own values to erase the painful memories of their home. But left to their own willpower and strength, too often they end up repeating many of the same mistakes their parents made which makes them feel guilty or ashamed.

When this happens, the majority of them wind up in the second group —giving up on the idea of family altogether. They disengage from long-term, committed relationships in an attempt to protect themselves from the inevitable disappointment of dysfunction and unhealthy relationships.

I genuinely understand why people make this choice. I do. Committing to love and care for others makes us incredibly vulnerable. Most people don't like being vulnerable...especially not in Texas.

When you combine all the emotions, suspicion and mistrust many people carry towards the church, the phrase "*spiritual family*" becomes a double whammy. It's like combining the IRS and the DMV or dieting and going to the dentist.

No thanks, I'll pass.

But I believe this desire to belong, to be loved, to be placed in a family is so strong, we can't deny it. Even when we give up on it, we can't stop thinking about it. We can't stop longing for it. It's hard-wired into our system.

It's easy to look at people in church from a distance and think their families are perfect. We look at their Christmas card with everybody in their matching outfits and they all look so happy and loving, but we're not getting the full picture. The picture doesn't tell us Mom and Dad were arguing in the car on the way over and the kids were screaming and pouting. The only peaceful moment in the whole afternoon could have been the second they all said "*Cheese!*"

We know God is perfect and so we think He only makes room for perfect families in His Church. It makes sense to think this way...until you actually read the Bible. If you think your family is messed up, read the book of Genesis. It will make you feel better.

Brothers murder each other and keep it from their parents. Children mock their dad for passing out drunk while he's naked. Husbands lie and tell opposing kings their wives are their sisters. A wife tells her husband to sleep with the maid so they can have a baby—he does and then she hates him for it. One family promises their daughter in marriage in exchange for seven years of labor and then pulls a switcheroo on the wedding day.

Reality TV is tame compared to the book of Genesis. All this happens in the first twenty chapters to some of the most iconic figures in Scripture. And these are just the PG-13 stories.

No matter what's happened in your family, God's not shocked by it. He's not wondering whether or not you're beyond hope or restoration. In fact, He loves stories like these because they give Him the opportunity to show His goodness and His mercy.

During one of the darkest moments in the history of God's people at the end of the Old Testament, God makes an incredible promise. He said this promise had to come before the great and awesome day of the Lord, a picture of His return and the culmination of history.

God promises to send the spirit of Elijah, which would turn the hearts of parents to their children and children to their parents. God said if this doesn't happen, this land would be destroyed. That's how critical the health of the family is to God.

This promise was fulfilled in Jesus who demonstrated what the relationship between a Father and a child should look like—perfect love, perfect obedience, perfect peace. Jesus didn't primarily relate to God as Judge, Boss, Creator or Law-Giver—first and foremost, He was Father.

Through His atoning death on the Cross, Jesus restored the breach between God and man and made it possible for us to have peace with God. But He also modeled what it looks like to relate to God as our loving Father. He gave us a clear picture of what God's family looks like.

The Culture of God's Family

Every family has a culture—defining values, characteristics, practices and traditions. Some cultures are life-giving and healthy while others are oppressive and toxic. My greatest desire is for your family, my family and our spiritual family to be healthy. But this won't just happen. We have to be intentional about it and we need a model—a picture of health to show us what a family is supposed to look like.

The culture of God's family is built around love, humility, forgiveness and honor. When we understand this and value what He values, we benefit from this culture and find great fulfillment by contributing to it. But if we have unrealistic expectations or if we attempt to redefine His culture with our own set of values, disappointment and frustration will be unavoidable.

1) LOVE

Love isn't one of God's character traits, it's fundamental to His nature. God isn't loving—He *is* love. We can't understand love apart from Him. When the Bible talks about how we recognize God's family it always begins with the clear demonstration of this love—both for others in the family, our neighbors and even our enemies.

Remember, *"the love chapter"* wasn't written for weddings, it was written to a church, a family of believers who were failing to model the culture of God's family. The Bible defines the ultimate demonstration of love as Jesus' death—while we were enemies and aliens to God, Jesus died so we could be reconciled to know and love Him. This supreme act of love should define and impact how we treat others.

Jesus said the world would know we were His by the way we loved one another. This is an incredibly high standard. Honestly, it freaks me out. In my own strength, there's no way I can live this way. That's why I don't set the values of God's family—I follow them.

When you understand how loved you are, you no longer have to earn love or prove your own worthiness in order to secure that love. Fear, pride and anxiety all result from a lack of love and acceptance. When you are confident in the unconditional love God has for you, you are free to stop obsessing over yourself.

LOVE ISN'T ONE OF GOD'S CHARACTER TRAITS, IT'S FUNDAMENTAL TO HIS NATURE. GOD ISN'T LOVING—HE *IS* LOVE.

2) HUMILITY

So much of our pain and discomfort in life comes from this attitude of entitlement. If you're a parent, you know the battle cry of every child at some point becomes, "*It's not fair!*" What they're saying is one of their siblings or friends got something they wanted…something they believed they deserved, whether it's a toy, a sleepover or an ice cream. The dark reality is that our hearts are never satisfied—we could get all three and before long we'd start to focus on something else.

Another distinctive of the culture of God's family is humility. Humility doesn't mean you think less of yourself; it means you think of yourself less. You're no longer obsessed with you and what you want. You're free to value and love others, to prefer them and to enjoy their success, their joy and their peace above your own.

This is one of life's most mysterious paradoxes—the more you make your life about you, the more miserable you become. Especially when you always get what you want. But when you make your life about serving Jesus and pleasing Him by loving and serving others, you end up with a joy and peace you never thought possible.

ANOTHER DISTINCTIVE OF THE CULTURE OF GOD'S FAMILY IS **HUMILITY.**

As long as you hold on tight to what you have or don't have, what you've earned, what you deserve, you'll ensure your own misery even in the presence of your Father. You'll be the older brother from Luke 15—and our churches are filled with them. He's one of the most tragic figures in Scripture.

3) FORGIVENESS

Without an accurate picture of yourself, you'll feel entitled to what you believe you deserve. But when you realize how much you've been forgiven, you're able to forgive others. If you don't think you need the grace of God, you'll be very slow to give it to others, which will make self-righteousness easy and forgiveness really hard. I don't recommend this option.

This is incredibly important because in a family, forgiveness isn't an option —it's a daily necessity. Feelings get hurt, stuff gets broken, accidents happen and life gets messy. If you keep track of what others have done to you, your list will grow long and your heart will grow bitter.

If you're willing to freely forgive as you've been forgiven, you'll be able to overcome offense, your relationships will endure and grow strong and you'll live at peace with all different kinds of people.

4) HONOR

Out of all these characteristics, maybe the most rare or endangered is honor. Have you ever seen a kid call his dad by his first name? I'm not talking about a 40-year-old adult, I mean a kid. It's weird. I wince when I hear it because I grew up with, "Yes, sir" and "No, ma'am" which are becoming increasingly rare.

As a culture, we don't respect authority and we don't trust institutions. In pop culture, Dad is portrayed as a clueless goofball and pastors are manipulative con-artists. This makes trusting God and embracing His models of both the family and the church completely countercultural. The idea of honoring these roles don't come from church tradition and religion—we find them throughout God's Word.

"Let the elders who rule well be considered worthy of double honor, especially those who labor in preaching and teaching."[2] In the New Testament, the term

2   1 Timothy 5:17 (ESV)

"elder" is used almost interchangeably with "pastor." We're not just called to honor them, we're called to imitate them too. *"Remember your leaders, those who spoke to you the word of God. Consider the outcome of their way of life, and imitate their faith."*[3]

Not only are we supposed to honor our spiritual authority, but our natural ones as well. On several occasions Jesus reminded the people of God's command in Exodus to honor their father and mother. Ephesians 6 goes even further: "'Honor our father and mother'—which is the first commandment with a promise—'so that it may go well with you and that you may enjoy long life on the earth.'"

In God's family, the expectation is for pastors and leaders to be honored as well as our parents. But they're not the only ones. "Love each other with genuine affection and take delight in honoring each other." In other words, honor isn't something we give to a select few begrudgingly, but it should be the norm of our environments.

There should be honor and respect in abundance in our environments. People matter to God—He loved them and sent His Son for them. The least we can do is treat them with respect, encourage them and recognize their contributions.

"Yeah...but what about unhealthy leaders?"

You might be thinking, *"Jeff...of course you're going to make a big deal out of this. You're a pastor...and a dad."* This isn't something I only expect out of others. I do everything I can to practice it. Not because I thought it would help me get ahead, but because it pleases God.

When we came and planted Milestone Church I went to pastors who had served in the city and honored them. I was so grateful for their leadership and their example, I wanted to simply take them to lunch to say thank you

3   Hebrews 13:7 (ESV)

and give them a gift card. Some of the most well-known pastors said it was the first time anyone had done that for them. I couldn't believe it. Not because I did this small gesture…but because no one else had.

I believe we have a responsibility as pastors and leaders to model this. Leaders go first. We have a responsibility to love and honor other pastors and churches in the area because the body of Christ is the family of God. How we honor one another demonstrates how we view God.

Of course there have been abuses. Some leaders have taken this to an extreme and tried to exert undue influence over others. Honoring our spiritual leadership isn't an invitation for them to tell us where we should live, whom we should marry or what job we should take. These are issues of individual conscience.

Honoring spiritual authority isn't about titles or constantly reminding someone of their position in a hierarchy or forcing them to address you by a certain title. That's poor leadership. Margaret Thatcher once said, "*Being powerful is like being a lady; if you have to tell someone you are, you aren't.*"

You don't have to live this way. If you choose to avoid it, and if life works out just right, you may save yourself from getting hurt by leadership. But you'll also miss out on an incredible gift God has given us.

If we're wise we'll seek their counsel and be grateful for trusted counsel who care enough to pray and process through important life decisions with us. I'm so grateful for the men of God who have loved me and provided this invaluable role in my life. It inspires me to serve others with the grace and love they've served me.

When you experience this kind of spiritual family, you realize it's not about titles or position. True authority and leadership serves, gives, empowers and finds its greatest joy in developing others who will go farther faster.

Those kind of leaders don't have to tell anybody to honor them. The people they're leading will insist on it.

Healthy Families Grow

Anything that is healthy grows, and growth always brings change. Some people have argued that a church must choose between being large and impersonal or small and close-knit. I don't believe these two are mutually exclusive. I believe it's possible to be a large, growing church filled with many new people while at the same time experiencing loving, meaningful relationships throughout the congregation.

Spiritual family doesn't mean you sit back and enjoy each other's company any more than a happy married couple stays at home and enjoys each other's company for the rest of their lives.

In a healthy family, everyone is overjoyed with the birth of a new child.

In a healthy spiritual family, everyone is overjoyed any time a son or daughter comes home to the loving arms of the Father and is added to the family.

In order to experience spiritual family, you first have to get a conviction —a firm belief—that you don't choose or join a church…God places you in a body in the way He chooses.

If you don't believe this, you'll find a reason to be upset, offended and dis-appointed, not just with Milestone Church, but with any church where you end up. There are no perfect churches…and if there were, they'd cease to be perfect when we joined them.

You have to be willing to embrace the culture of God's family—love, humility, forgiveness and honor.

And you have to be ready to experience change. Your small group will change. Your relationship with me will change. Service times, worship pastors, teachers, leaders, facilities, programs…they're all subject to change. But our commitment to Jesus and His Church stays the same. This frees us up to fully commit to what God's doing, to live in the moment, and to enjoy everything He has for us with the people He's called us to walk with.

And once you taste it you'll realize that's some delicious apple pie.

SPIRITUAL FAMILY

Key Points

- In our current culture, many people approach their local church with the same level of commitment with which they purchase their groceries: I'm going with whoever gives me the best deal. It's the way capitalism works, but it's not how God designed His Church.

- When God thinks about people, He always frames those thoughts in the context of relationships, and the primary context for every relationship is family. Jesus is fully God, uncreated, without a beginning or an end, and yet the Bible intentionally uses phrases like *"the Son of God," "the Son of Man,"* and *"the firstborn among many brothers"* to describe Him.

- There are many words we could use to describe family, but convenient and inexpensive don't show up anywhere on the list. Family is costly—it requires all of our resources—time, mental, spiritual & emotional energy, talents and of course as every parent realizes…lots of money.

- None of us are meant to be alone. And when we are alone, His greatest desire for us is to come home. All throughout Scripture God describes His great care for the orphan and the widow—those who've been separated or cut off from family. This is the culture of God's family: to go and look for those without family and to bring them home to be welcomed into His.

- When you believe God placed you in a body of believers, to serve and love Him as you serve and love others, not because it is easy or you always feel like it, it has a massive impact upon the culture of the church. You don't see the church as an organization, a religious gathering, a business, or a network. You see it as a family. This changes everything.

- When you believe you don't choose a church the way you choose a place to shop, you won't leave the first time you get offended. And you will get offended. Your feelings will get hurt. This isn't unique to the church—the same is true at work, in your marriage, in your family, or in any relationship with any other imperfect person.

- No matter what has happened in your family, God's not shocked by it. He's not wondering whether or not you are beyond hope or restoration. In fact, He loves stories like these because they give Him the opportunity to show His goodness and His mercy.

- Through His atoning death on the Cross, Jesus restored the breach between God and man and made it possible for us to have peace with God. But He also modeled what it looks like to relate to God as our loving Father. He gave us a clear picture of what God's family looks like.

- The culture of God's family is built around love, humility, forgiveness and honor. When we understand this and value what He values, we benefit from this culture and find great fulfillment by contributing to it. But if we have unrealistic expectations or if we attempt to redefine His culture with our own set of values, disappointment and frustration will be unavoidable.

- Anything that's healthy grows, and growth always brings change. Some people have argued that a church must choose between being large and impersonal or small and close-knit. I don't believe these two are mutually exclusive. I believe it's possible to be a large, growing church filled with many new people while at the same time experiencing loving, meaningful relationships throughout the congregation

Discussion Questions

- Would you say you have chosen a church based on preference or have you trusted God to place you in a family of believers?

- What family values and culture did you have growing up? Would you consider those similar or different to the values and culture of God's family? In what ways?
- Whenever God wants to do something significant, He always starts with a family. Why do you think God places such value on family?

Practical Steps

- The culture of God's family is built around love, humility, forgiveness, and honor. Write down one tangible way you can strive to support each of these values within your own church and family this month.
- Search your own heart for any unforgiveness you may be harboring against an individual or family member. Make a plan to reach out and forgive this person.
- Find five people in your spiritual family this week. Encourage them and tell them you notice and honor their contributions.

CHAPTER ELEVEN

DEVELOPMENT IS WORTH IT

Value #4: Development

We value a lifestyle of worship that leads to the ongoing process of development in the life of every believer.

We are all works in progress. We're not who we once were, and we're not yet who we will become. We should be able to see this ongoing process of development in the life of every believer as we grow closer to God.

Religion leaves you empty. You may learn some rules and some new words and phrases. You may learn how to act during a service, what you should say and what you shouldn't say, but in the end, nothing on the inside changes.

But when we fully engage with God, when we give our whole hearts and every area of our lives, we don't just "worship" during a service, we live a lifestyle of worship. Whatever we do, we do it to honor God and to show Him that we love Him. When we live this way, we'll never stop growing.

I wasn't born in Texas, but I got here as soon as I could.

—Novelty T-Shirt/Bumper Sticker

It seems like everybody is moving to Texas.

Demographic studies show large numbers of companies, families, entrepreneurs and internationals are headed to our great nation. Currently, someone moves to the Dallas/Forth Worth area every four minutes. Projections show this trend will continue in a dramatic way over the next 10 years.

I didn't need this research to know this—I see the reality of it all around our community. Everywhere you look there is construction—homes, businesses, roads—in order to accommodate the people moving into the area. To sustain this growth, architects, engineers, financial institutions, construction crews, and heavy equipment develop landscapes and resources into places where people work, live, go to school and do life.

And now many of these newcomers are finding a home at Milestone Church —so much so, that the number of new Texans has outnumbered the natives in our monthly gatherings for new members for quite some time.

I love it.

I love the fact that God is adding people from places like the Northeast and California to our community. We're a more diverse and more representative reflection of God's people because of it.

On one hand, this development and growth are a testament to the strength of the local economy and the quality of life this region affords. But at the same time, this kind of development comes with an understanding: expect delays. It's part of the process.

Increased traffic eventually means roads have to be widened. This can't happen unless you put crews to work, which leads to significantly longer commutes and frustrated drivers. All these people need homes to live in, schools for their children, hospitals, restaurants, gyms and every kind of store you can imagine. This influx of construction means more trucks and heavy machinery on the roads, and you're far more likely to catch a stray nail in your tire as you're driving through your own neighborhood.

In the short term, spending all of this energy on the infrastructure which the growth requires is painstakingly slow and inconvenient. But there's no growth without it. Expect delays.

For a region, development for a better tomorrow comes at the price of inconvenience, sacrifices and a lot of hard work today.

The same is true of people.

Build Big People

Over more than three decades of ministry, Jack Hayford has demonstrated what it looks like to care for and develop people. He planted The church on the Way in Van Nuys, California, founded a college that has become a university, served as a pastor to pastors and took on an international leadership role within his network. Somehow, in addition to leading a family that grew to include all kinds of grandkids and even great-grandkids, he found the time to build bridges across large sections of the body of Christ.

It's hard to argue with his legacy but what's so startling to me is the simplicity of his approach. His early ministry years took place in the midst of massive cultural shifts and before church growth became a science and mega churches became a normal part of the landscape.

Pastor Jack said he never set out to build a big church. Instead, he prioritized building big people. He believed if you focused on building big people, then sooner or later, those people would build something great. Building a big church can make you famous and important, but he decided developing people wasn't about focusing on the success of the pastor; it was all about trying to help people win.

It worked. By investing in people, Pastor Jack's influence and impact on the body of Christ, both in his area and to the ends of the earth, has been profound.

This sounds simple, but it doesn't just happen. You have to make it a priority over a long period of time. It's not without its challenges either.

Expect delays.

It requires a great deal of emotional energy, patience, and the ability to see beyond the current circumstances to the potential of the people you're walking with.

Although he's modeled it beautifully, Jack Hayford didn't create this approach. He got it from Jesus. I believe developing people to be big and to live great lives is something God designed to be a fundamental part of His Church. The purpose of the church is not to relay information—it's to transform lives.

Everything That's Healthy Grows

Somewhere along the way I picked up this phrase, "*Everything that's healthy grows.*" I know I've already mentioned it, but I believe it's worth repeating.

It reminds me of Jesus' words to His disciples in John 15 about the vine and the branches. We're created to grow, to bear fruit, to become the unique masterpiece God created us to be and to accomplish everything He has for us.

This doesn't just happen. If you're a parent, you understand what I mean. I think about this every year when the Christmas cards come. When you see all those pictures of your friends and family you realize how the toddlers you remembered are heading into junior high. Sometimes it's hard to even recognize them. That strange sensation you experience is shared by your friends and loved ones when they're looking at your card.

It doesn't jump out at you because you're with your own kids every day. Since your friends last saw your kids, you've been potty training, teaching them to ride a bike, shuttling them around to 52 different activities, taking them to get new clothes, and playing catch in the front yard. This required a ton of time, energy, patience and intentionality—but it develops them and helps their growth.

Helping new followers of Christ, no matter how old they are, is a lot like being a parent. You just replace potty training, bike riding, homework & tee ball with learning to love God and people through reading the Bible, renewing your mind, financial stewardship, leadership skills and marriage and parenting development. In both cases, the goal is simple: take the next step.

It's a little crazy, but it's true. Being a pastor and being a parent are fairly similar. But before you get upset, I want you to remember I didn't come up with this. The Apostle Paul, in my opinion a fairly reliable source, called himself a "father" to the Corinthians. That may not be too hard for you to grasp, but did you realize he compared himself to a *mother* in his letter to the Thessalonians?

It's true. And by the way, he's right. Paul was primarily referencing the defining, disciplinary role of a father and the loving, encouraging role of a mother. Now I realize these traits can and should be employed by both Mom & Dad, but this isn't a gender discussion—it's about development.

Development requires discipline and encouragement whether it is coming from a coach, a mentor, a boss, a parent or a pastor. Take the next step.

You never outgrow this. It's true both physically and spiritually. Research has shown prolonged inactivity creates a significant danger to our long-term well-being. In fact, over a period of time, simply sitting at a desk can create the same level of risk to your health as smoking cigarettes! The latest studies tell us the average person needs to take around 10,000 steps per day to maintain a healthy lifestyle.[1]

It's the simple process of life. Everything that's healthy grows—growth always requires taking the next step.

One of the things I appreciate about my community is that the overwhelming majority of the people want to be developed. They want to grow, they want to increase their capacity, they want to be more effective leaders, spouses and parents.

Like I said before, in the early days of Milestone we wanted to do something for the men, so we went back to an old church staple: the pancake breakfast. We didn't get a great response. Guys weren't looking to load up on carbs and sing, "*Our God is an Awesome God,*" with an acoustic guitar.[2] They wanted help. They wanted to be stronger for their families, more effective in their career and more fulfilled in their lives.

I couldn't have been more excited.

We started to meet on a weekly basis with men, to see what the Bible said about leading, and to pray and encourage one another. We also used practical resources like the Strengths Finder assessment and the DISC test to help

---

1   Rath, pp. 21, 49.
2   There's nothing wrong with either of those things. I've done both many times over the years and God has used it. But our methods change over time.

them grow in their understanding of how they're wired and how they could most effectively use their gifts and abilities in the workplace.

This approach to development was the foundation for our small group strategy—not another meeting to add to the calendar, but an intentional way to help people grow. And from the beginning our clear intention was to develop in each one of these leaders a greater capacity to lead themselves. Again, this is another one of those great ideas we didn't come up with. We got it from 2 Timothy 2:2 *"And the things you have heard me say in the presence of many witnesses entrust to reliable people who will also be qualified to teach others."* (NIV)

> IT'S THE SIMPLE PROCESS OF LIFE. **EVERYTHING THAT'S HEALTHY GROWS**—GROWTH ALWAYS REQUIRES TAKING THE NEXT STEP.

We knew men were a key part of this approach. Our goal wasn't to exclude women or children. In fact, we knew the best thing we could do to help develop them was to start with the men in their lives. If a man's engaged spiritually, if he's being developed and coached to lovingly lead his family, it creates health for the entire home. But if Mom and the kids are bought in while Dad taps out or reluctantly gets dragged along, you don't see the same level of transformation in the family.

As a church family, we realized that in order to sustain the level of growth we believe God wanted to entrust us with, we were going to need a large core of mobilized leaders who'd been empowered not merely to show up, but to carry weight. Not an insider's club with blazers and secret handshakes, but a group united by a clear vision and a greater level of buy-in to the mission of Milestone. It wasn't a social club. There was a clear process that began with the development groups that allowed for new men to join.

We called this group, "LEAD 3:15" as a reference to 1 Timothy 3:15: "...*if I am delayed, you will know how people ought to conduct themselves in God's household, which is the church of the living God, the pillar and foundation of the truth.*"

In the passage, Paul is empowering Timothy to delegate the leadership of the church to others who've proven themselves capable of upholding the standards and values of the church God has in mind. Paul's language emphasizes how central this role is to God's purpose and plan and the incredibly high view of the mission of the church that this role required.

Our Lead 3:15 is a group of leaders who have been developed, are regularly serving and leading, are faithful givers/investors and when the church has a new initiative or a critical decision, outside of our elders, they're the first group I call. I want to empower them, inspire them and mobilize them, because I know in so many ways, this group sets the tone for the church as a whole.

Don't hear what I'm not saying—remember, people matter to God. All people. Not just the ones in Lead 3:15. The reason this group exists is so as a church we can more effectively love and develop the new people who come to Milestone Church. That's not the responsibility of paid staff—it's ministry given to all Christians. But they need to be developed to have the confidence and the ability to do it effectively. As they're walking deeper into what God has for them, they can teach others to take the next step too.

I believe this so strongly. Milestone's hope for the future hinges on our ability to develop people. This reality is not lost on us. We communicate this in every department. We keep the goal in front of us. We allocate energy and resources toward this end.

We created NEXT, our internship program, not just for people who are considering vocational ministry, but for anyone who wants to prepare themselves for what God has for them, no matter what age or season of life they're in. Paul told Timothy that he needed to be diligent in applying himself, to give himself completely to the process, so that his progress would be clear to everyone.[3]

This was spoken initially for Timothy in his role, but I believe this is a challenge for every follower of Christ. We should give ourselves completely to what God wants to do in us. And people should be able to see we've been growing.

Take the next step.

Developing the next generation isn't one of those things buried on my to-do list. I think about it every day. It's always right in front of me. I get emotional when I start to talk about it. As long as I'm in the game, I'm going to give everything I have to those coming behind me so I can help them become who God has called them to be and give them every opportunity to fulfill God's purpose and destiny for their lives.

Just writing these words gets me fired up.

When I come to the end of my life, I'm going to measure my impact not in trophies, awards, vacations or my investment portfolios. If we take the Bible seriously, our legacy is measured by the impact we have in the lives of people.

We don't get to choose our legacy. I don't know about you, but I've never seen someone speak at their own funeral. I'm not trying to be morbid, but I want you to see how central this issue of development is for each of us.

---

3   1 Timothy 4:15-16

The Biblical Term for Development

Paul taught Timothy to develop reliable or faithful leaders who could develop others. It's a brilliant strategy, but Paul didn't invent it either. It was passed on to him from faithful men who got it from Jesus. There's a name we have for these guys—"*disciples*." This was what Jesus invited His followers to become. It was the common term for a follower of Christ.

The Bible uses this word more than 250 times—by comparison, the word "*Christian*" only appears in passing three times.[4] I don't have anything against the word and proudly self-identify as one, but I think you'd have a hard time arguing it contains the same depth and significance as the word "disciple."

Discipleship is no small thing. It's not casual, comfortable or coincidental. There's a greater level of commitment, a clearer connection to the mission of Christ inherent in the word. When I think of developing leaders to honor God through loving Him and loving people, to more effectively carry weight, to handle their responsibilities and become more of who they were created to be, it's clear the Bible calls this process "*discipleship*."

Dallas Willard was one of the world's leading authorities on the subject. He believed the closest word in our language to the ancient concept of discipleship was an "*apprentice*."

> ...*a disciple, or apprentice, is simply someone who has decided to be with another person, under appropriated conditions, in order to become capable of doing what the person does or to become what the person is...And as a disciple of Jesus I am with Him, by choice and by grace, learning from Him how to live in the Kingdom of God...I am learning from Jesus to live my life as He would live my life if He were I. I am not necessarily learning to*

---

4   Acts 11:26b ("The disciples were first called Christians at Antioch"), Acts 26:28 (King Agrippa asks Paul, "Do you think you can persuade me to be a Christian...") and 1 Peter 4:16 ("However if you suffer as a Christian...")

*do everything He did, but I am learning how to do everything
I do in the manner that He did all that He did.*[5]

Willard believed this was the critical issue facing the church—not moral failures, financial abuses or challenges in the culture—but the inability for the local church to make disciples. Think about that for a moment. Out of all the things he could have chosen, he picked the lack of discipleship.

Ed Stetzer, the President of LifeWay Research, agrees with this assessment. His organization interviewed thousands of church members who identified themselves as committed followers of Christ. They found that less than half of them had ever been discipled and less than forty percent had discipled someone else.[6] Stetzer calls this a discipleship deficit—it's hard to argue with the numbers.

It's hard for me to understand. I'm not sure why you'd want to go to church and not be developed. Maybe I'm just weird. I do realize most people enjoy their comforts and freedoms; they like keeping their options open, and they're not nearly into the mission of God as we are.

Maybe I'm oversimplifying it.

But why would you buy golf clubs if you're never going to hit some balls or head out on the course? Why would you go to a restaurant if you're not going to eat a meal? Why would you take piano lessons and never sit down and play?

And why would you go to church if you're not going to develop a relationship with Jesus and become everything He created you to be?

Take the next step.

---

5   Willard, p. 282-3.

6   Statistics came from this seminar, http://www.qideas.org/video/the-future-of-discipleship.aspx (accessed 3-11-2014)

Covered In Dust

This process of discipleship was common in Jesus' day, but it looked a little different than the way He modeled it. For young Hebrew boys, they sought out a prominent rabbi (*teacher*) and followed a few paces behind him wherever he went. They would carefully watch, listen and observe everything he did. In the process he would observe them and the way they interacted with each other. Because of their proximity to him and the desert climate of the Middle East, these aspiring disciples would end up covered in the dust that flew up from the rabbi at the end of the day.

After a period of time, the rabbi could extend a formal invitation for one of these boys to become his apprentice, his disciple. Once he was sufficiently impressed he would invite them to "*Follow me*." This was always an honor, but to be invited by the most revered leaders was an extraordinary gesture and privilege.

The process was not too dissimilar from the way many parents maneuver and jockey to get their kids into the best schools or on the most prestigious youth sports teams. What was dissimilar was the way the greatest rabbi, the most gifted teacher in the history of the world, flipped the process on its head. He didn't wait for the most talented and celebrated young men to follow Him. Instead, He went and called fishermen and tax collectors and sinners and the unclean. "*Follow me*."

For three years He poured everything He had into them, even though they rarely understood, constantly underperformed, regularly complained about petty things, and generally missed the point. He wasn't solely thinking about their spiritual maturity—His goal was so much greater. He was investing in His followers so they in turn could invest in those who would come later. His entire strategy hinged on the success of this approach.

What an incredibly risky move. But it demonstrates how highly Jesus valued discipleship. Everything was riding on it. And yet, just as it was 2,000 years ago when He walked the earth, in many places it's still undervalued and misunderstood today.

Perhaps more than anything else, this is why Milestone exists to this day. We wouldn't be here without it. We've embraced this approach with every part of who we are. We're not the most creative church. We're not the most talented. We don't have the best facilities…but we love people and we'll do everything we can to develop them.

It's important to add that Jesus' emphasis on discipleship did not communicate disdain for the crowds of people who followed Him from a distance. He was moved by their needs, demonstrated compassion for them and asked His disciples to feed them. In the same way, we love people—not just disciples. While we believe discipleship is a natural progression in the life of a follower of Christ, we do not believe it creates a hierarchy of spiritual maturity or a standard beyond simple faith in the finished work of Jesus Christ to be accepted into the people of God.

The Master Plan

One of the books we've used in our development groups from the very beginning is "*The Master Plan of Evangelism*," by Robert Coleman. Here's how he describes this approach.

> *It will be slow, tedious, painful, and probably unnoticed by people at first, but the end result will be glorious, even if we don't live to see it. Seen this way, though, it becomes a big decision in the ministry. We must decide where we want our ministry to count—in the momentary applause of popular recognition or in the reproduction of our lives in a few chosen people who will carry on our work after we have gone.*[7]

---

7   Coleman, p.35.

Coleman packs a lot of truth into those three sentences. This strategy isn't a sixty yard touchdown pass that ends up on SportsCenter. It's three tough yards up the gut.

But if you give your life to it, every six months or so you look up and see all the lives that have been transformed. Coleman says it this way: *"Men were his method."*[8]

When Milestone first started, we had a whole group of our core volunteers who worked at Chili's to make a little extra money. One day I went in for lunch and the manager stopped me and paid for my lunch. As I was finishing my meal, he slid into the booth, and said, *"I don't know where you're getting these people, but if you have anyone else, you can send them our way, and because of the caliber of individuals I've seen, I'll hire them sight unseen."*

To this day it's one of the greatest compliments we have been given. I realized this was the best way I could serve my region and make a difference for the Kingdom.

Planting a church in the metroplex is like being a songwriter in Nashville. If we didn't develop leaders, we wouldn't exist. In our area there are close to ten churches with more than 10,000 people. No one was coming to our church for the incredible play area in our children's ministry. Down the street you can find the church version of Disneyland, complete with retinal eye scan, a faux Starbucks and Barnes and Noble-style bookstore. Our ambience wasn't bringing anybody through the door.

I'll never forget the time early on when we saved enough money to travel around the world to attend the Hillsong Conference in Australia. This was before they had these events in several cities in the U.S. If you wanted the experience, you had to make the trek. It was a major investment and I was expecting big things.

---

8   Coleman, p.109.

You can imagine my surprise when I realized that two of the keynote speakers were pastors from my city. I didn't have to fly Down Under—I could have hopped in my car and driven to their church. I was flying around the world to get new insights on how to lead my church while the conference organizers were looking in my own backyard.

Don't feel bad for me. It was worth the trip to realize how vital this distinctive was for Milestone. I'm not counting on it, but if somehow we get miraculously cool or wind up on *Outreach*, the reason won't be a moment of genius or the latest ministry trend.

It will only happen because we are developing and discipling leaders. In other words, we are helping each person take their next step.

What You Can Do

One of the biggest reasons for the lack of development or discipleship is a failure to understand what it practically looks like. It's not about gaining more knowledge; it's not necessarily about listening to more preaching or joining a program. First and foremost, it's a heart change. This process starts with a heart that says, *"God, I want to become everything you've created me to be."*

Don't hear what I'm not saying. This has nothing to do with your standing with God. We have peace with God, not because of our own righteousness, but because we receive it by grace through faith. This is the historic doctrine of justification—when we give our lives to Jesus and receive His righteousness by faith, God no longer looks at our righteousness (our moral record), He looks at the perfect obedience of His Son. We didn't earn that. Nothing can be added to it and nothing can be taken away. It's a gift we've been given.

When we understand this incredible love and the goodness of God, our response is overwhelming gratitude. One of the clearest ways we express this gratitude is through a desire to love and honor God in return by obeying

Him and becoming more and more the person He created us to be. This is the historic, Christian doctrine of sanctification.

It's critical for you to understand discipleship and development are a function of sanctification and not justification. Justification secures your right standing before God and ensures you'll live forever with Him in eternity. There will be many Christians in heaven who never entered the process of sanctification who are just as beloved by the Father.

But why would you want to stop there if you could grow deeper in Christ? If not only the greatest rabbi who ever lived but God Himself, the Creator of the Universe, the King of Kings and the Lord of Lords didn't wait for you to follow Him, but instead came looking for you and called you to follow, at one point would you say, "That's good enough."

This is certainly a value for us at Milestone, but by no means are we implying we're the only church in our area that's making disciples. But if you're sufficiently convinced and you're asking, "*Jeff, how do I get developed? How do I become a disciple?*"

I want to give you some practical help so you can take your next step.

1) Get in the Growth Track

This may sound basic, but everyone has to start somewhere. Our Growth Track starts with Discovery 101, an overview of the visions/values/history of Milestone with a time for questions and answers. For some it's a time to get connected to Milestone, but for many, their next steps include the critical foundational steps of giving their lives to Christ and water baptism. At each point along the way we encourage each person to take the appropriate next steps.

Dream Team 201 builds off of our values and history to give you practical ways to serve in our various ministry environments. I believe you learn more about discipleship through serving than in a classroom, and we want to give you the opportunity to start serving others out of your love for Christ as quickly as possible. It's also a great way to get connected relationally.

The third part of our Growth Track is Foundations 301, which combines foundational teaching with our pastoral staff and small group involvement with volunteer leaders.

2) Join A Development Group

I've mentioned several times how critical these development groups have been in our growth as a church. Whatever season you're at in life, we have one for you—students, young adults, single moms, first time moms, businessmen, couples, left-handed thirtysomethings who like exercise but don't care about organized sports who try to eat organic but occasionally cheat for ice cream and popcorn at the movies who…okay, that last one was a stretch but you get the idea.

In these groups we encourage, challenge, support, pray, cast vision and coach you into a deeper walk with Christ. Like we described in Chapter 8, discipleship and spiritual family aren't excuses to violate boundaries or exert undue authority, but we can't develop ourselves. We need to get connected in relationships and be honest with where we're really at. I've seen so many people make poor choices that had lasting consequences because they first distanced themselves relationally.

3) Be A Disciple

You can make it through the Growth Track and be in a development group for years…but if you don't choose to be a disciple, it's going to be difficult for you to grow. It doesn't just happen. There are so many forces working against you becoming the person God created you to be.

The Bible spends a good amount of time on three in particular: your flesh, the world and the enemy. Your flesh is your selfish nature—if you're in

Christ you've been given a new nature, but the old one clings on for dear life. It tries to block you at every turn. That's why Jesus said we had to pick up our cross daily and it's the wrestling Paul talks about in Romans 7. Don't be discouraged by the struggle—if you weren't alive in Christ you wouldn't struggle. Your flesh would just beat you down.

YOU TEACH WHAT YOU KNOW, BUT YOU REPRODUCE WHAT YOU ARE.

The world describes systems in our culture: greed, lust, pride, the desire for luxury/power, etc. They're like default settings; no one has to be reminded to live this way, it's the way the world works. To resist them you have to renew your mind. It's what John is talking about in 1 John 2:15 when he writes, "Do not love the world or anything in the world. If anyone loves the world, love for the Father is not in them." Being a disciple is as counter-cultural as it gets.

The third force working against you is the enemy—Satan and his forces. His primary weapon is deception—a never ending barrage of lies designed to twist our perspective and make us offended, mad, angry and separated from God and the people He's placed in our lives.

A disciple who is committed to God's Word, to mission, to spiritual family, to development and to generosity has every opportunity to win in each of these struggles. As they win, they start to change on the inside. Remember, it happens slowly—expect delays. As Coleman said, it's tedious, slow and largely unnoticed…but in the end it's glorious.

That's why I compared it to parenting. It's a grind. You've got your sleeves rolled up and you're working on the same issue over and over and it feels like it's never going to end and then one day you look up and there's a massive growth spurt. And just like parenting, the old line "Do as I say, not as I do!" won't get you anywhere.

You teach what you know, but you reproduce what you are. Paul tells the Corinthians, *"Follow my example as I follow the example of Christ."*[9] That's discipleship.

4) MAKE DISCIPLES

This is the final step—but it's one you never stop taking. As long as you are alive, you're called to make disciples. According to Stetzer this is the place the fewest number of followers of Christ make it to. The assumption is often that this is rarified air—the job of pastors, preachers and maybe a few SuperChristians. I want to straight up murder this assumption.

I believe every follower of Christ can and should do this. Kids can do it. Moms can do it. Empty nesters can do it. Dads whose lives are filled with work and family responsibilities can do it. All it takes is the willingness and the confidence that comes from walking with Jesus. He couldn't have made it any more clear—He sent us to do it and He said He gave us all of His authority.

Sometimes people get tripped up in the details, but it's not that complicated. Start with the people around you. *Who needs to be developed?* You're not trying to answer every question or make them theological experts—your goal is simple. *What is their next step?* In order to help them, you have to be committed to the process yourself—not perfect, but making progress.

Making disciples is like being a player coach. You're in the game yourself, but you're on the lookout for people with untapped potential. You can't look for finished products—you have to look past the raw edges to see what they

---

9   1 Corinthians 11:1 (NIV)

could be in Christ. People like Patrick & Eddie I told you about in Chapter 2. People like Patrick's friend Ron.

Ron played golf in college at TCU and had been chasing his dream by trying to get on the PGA Tour. When that didn't work out he ended up doing the next best thing…waiting tables. It was not exactly his life's passion. Although his primary purpose in going to school was to pursue his golf dreams, he majored in Speech Communication with a business emphasis. Things took a dramatic turn not long after when he was given a share of a Harley Davidson dealership from his parents. The new business quickly became one of the flagship branches in the country and they were already looking to expand throughout the region.

His professional life had never been better, but his personal world was cratering.

> # PEOPLE ARE BEING DEVELOPED.
> # DISCIPLES ARE BEING MADE.

When Patrick got married I remember talking with Ron at the rehearsal dinner—he was emptying wine carafes faster than an entire family from Sicily. It didn't bother me because it was immoral; it bothered me because we were playing golf in the morning and he was on my team. I didn't want him to be sick when he was lining up the winning putt. A man needs to have his priorities in order.

I'm joking. Mostly.

After many invitations Ron finally showed up at Milestone and what happened next was nothing short of miraculous. He was married with a young daughter, and like so many other men in our area, he was experiencing all the things the world promised would lead to fulfillment; he was living the American Dream. And somehow...*it wasn't enough*. He found himself wanting more.

This led to a series of immoral decisions that threatened the future of his marriage.

Ron grew up faithfully attending church, but by the time he got to college he had stopped going. He didn't have a personal relationship with Jesus and he certainly wasn't a disciple. With his home life collapsing, he went home and held his daughter, and as he laid her back down in her bed he came to the conclusion he couldn't live this way any longer. He walked out of his home and moved in with relatives in the area. Not long after, his wife and daughter moved in with her parents.

From all appearances it looked as though this would be the painful end of this season of his life, but the story wasn't over.

In his brokenness he gave his life to Christ, but he realized there was no guarantee it would be in time to save his marriage. The divorce process was well underway and for the next six months his wife watched closely to see if the transformation was real. Ron continued to throw himself into the Word; he served anyone he could and he demonstrated a genuine hunger to be a disciple.

In time his wife came and gave her life to Christ, their marriage was restored and their family has grown to include three beautiful children. As they both continued to grow in their relationship with Jesus they served others and looked to be an encouragement to others with similar stories. Eventually Ron joined our team, has become a pastor and he and his wife lead Restore—our ministry environment for healing and recovery. Every week hundreds of people gather both to receive healing and restoration and to help give it as well.

People are being developed. Disciples are being made.

This is what the church was created to look like. Anybody can recognize a disciple who is mature and bearing fruit in Christ but to see that potential in the midst of patterns of dysfunction and brokenness, you have to be a disciple yourself. You've got to be in the game. You've got to daily remember how far Jesus has brought you.

Discipleship is not a system, it's not a book and it's not a class. Two thousand years later, it still works the same way: one follower of Christ helping another to take their next step. That's the target. I want to encourage you to try it.

We may help make them, but every disciple belongs to Jesus. He's the one who redeems, transforms and makes them new. He's the One who gets the glory.

We expect delays. We know it will be tedious, slow and largely unnoticed, but we also know that in the end it's glorious.

DEVELOPMENT

Key Points

- For a region, development for a better tomorrow comes at the price of inconvenience, sacrifices and a lot of hard work today. The same is true of people.
- I believe developing people to be big and to live great lives is something God designed to be a fundamental part of His Church. The purpose of the church is not to relay information—it's to transform lives.
- Helping new followers of Christ, no matter how old they are, is a lot like being a parent. You replace potty training, bike riding, homework & tee ball with learning to love God and people through reading the Bible, renewing your mind, financial stewardship, leadership skills and marriage and parenting development. In both cases, the goal is simple: take the next step.
- It's the simple process of life. Everything that's healthy grows and growth always requires taking the next step.
- If a man is engaged spiritually, if he is being developed and coached to lovingly lead his family, it creates health for the entire home. But if Mom and the kids are bought in while Dad taps out or reluctantly gets dragged along, you don't see the same level of transformation in the family.
- Milestone's hope for the future hinges on our ability to develop people. This reality is not lost on us. We communicate this in every department. We keep the goal in front of us. We allocate energy and resources toward this end.

- Discipleship is no small thing. It's not casual, comfortable or coincidental. There's a greater level of commitment, a clearer connection to the mission of Christ inherent in the Word. When I think of developing leaders to honor God through loving Him and loving people, to more effectively carry weight, to handle their responsibilities and become more of who they were created to be, it's clear the Bible calls this process *"discipleship."*
- This strategy isn't a sixty yard touchdown pass that ends up on SportsCenter. It's three tough yards up the gut. It's not going to land you on a magazine list of the fastest growing or most innovative churches in America. It won't get you 10,000 followers on Twitter. But if you give your life to it, every six months or so you look up and see all the lives that have been transformed.
- One of the biggest reasons for the lack of development or discipleship is a failure to understand what it practically looks like. It's not about gaining more knowledge; it's not necessarily about listening to more preaching or joining a program. First and foremost, it's a heart change.
- Making disciples is like being a player coach. You're in the game yourself, but you're on the lookout for people with untapped potential. You can't look for finished products—you have to look past the raw edges to see what they could be in Christ.
- We may help make them, but every disciple belongs to Jesus. He's the One who redeems, transforms and makes new. He's the One who gets the glory. We expect delays. We know it will be tedious, slow and largely unnoticed, but we also know that in the end it's glorious.

Discussion Questions

- Why is ongoing development an important part of a believer's life?
- Discipleship was a common process in Jesus' day, yet He modeled it differently than anyone else before Him. How did Jesus flip the process on its head and what was the end result?
- How are the doctrines of justification and sanctification different? Which of these doctrines encompasses discipleship and development?

Practical Steps

- Make it a goal this month to take a next step in your walk with Christ. This may include getting in the growth track (Discovery 101, Dream Team 201 or Foundations 301) or joining a development group.
- Seek out someone in your spiritual family that can help you as you grow in your Christian walk. No matter how far along we are in our relationship with Christ we all need trusted voices and anchor points to help us continue to develop.
- Remember every follower in Christ can make disciples. Start with the people around you and ask yourself, "Who needs to be developed?" Plan a meeting and get started!

CHAPTER TWELVE

GENEROSITY IS WORTH IT

Core Value #5: Generosity

We value the biblical principle of giving our first fruits to God and believe that generosity transforms our lives as Christ followers. When we give, we affirm our commitment to the ongoing mission of Milestone Church: reaching people and building lives. As we continue to give generously with our time, our talent and our resources, we believe we'll experience the joy of seeing God transform lives.

One of the most powerful things about generosity is the truth that it always makes a difference in the life of both the one who gives and the one who receives. Remember, when you give your tithe (10% of your income), you are acting in obedience and worship to God, inviting His blessing in all areas of life (Malachi 3:10).

The first time I went skiing I was in my early thirties.

A church member offered his condo so our youth pastor and our wives and I could go on a ski vacation. You've probably realized by now I'm a fairly confident guy who sees himself as at least moderately athletic. Naturally I assumed I would quickly master this new hobby.

When we arrived at the ski resort, we ran into a couple of young guys from the church and I informed them I would be putting on a clinic on the slopes. As I made my way down the stairs I gave them a little demonstration of my perfect form—complete with a matching "*woosh*" sound effect as I changed direction by shifting my knees.

The next morning I quickly realized that I might have slightly overestimated my ability. We went to the rental shop and I found my size, I put on my boots, they laid my skis down, I put my toes in first and then…snap, snap… I was ready to roll. The only problem was I couldn't go anywhere. I had to be pushed/pulled to the ski lift and that's when we ran into the guys again.

They had been so impressed by my bold claims and stair work in the lodge they insisted I join them on the lift that went all the way up to the blue and black diamond runs. I had no choice—I couldn't let them see their pastor had talked a game he lacked the skills to back up.

Brandy grew up skiing; she had the perfect outfit and was watching with interest to see what I would do next. She gracefully veered to the side—she wasn't going to miss what was about to happen. She knew where my pride was taking me.

Somehow the image of me gracefully gliding down the mountain never quite came to pass. Instead, I was six feet four inches of human train wreck. My arms were spinning one way while my legs and skis were spinning the other as I morphed into a helicopter of doom wiping out anyone unfortunate enough to be in my path. Eventually my skis, poles, goggles and hat were scattered like a yard sale all over the mountainside.

I spent my morning falling down the mountain a few feet at a time. I was in pain, sweating profusely and flat out miserable. About halfway down I contemplated walking the rest of the way…but it was much too far. Then I saw the emergency crew helping an injured skier back to the lodge and I thought about faking an injury so I too could ride the courtesy shuttle. I wasn't sure I could pull it off, so I soldiered on. Thirty or forty falls later I was at the top of the last hill. I could see Brandy and the rest of our group sitting in front of the hot chocolate hut, so I pointed my skis in their direction, closed my eyes and went for it.

A few moments later I realized I was going really, really fast and I had no idea how to stop. You don't need that skill when you wipe out every five feet. I decided in the interest of public safety I had to take one for the team so I jumped sideways to my right and totally ate it like the "agony of defeat[1]" guy at the beginning of the "Wide World of Sports" I watched as a kid.

To my surprise, I survived. I just laid there on my back in the snow looking up at the sky for about five minutes—exhausted, frustrated, angry, humiliated and confused. I needed encouragement. I needed some compassion. I needed someone to explain to me why this was a good idea. I got none of those. Instead, Brandy comes over, looks down at me and says: "*Get up! You're embarrassing me.*"

Are you kidding me? I'm halfway dead, eating dirty snow, living on the threshold of hell on earth and she's worried about being embarrassed? In that moment I wanted to permanently quit skiing, but Brandy insisted that I had to learn so we could take our kids later in life.

I swallowed my pride and it took all of my strength to come back the next day and take a lesson. But I did. And here's what I learned—the first basic

---

1   http://www.youtube.com/watch?v=P2AZH4FeGsc You'll see what I'm talking about 0:13 in. That's how it felt.

principle is to utilize the edges of the skis and the only way you can do this is to push your weight forward. Your shins have to be in the front of the boot. It didn't make sense to me but the ski instructor kept telling me to trust him. When I finally did, I discovered he was right.

By leaning into the hill and applying pressure in the direction you're headed, you create the tension necessary to slow your momentum, which allows you to safely, and even smoothly, make your way down the mountain.

The way forward is not to move away from the source of your fear; you have to lean into it.

There are elements of the Christian life that work the same way. If you try to pull back to play it safe you end up falling down. The only way to go forward is to lean into the very thing you're afraid of. It doesn't make sense—you have to trust by faith.

It's true with humility. It's true with spiritual family. It's true with serving. And it's definitely true with generosity and giving.

For You, Not From You

Yes. I'm going to talk about money but not for the reasons you might think. My motivation is not to get something FROM you; it's to get something FOR you.

I didn't include this chapter in the book to correct or persuade the people in our community to be generous. They already are. I have the incredible privilege to lead a church that doesn't merely aspire to be generous—they live it. The numbers demonstrate how much they value generosity. Our giving percentages have consistently ranked in the top five percent of all churches in the U.S. over the past few years.

As a country we're not very good at handling money. Our national debt is in the trillions. Here's how big that number is: even if you could count 10 numbers per second (which would be fairly impressive), it would take you 3170 years to count to one trillion. Personal consumer debt is at an all-time high. Money is always in the top three reasons behind relationship challenges.

Recently I was talking to a doctor who practices in a wealthy community. He told me the clear cause behind the majority of sickness in their area was stress. And the leading cause of stress is money.

No one wants to do a terrible job of managing their money; no one wants it to tear their family or business apart, or to create unbearable stress, but this is how so many people in our world live. Most people feel like if they had more, their problems would go away, but the research doesn't bear this out. It goes the other way—the more you have, the more you worry about it and the less generous you become.

Jesus talked a great deal about money. The Bible is filled with insights and perspectives about how God feels about the way we handle our resources. Paul talked about it a great deal. In 2 Corinthians 9, Paul makes it clear that when we give generously, God continues to provide for us so we can be generous "*on every occasion.*" But when others receive the benefits of our generosity, they don't simply thank us, they end up thanking and praising God. It's important for us to realize the truth from the passage—the people wanted to give—Paul wasn't begging them to do something they were opposed to.

Paul trusted God to be his source, but he was constantly inviting the people he pastored to be exceedingly generous. In his letter to the Philippians he told them he had learned how to make do with a little or a lot, to be content in every situation. He didn't write those words while he was on vacation at a nice resort or on beach somewhere. He wrote them while he was in prison.

I think many people would like to be more generous. It's an aspiration or an honest intention. It's just not a priority. They want to give, but they also want to be comfortable.

Some people think the Bible says money is "*the root of all evil.*" It doesn't. It uses that phrase to describe the "*love of money.*" And unfortunately, the numbers show the majority of people love money more than they love God. That's why Jesus said you can't serve two masters—you can't worship God and worship money.

Many Christians talk about generosity the way I talked about skiing—they talk a big game among their friends, but they can't live it out. When they face their fears, they choose to play it safe instead of leaning into what they're feeling by faith.

You can say you're generous, but the numbers don't lie. Your bank ledger will always show what matters most to you.

If you want to know what someone truly values, what they love the most —follow the money. That's what Jesus was saying—where your heart is, there your treasure will be also.

I've seen money wreck marriages, families, friendships, businesses, schools and churches. I don't want that for you. Money is not evil. It creates a lot of opportunities and is a great tool.

But it's a terrible god.

It All Belongs To God

Money is a terrible god—but nothing is more worshipped in our world. In America, money talks, cash is king, everybody has a price, it's all about the "Benjamins" and you never count your money when you're sittin' at the table.

Kenny didn't know you don't have to count it anymore—you just check your account online.[2]

We may sing, *"Can't buy me love,"* or tell people, *"Money can't buy you happiness..."* but it sure seems like most people are willing to give it a shot.

Now I could try to inspire and convince you to give to a worthy cause with great promises of what you'll receive in return. Or I could tell you some incredibly sad stories about people who are far less fortunate than you. I could pull out some Scriptures and guilt or shame you into giving. Or I could scare you into what could happen if you don't give.

But every one of those approaches would be playing it safe. They're proven strategies in fund-raising. They work, but they don't deal with the real issue in our hearts and our minds that keep us from being truly generous.

What we really need is a change in our thinking; a radical, cross-cultural, paradigm-busting shift in the way we view this issue.

WAIT! Don't put the book down or set it aside. Let me explain.

I know this sounds terrifying but remember, if you try to play it safe, you crash. If you lean into the very thing you're afraid of, you gain momentum and move forward.

America is the land of opportunity, where anyone who is willing to work hard can have whatever they want...if they want it badly enough. They can work, climb, scratch & claw their way to the top. We celebrate this idea through TV shows featuring house flipping, talent searches and great ideas from aspiring entrepreneurs. Our best-selling book lists are filled with promises of better lives through healthy living, financial breakthroughs and personal improvement.

---

2   This is just the tip of the iceberg. There are so many songs about money—I'm sure there's one or two bouncing around in your head right now. It seems like half of them are just repeating the word over and over to different tunes.

This is the "*American Dream.*" People come from all over the world in pursuit of this promise.

> EVERY GOOD THING IN OUR LIFE IS A GIFT, A DEMONSTRATION OF GOD'S LOVE AND GENEROSITY.

We pull ourselves up by our boot-straps. We do whatever it takes to get the job done. We work hard for our money…and we deserve to enjoy ourselves.

There's only one problem—this may be what we believe, but it's not what the Bible says.

> *Don't be deceived, my dear brothers and sisters. Every good and*
> *perfect gift is from above, coming down from the Father of the*
> *heavenly lights…*[3]

These words come from Jesus' younger brother, James, in his letter to a group of believers. You've probably heard the idea "*every good thing comes from God,*" but I'm guessing you haven't seen it in this context. There's a reason the passage starts with, "*Don't be deceived…*" He knew we would be tempted to feel like we were responsible for the good things in our lives. If we allow ourselves to believe this, we'll see ourselves as our source, which leads to a profound sense of entitlement.

Entitlement says we deserve everything we have. Actually, entitlement says we deserve MORE than what we have. It's owed to us. This makes gratitude, humility and genuine generosity nearly impossible. And this attitude is rampant in our culture. Somehow we believe as Americans that we're owed

---

3   James 1:16-17a (NIV)

a certain standard of living—whether that responsibility lies with our parents, our boss or the government.

From the beginning of Scripture all the way to the end, the clear consensus, the undeniable perspective is that we're not owed anything. Every good thing in our life is a gift, a demonstration of God's love and generosity.

David was from a modest, rural family. When his dad gathered all his sons as potential candidates in a surprise audition for the next king, he completely forgot about his son out in the field playing the harp. But David didn't let that stop him—he kept working hard at his job protecting the sheep—he killed lions and bears and anything else that went after them.

Later when he ran the seemingly insignificant errand of bringing food to his brothers at the front lines of a war zone, he seized his opportunity and became a national hero by killing Goliath, the giant champion of Israel's hated enemies. Over the course of his life, he went from famine to feast and back again—by the end of his life his family and his kingdom had so much money it's said his son Solomon was one of the wealthiest men who had ever lived.

David would have been the ideal American—he experienced the exponential version of the American Dream. But that's not how he saw things:

> The earth is the Lord's, and everything in it, the world and all
> who live in it;[4]

David didn't see himself as a self-made man like we may have in his situation. His perspective was essentially, "It all belongs to God." I believe he's exactly right.

Now you might be thinking, "*Seriously, Jeff? God didn't get up today and go to work for me, he didn't make that sale or finish that project or go on the business trip in my place.*" That's true. He didn't, but what He did was create you, give you the gifts, the intellect, the talent, and the opportunity to produce for

4   Psalm 24:1 (NIV)

your company. This resulted in you getting a paycheck, which allowed you to pay for the food you ate today, the car you drove to work, the clothes on your back and the roof over your head.

Think about this: there are more than 7 billion people on the planet today and about 315 million of those live in the U.S. The average American family makes about $50,000 a year. Not bad, but certainly not rich, right? If you made $50,000 in 2014, 99.69% of the world's population made less than you did.

If you take 2014 out of the equation and compare yourself against everyone who's ever lived, that number goes way up. A modest standard of living on today's scale is far more comfortable and luxurious than what royalty experienced several hundred years ago. They couldn't go to the grocery store or the drive-thru to get something to eat; there was no air conditioning, no airline travel, no white collar industry and no way to do much of anything productive after the sun went down.

When we compare ourselves against our neighbors with the bigger house, the newer car, the multiple vacations per year or the lake house we're still saving for, we don't feel rich. But when we compare ourselves against the sum total of people who have lived throughout history, we can't deny it. We're wealthy. Loaded. Like Scrooge McDuck doing the backstroke through a mountain of gold coins.

How do we explain this? I'm not saying you don't work hard. I'm certainly not suggesting your salary isn't fair or appropriate according to industry standards. But I'm telling you, if you believe what the Bible says, every good gift comes from God, and it all belongs to Him. You can't take credit for what you've been given. And oh, by the way, Jesus said to whom much is given, much is required.

So what do we do about it? We'll get practical in a minute, but remember, the first thing we need is a radical perspective shift. The Bible is filled with them on this subject, and here's another one. You may want to brace yourself.

Command those who are rich in this present world not to be arrogant nor to put their hope in wealth, which is so uncertain, but to put their hope in God, who richly provides us with everything for our enjoyment.[5]

The Apostle Paul is challenging his young pastor, Timothy, to command those who are rich—(that's us, remember?)—not to be arrogant and not to put our hope in our wealth.

Not a suggestion. Not a hint. A command.

This isn't rotating your tires every three thousand miles, flossing after every meal or restricting your diet to local, organic, farm-raised fruits and vegetables. Those are suggestions only the extreme follow.

This is a command—you don't negotiate, you don't think it over, and you don't get a vote.

Once again, the Bible emphasizes this because God understands this is the natural trajectory of our hearts. When we start to have things, things start to have us. Our stuff fills us with pride and makes us feel powerful. If we're not careful, we'll start to tie our hope and our joy to what we have and our ability to acquire it.

Whether you're spending hundreds or millions, this approach doesn't work. It won't make you generous; it will make you greedy. You won't be able to gratefully celebrate and enjoy what you've been given. You'll anxiously obsess over what you've failed to receive.

This has become increasingly difficult with social media. Your friends have always been going on vacation to exotic places and buying stuff you really want—you just didn't see pictures and posts about it all the time.

---

5   1 Timothy 6:17 (NIV)

I love to encourage parents to train their children about money. Let's face it—kids are like a money pit. It's expensive to have babies, but those costs only rise exponentially as they continue to grow—and mine aren't even in college or getting married yet! If you have kids in your home, I'm guessing you never had to teach them to fight over toys or to grab something from their friends and shout, "*Mine!*"

Your kids won't teach themselves how to handle money—somebody else has to do it. You may want to keep this in mind—if you don't teach them, their friends or culture will step in and do it for you, but you probably won't like the results.

Money makes most people emotional. It creates passion and intense discussions, which is a polite way of saying "fights." But like very few things in our world, money is supremely quantifiable. It all comes down to numbers. It's hard to quantify pain or love, but you can count money.

Isn't the "Tithe" an Old Testament Thing?

God gives us a simple way to count. It's a source of controversy, it's a constantly debated concept, but in light of this larger discussion, it's extremely generous. The Bible makes it clear it all belongs to God—you don't have to be a math major to realize giving Him ten percent off the top is a bargain.

We call this act of worship the "*tithe*" because the word means "tenth." This practice of giving God the first ten percent of our resources can be traced back to at least as far as Abraham,[6] before the law was given to Moses. I think you could make the case this was what Cain and Abel were doing all the way back in Genesis 4.

Some people who've spent a lot of time in church or reading on the internet like to argue tithing is an Old Testament law and therefore should be treated the same way we treat the ceremonial minutiae of what we should wear,

6   Hebrews 7:1-10

what we should eat and how we should conduct ourselves during feasts and celebrations.

In other words, we ignore them because they served their purpose during the old covenant and they're no longer relevant to us today. There may be an excuse I've never heard as to why we don't have to tithe, but most of the time, it's the same old songs over and over. Here's how these "tunes" go:

- Don't quote the law to me. Jesus fulfilled the law, He paid it all, so there's nothing left for me to pay. I'm not under the law; I'm under grace.
- I give whatever God leads me to give.
- Salvation is free—it can't be bought. God doesn't need my money.
- The church just wants our money…they don't ask us to do anything else from the Old Testament.
- The tithe went to take care of priests, and in this day we're the priesthood of all believers, so I tithe to myself.

Don't hear what I'm not saying—research is healthy, obeying from a place of conviction and not merely following the status quo is commendable, but let's be real. Statistics tell us less than thirteen percent of Christians tithe.

By those numbers, tithing doesn't make you a mindless drone…it makes you a radical rebel.

And there is an element of truth in each of these statements. Jesus did fulfill the law on our behalf, He paid it all, He lived the life we couldn't and died in our place on our behalf.

So…we can't trust Him with 10 percent of what He gives us?

It is a beautiful, inspiring thing to say you're willing to give whatever God leads you to give.

But when you look at how Jesus treated the moral law, He always took what God said to the extreme. An eye for an eye became love your enemy, turn the other cheek and go the second mile. Don't commit adultery became don't have a lustful thought. Don't murder became don't use harsh words in talking with your brother.

If you apply this same method to giving, you're waving goodbye to ten percent a long time ago.[7]

And the truth is, the tithe is just a starting place, but most people use this as a rationale to tip, not tithe. At Christmas or for a project, they'll kick in the cash they have in their wallet or write a check that feels generous and safe. That's a long way from taking the top ten percent, right off the top, no questions asked.

People like to feel needed. Standing up and saying God needs your money is a proven method for raising money, but it doesn't hold up to the perspective of Scripture. God doesn't need anything. He's unlimited in His resources.

God doesn't ask us to give for His benefit—He does it for us. When we give our resources, our hearts always go with our money.

As we give to support what God is doing in the earth, our passion and our connection to the mission grow. This process also knocks down the other things we could spend the money on that are constantly calling out for our attention and our money.

And because God doesn't need anything, and He's promised to build and provide for His Church, I don't look at people as the source. I'm sorry if you've been hurt in this area. I know it can be a source of great pain, but

---

7   Whenever Jesus addresses giving, He assumes it's a natural part of your worship. The one time He addressed tithing specifically, He was correcting the Pharisees for doing it with the wrong motivation. He could have told them to stop doing it, but instead He says they should do it with the right heart. (Matthew 23:20)

we can't let our experience determine whether or not this is how God has called us to live.

When God tells us to live a certain way, when He gives us a clear boundary line, His intention is not to beat us down or keep us from experiencing something so amazing we'd love it more than Him. He does it to protect us as a loving Father. He wants us to trust Him.

Very few things in life demonstrate what we trust more than how we handle our money. That's why our founding fathers put that little phrase on our money ("In God We Trust")—we just don't see it as often now that most of us no longer carry much cash.

Unfortunately most of us are more like Simon the Pharisee than the woman who dumped the alabaster jar on Jesus' head and washed His feet with her tears.[8] Simon had an excuse for not being generous, but the woman was so overwhelmed by the goodness of God she couldn't stop herself.

I feel like it's important for you to hear me say that I realize there are people at Milestone who don't tithe. Some are working through it, some have been hurt by how it's been taught or the painful experiences of loved ones, and some don't want to discuss it. And that's okay with me. We still love you and want you to be a part of our community. Take the time you need to sort it out.

Remember—I'm not doing this for me. I'm fully confident God will meet all of our needs. I want this for you. We're not going to stop bringing it up.

What Is A "First fruit" and Why Does It Matter?

In Proverbs 3, the Bible is unpacking what makes a person wise. In verse three we're instructed to tie love and faithfulness around our necks and write them on our hearts, meaning those traits should characterize how we treat

---

8   If you're not familiar with the story you can find it in Luke 7:36-50.

the people in our lives. The next verse promises if we do this we'll earn favor with both God and people.

It's funny...I've never had anyone argue whether or not that passed away with the old covenant.

Verses five and six are well known and are probably familiar to you:

> *Trust in the Lord with all your heart and lean not on your own understanding; in all your ways submit to Him, and He will make your paths straight.*[9]

These are such beautiful and poetic words. This passage sounds great as a song and it makes a powerful and inspiring reminder on everything from wall murals to coffee cups. Over the years I've seen this in all kinds of places, but it's one thing to memorize it and something totally different to live it out.

It's fairly un-American. Leaning on our own understanding and refusing to do what somebody else tells us when we don't agree is how we do things. It goes on to say we shouldn't be wise in our own eyes. This whole passage is about how we learn to love God and people well, trust Him more than we trust ourselves, and learn how to guard our hearts.

Guess where this inevitably leads us? How do you know if you're trusting God in your heart?

> *Honor the Lord with your wealth, with the firstfruits of all your crops;*

There it is.

This term *"first fruit"* means the very first part, the place of honor, the part you've already spent in your mind before you get it. This can be hard for us

9   Proverbs 3:5-6 (NIV)

to grasp—we're not big on delayed gratification today. If we want something, we finance it. But back before people lived off consumer credit, when they didn't have something they really wanted, it became the first place their new resources went.

God says, *"That's the part I want."*

This is consistent with how He relates to us. He doesn't want to be second place in our hearts—not because He's insecure but because it's the way He designed us. Whenever we put anything in front of Him—money, career, fame, a relationship, our family, or material things—our souls end up broken. The first commandment essentially says, *"Don't put anything in my place."*

I remember learning this as a kid. Whether it was my allowance, money I got from mowing a lawn or one of my other teen jobs, before it went in the bank, that first piece was set aside. I still live this way today—I take the suspense or the temptation out of the equation. I'm not offering a crop or a piece of livestock; my harvest comes in the form of electronic currency, and the first place it goes is to the Lord.

I'm not saying you have to do it this way—this is my personal conviction. Some people like to write a check instead of wiring it because they like the personal act of participating in the process each month. I get it.

I also realize when you're first starting to live this way, leaving it up in the air brings procrastination or other priorities into the equation. Fear starts to creep in. You tell yourself, *"Things are tight this month. We'll start next month."* You mean well and you want to do it, but next month turns into next year. All of a sudden the arguments people make about why we don't need to do this start to sound pretty convincing.

Through the years I've heard so many people say, *"I can't afford to tithe."* But first fruits keep it really simple. They're always there. Now you may live in your tithe, drive your tithe, eat your tithe or send your kids to school with your tithe, but that first ten percent is going somewhere.

There is no ambiguity in numbers. There's no fuzzy math. The ledger will show you what matters most. Remember—God doesn't need your money —He wants your heart.

Let me show you what I mean.

Imagine there are two families who attend Milestone (or any church) who make the same amount of money and have similar expenses. Both families love God and serve people, participate in events during the week and have great relationships throughout the church community.

Family 1 tithes every month and on top of that gives to missions and to support various projects like new campuses or single moms. They don't determine their willingness to give based on what they get in return. They give because they love Jesus and are grateful for all He's done in their lives. Every month, when that paycheck comes in, that first ten percent goes to God.

Family 2 gives when they have a surplus and a few times during the year like Christmas and Easter. They occasionally participate in missions' projects and special events, but their son is playing select baseball, their daughter competes in gymnastics and they've just learned about a great deal on a lake house that's too good to pass up.

I've seen this scenario so many times I can tell you what happens next. From a distance, both families look equally committed. You can't tell a difference. But over time, we will see less and less of Family 2. Not because they're bad or they don't love God or the church, but because their hearts are divided. If they get that lake house, they're going to use it. When their kids have com-petitions on the weekend, which is becoming more and more normal, they'll be gone.

Before long, six months have gone by. They feel bad for not coming and they wonder what others are thinking about them. A small insignificant event in their mind becomes the evidence that no one cares about them. The circumstances don't create these heart issues—they simply reveal the condition that has been there all along.

Family 1 will also have to manage their children's activities, they may have a great opportunity for a lake house, they may even go through a major financial crisis—but because of the commitment they've made in their hearts, they'll process it differently.

They're not better or more loved by God, but these choices create boundaries that frame how we process through decisions. It's just the way it is. That's what Jesus was talking about when He said where your treasure is, your heart will be also.

When something is important to you, you don't constantly re-evaluate your decision. You don't constantly second-guess or put it off. You settle the issue in your heart and move forward.

I'm A Steward, Not An Owner

From the Bible's perspective, every resource we have is from God. He owns it all whether we're talking about our money, our material possessions, our talents and abilities, our energy or even our time.

We only enjoy the benefits of these things because He's entrusted us with them. One day, before too long, we'll stand before Him and explain what we did with what we were given.

How we answer this question won't determine whether or not we'll spend eternity with God—that depends on how we answer His first question: "*What did you do with my Son?*" But this important distinction doesn't diminish how this expectation should fundamentally change the way we live on a daily basis.

Jesus loved to use this set up in His parables. On several occasions He told His disciples about a king who went away and left His kingdom to His servants, or a master, or a man who owned a vineyard. With each telling, the purpose was clear. He was pointing back to the way God framed the world in the Garden—God created it, He owns it, and He entrusts it to His children to develop it for the benefit of all.

"Be fruitful and increase in number; fill the earth and subdue it," in Genesis 1[10] becomes *"Do business with this until I come back,"* in Luke 19.[11] It's the same idea—it's the principle of stewardship. It still hasn't changed.

A steward understands his primary responsibly is to honor the one he serves through faithfully developing what he's been given. The only way this is possible is through great generosity. Sometimes this can be very difficult when you're serving a hard master—anybody who ever had a tough boss knows what I'm talking about.

However, this scenario doesn't apply to us. We serve an incredibly generous, loving, kind and caring Master. Giving generously and sacrificially is part of His nature. He does it when He doesn't have to. He does it when it doesn't make sense. He does it when nothing is promised to Him in return.

God doesn't give hand-me-downs and leftovers—He gives His absolute best. While we were His enemies, when we were disobedient and selfish and hard-hearted, God gave us His best. Not merely the earth, not an angel, not a great man—He gave us His Son Jesus.

The Bible tells us this unimaginable generosity is the definition of what true love is—meaning, everything that aspires to be called *"love"* has to meet this standard.[12]

---

10   Genesis 1:28a (NIV)
11   Luke 19:13b (NASB)
12   Romans 5:8, 1 John 4:9

That will blow your mind if you think about it. It will also drive you crazy.

How in the world can someone say they're a follower of Jesus without being generous? When you follow someone you become more like them, not less. More and more you start to look, sound, talk and think like them. That's why I can't understand someone who's been *following* Jesus for decades who doesn't tithe, doesn't give and doesn't care.

> # GOD DOESN'T GIVE HAND-ME-DOWNS AND LEFTOVERS —HE GIVES HIS ABSOLUTE BEST.

God sends His Son to be betrayed, broken and beaten on our behalf and we're arguing over whether or not we have to give a full 10 percent, whether it has to be gross or net, or whether it has to be the first money we give or just at some point during the year? Are you joking with me?

I know I'm on my soapbox now and I'm full-on venting, but I can't help it. This drives me crazy.

There's a simple explanation—it's bad stewardship. It doesn't matter if it's fear, or greed, or a misperception that causes you to see yourself as the owner. Being a bad steward is miserable—you never feel like you have enough, you feel like you're missing out on what everyone else is experiencing and most of the time you attach people to your problems ("*He did this,*" and "*They did that,*" etc.).

Being a good steward is its own reward. It fills you with a sense of joy and peace you can not get any other way. Did you know that God created us to receive through giving? That's why Jesus said it's better to give than receive[13]—that wasn't Santa Claus.

If you're a parent like I am, every day you're faced with a long list of daily responsibilities—work, drive the shuttle service for your children, help with homework, manage relationships, change diapers, make meals, get the kids ready for bed, spend time with your spouse, eat, sleep, pray, read your Bible and if there's time…relax for a moment.

Every one of these issues is a stewardship issue that requires your generosity. Sometimes that means saying "*No*" to things you can't fit in this season. And remember, saying "*Yes*" to one thing usually means saying "*No*" to something else. A good steward realizes this and prioritizes accordingly.

Good stewards are also free from comparison. They are not being judged by what anyone else does, but by what they do with what they're given. Good stewards realize the goal of their giving is not equal gift, but equal sacrifice. The whole world has remembered the generosity of a poor widow who gave a few pennies while most Christians who read their Bibles daily don't remember that the Queen of Sheba gave King Solomon millions of dollars worth of gold to build the temple.

It's a heart issue. I love how the Message phrases Jesus' words about the widow.

> *The truth is that this poor widow gave more to all the collection than all the others put together. All the others gave what they'll never miss; she gave what she couldn't afford—she gave her all.*[14]

If you train your heart at an early age when equal sacrifice is small, it's much easier as you get older to continue to be a good steward when your gift is much larger than it used to be. This is why it's important for children and students and young people to embrace this from an early age.

---

13 Acts 20:35
14 Mark 12:43-44 (MSG)

What's most important to good stewards is the joy of their Master. More than anything else in life, they want to hear Him say, "*Well done, good and faithful servant! You have been faithful with a few things; I will put you in charge of many things. Come and share your master's happiness!*"[15]

How Does God Treat A Faithful Steward?

The middle sentence of this verse (Matthew 25:21) highlights a discussion that's created no shortage of controversy.

One group argues this is one of many examples from Scripture that proves God is looking for people He can entrust with unlimited wealth to accomplish His purposes. They reduce the Christian life to a series of principles, when, if correctly understood and practiced, lead to limitless resources.

According to this overemphasis on prosperity, financial abundance is *the* sign of spiritual maturity and the blessing of God. They primarily read Scripture through the lens of finances, and the truth is that the Bible has a lot to say about this issue. Taken out of context, there are plenty of passages[16] and stories of people that appear to support this perspective.

For the most part, this perspective is an extreme reaction to an older view that elevates and promotes not just simplicity, but *poverty* as a Christian virtue. They get there from different routes—some use a hard literal reading of The Rich Young Ruler,[17] others read into James 2:5 that somehow God chooses and honors some people to be poor in this life as preparation for a special reward in the next life, while still others downplay "*the love of*

---

15   Matthew 25:21 & 23 (NIV)

16   Not unlike the popular book from a few years back *The Secret*, prosperity theology suggest if you have enough faith you can get whatever you want and God will make it happen for you. To get there, they claim every promise of Scripture at any time, made to any one can be yours if you believe. They love Deuteronomy 8:18, Psalm 34:10, Philippians 4:13 and any Scripture that reads like a blank check. They also point to characters like Abraham, Jabez, Solomon, Joseph & everyone else you find in Hebrews 11. But for some reason they never mention the last five verses of that famous chapter. Weird.

17   Matthew 19:16-22, Luke 18:18-23

money" out of 1 Timothy 6:10 to simply conclude money is the root of all evil. For years and years monks and priests willingly took a vow of poverty like a vow of celibacy, and so tradition began to attach a greater measure of spirituality to being poor.

I believe equating prosperity or poverty as a clear sign of maturity in Christ is a mistake. Both views are extremes. They're like a big ditch on either side of the road.

As we've seen, the issue is not how much you give but your heart as a steward. Whether you find your righteousness before God in how much you have or how little you have, in both cases…you're wrong. God's approval and love for you comes from your position in Christ alone.

Whenever Jesus talked about good stewards—the reward for doing well was always being entrusted with more. The "more" isn't always money or tangible resources—it also includes more joy, responsibility, peace, faith and other non-material rewards.

You can't deny the principle of sowing and reaping in Scripture—from the Old Testament to the New—those who sow generously reap well and those who hoard what they've been entrusted with eventually run out. Paul writes simply, "*Whoever sows sparingly will reap sparingly, and whoever sows generously will reap generously.*"[18] Later he goes so far as to say that if this principle is disrupted it actually mocks God.[19] When it comes to the tithe, God actually says, "*Test me in this…*" and promises to open the floodgates of heaven and pour out a blessing so big we couldn't even take it all in.

But none of us should be quick to turn stewardship into a purely transactional relationship based on merit. If we do, we're missing the point.

---

18   2 Corinthians 9:6
19   Galatians 6:7

That's like one of our kids coming to us on the basis of getting an allowance for services rendered. They would never be able to earn their keep by emptying the dishwasher or letting the dog out.

In the same way, being a good steward doesn't make us even with the one who gave us everything. Jesus said His followers would reap even where they haven't sown as they received the rewards others worked for.[20]

God wants to bless you. This does not mean He's writing you a blank check—it's actually even better than that. Being a good steward means learning to enjoy what God enjoys—the joy, life and encouragement that comes from viewing life through, *"How can I be a blessing?"* more than *"How can I be blessed?"*

Practical Steps

If you're still reading along with me you're probably thinking, *"Okay Jeff, I get it. Just tell me what to do!"* Sounds like you're ready to strap on those skis, get off the bunny hill, lean into it and take off down the mountain.

1) TITHE & FIRST FRUITS

It all starts here. This isn't a PhD, reserved for the super-committed. This is Biblical Generosity 101. It's the basics. You go up from here. The simplest way to begin is to set aside the first ten percent of your income every month and give it to God. Because I believe you don't pick a church but God places you in one, I believe that ten percent goes to the church. I don't believe this because I'm a pastor and this is how I draw my living, I believe it because of what the Bible says about the role of the church. It's God's Plan A and He has no Plan B. I believed this long before I was a pastor and if I ever do anything else, the first fruits of any income that I have will go straight to the church God places me in.

---

20   John 4:38

2) GIVING TO MISSIONS, PROJECTS & THE POOR

In addition to the tithe/first fruits, the Bible talks a great deal about giving offerings and taking care of widows, orphans and the poor. As I mentioned before, I believe single moms are the widows of our day so we give generously and consistently to support them. More than a billion people in the world don't have access to clean water—this kills more people every year than all the wars in the world combined so we give to organizations that drill wells to give people access to water. And because of our commitment to the life-transforming power of the Gospel, we give generously to missionaries and church plants all over the world.

Since we value spiritual family, I also think it's important to participate and give when our community gets behind a project. There are some projects I'm more motivated about than others, but when someone on our team or in my small group is passionate about something, I want to be involved. I don't want to miss out on what's happening because I'm part of the family. Because our treasure and our heart are connected, when you start to give to something, it's amazing how you start to care and pay much more attention to it.

Building projects don't have the same sizzle and high emotional buy-in of some of the other projects. They can even become a cause for criticism and scrutiny as if somehow the substantial money required for building facilities would be better used if given to the poor. Is it possible for churches to build in excess at the expense of caring about their communities and the needs of others around the world? Sure but you could say the same about a business, a school or a home. The issue isn't how much you spend on what you build. The issue isn't even how much you spend on a building. The issue is whether or not you are living generously and being a blessing every opportunity you can.

I value and believe in giving to the poor but as we have seen from several experts on this issue you can't solve global issues simply by taking the money you'd put towards a building and writing a check to an impoverished people group.[21]

Here's the bottom line: buildings can be incredibly valuable in creating environments for people to experience the presence of God and participate in genuine, life-giving community. I have done church in a furniture store, hotel ballrooms, cafetoriums, old churches with cracked foundations and dangerous electrical wiring and converted grocery stores. A building can't build a church—but when your facilities become an extension of your strategy, your ability to create a greater impact goes up.

Whether we like it or not, it's a fact. I'm not looking to build monuments to ourselves or as a legacy to what God did in our generation. I'm looking to build lives in people—especially the next generation—and buildings help us do this.

3) GET DEVELOPED/CREATE A CULTURE OF GENEROSITY

As a culture, we're severely underdeveloped in this area. Our government, our communities and even a lot of our businesses could use some basic development in sound financial practices. We offer stewardship small groups with budget coaches several times a year and we have started these in our student ministry as well.

I would encourage you to create a culture of generosity in your home—if you're single and you have roommates, talk about it with each other. Think of ways to be good stewards and to spur each other on towards increasing generosity. If you're married, I don't have to tell you how important it is to communicate honestly about this subject. Ignoring the issue might let you relax for a couple of weeks but it won't solve the problem. If you have children, it's critical you help them learn to cultivate gratitude and responsibility so they can fend off the self-centered, entitled attitude of our culture.

---

21 Both "When Helping Hurts," by Corbett & Fikkert and "The Spiritual Danger of Doing Good," by Peter Greer discuss this issue in brilliant detail. If you've ever wondered about this, they're worth checking out.

4) Give Where It Hurts the Most

Genuine, heart-felt generosity looks different during various seasons of life. Most young adults don't have a lot of discretionary income lying around, but they usually have time. As you get older and carry more responsibility, you tend to have less time but more money. Depending on your personality, some people love to get out and work on a project, while others prefer to spend their time quietly with loved ones.

When we talk about generosity, there are always people who say, *"It's more than just money!"* There are others who say, *"Who do I make the check out to?"* I appreciate the willingness to give in both situations. But generosity doesn't mean we give on our terms. Remember the widow's mite—*"all the others gave what they'll never miss, she gave what she couldn't afford."*

That's why I think it's healthy and important to discover which resource is the most difficult for you to give and then make it a practice to prioritize this kind of giving. This will help to ensure your generosity is challenging you and causing you to trust more deeply in Jesus.

GENEROSITY

Key Points

- The only way to go forward is to lean into the very thing you're afraid of. It doesn't make sense—you have to trust by faith. It's true with humility. It's true with spiritual family. It's true with serving and it's definitely true with generosity and giving.
- Money is not evil. It creates a lot of opportunities and is a great tool. It makes a terrible god.
- Entitlement says we deserve everything we have. Actually, entitlement says we deserve MORE than what we have. It's owed to us. This makes gratitude, humility and genuine generosity nearly impossible.
- From the beginning of Scripture all the way to the end, the clear consensus, the undeniable perspective is that we are not owed anything. Every good thing in our life is a gift, a demonstration of God's love and generosity.
- When we start to have things, things start to have us. Our stuff fills us with pride and makes us feel powerful. If we're not careful, we'll start to tie our hope and our joy to what we have and our ability to acquire it.
- God doesn't ask us to give for His benefit—He does it for us. When we give our resources, our hearts always go with our money.
- He doesn't want to be second place in our hearts—not because He's insecure but because it's the way He designed us. Whenever we put anything in front of Him—money, career, fame, a relationship, our family, or material things—our souls end up broken.

- You may live in your tithe, drive your tithe, eat your tithe or send your kids to school with your tithe, but that first ten percent is going somewhere. There is no ambiguity in numbers. There is no fuzzy math. The ledger will show you what matters most.

- He owns it all whether we're talking about our money, our material possessions, our talents and abilities, our energy and even our time. We only enjoy the benefits of these things because He's entrusted us with them. And one day, before too long, we'll stand before Him and explain what we did with what we were given.

- God doesn't give hand-me-downs and leftovers—He gives His absolute best. While we were His enemies, when we were disobedient, selfish and hard-hearted, God gave us His best. Not merely the earth, not an angel, not a great man—He gave us His Son Jesus.

- Good stewards realize the goal of their giving is not equal gift, but equal sacrifice. The whole world has remembered the generosity of a poor widow who gave a few pennies while most Christians who read their Bibles daily don't remember that the Queen of Sheba gave King Solomon millions of dollars worth of gold to build the temple.

- The issue is not how much you give but your heart as a steward. Whether you find your righteousness before God in how much you have or how little you have, in both cases…you're wrong. God's approval and love for you come from your position in Christ alone.

- God wants to bless you—this doesn't mean He's writing you a blank check—it's actually even better than that. Being a good steward means learning to enjoy what God enjoys—the joy, life and encouragement that comes from viewing life through, *"How can I be a blessing?"* more than *"How can I be blessed?"*

Discussion Questions

- Why do you think the Bible says that the love of money is the "root of all evil"? What is the American culture of entitlement?

- What does the term *"first fruits"* mean and how does it help us understand the biblical call to tithe?

- What is the difference between a steward and an owner? What does the Bible say about faithful stewardship?

Practical Steps

- The first step in generosity always starts with firstfruits and the tithe. Set aside the first ten percent of your income and give it straight to the church God has placed you in. In addition to your tithe give generously when your community gets behind a project.
- Get involved and get developed in the area of generosity. Find a stewardship class to participate in and cultivate a culture of stewardship and generosity in your home.
- Give where it hurts the most. Contemplate the resource that is most difficult for you to give and make it a practice to prioritize this kind of giving.

CHAPTER THIRTEEN

DNA PART ONE:

Who We Are At The Deepest Level

I love to hunt. I'm passionate about it. It does something for my soul.

This becomes quickly apparent when you walk into our pastors' room at the church. There's a collection of six or seven deer heads, a prong-horned antelope and an elk so big it looks like a triceratops. I like to take our creative, artistic guys and let them sit under the deer heads—it helps calibrate their manhood.

If you ask me, you can't be a full-blooded Texan until you draw blood on big game.

Hunting is so much more than killing or shooting. I enjoy the stillness of it. I like the idea of getting away from the busyness of life, slowing down and unplugging from technology. When you are in the middle of nowhere with no signal, your phone turns into a clock.

You have to be quiet for long periods of time. There's really no one to talk to. I end up praying and spending time with Jesus. Waiting patiently for one of these incredible beasts develops a level of respect and gratitude for them. When they emerge from the bushes or wander into your area, you get nervous and excited. It takes discipline to calm the butterflies and the shaky hands this moment produces.

Some people think hunting is cruel or abusive towards the animals, and it sounds completely counter-intuitive, but most hunters I know have a profound love and respect for nature. They're emotionally and financially invested in the long-term sustainability of the species of animal they hunt.

We're not trying to wipe a species out—it's not like we're hunting endangered species like California Condors, Spotted Owls, Leatherback Turtles or Red Wolves.

I remember when I was in college and the movie *Jurassic Park* came out. It seems like every boy becomes fascinated with dinosaurs at some point in his life. Even though they were computer generated, seeing them on the big screen took my breath away.

I was jealous of the head of security. He had the job to venture out from the compound to hunt down the velociraptors. I know the brother got killed,[1] but for a few moments he lived the ultimate hunting experience. Now before you accuse me of simply wanting to kill stuff, remember how the story went.

Scientists had discovered the DNA strands of dinosaurs from blood trapped in prehistoric mosquitoes and as long as they had the genetic codes, they could create as many new dinosaurs as they wanted to. Whether or not this is even remotely possible in reality, the notion is plausible enough to create a compelling story. That's how powerful DNA is.

---

1   I didn't call SPOILER ALERT here because the movie is more than 20 years old. At some point, that's on you. It's a movie about dinosaurs...what did you think was going to happen?

DNA stands for deoxyribonucleic acid and it is the genetic instructions used in the development and functioning of all known living organisms. Life is impossible without it. They are the instructions, the playbook to the trillions of cells in our bodies. It's made up of some of the most common elements on earth like hydrogen, oxygen, nitrogen and carbon, but what makes it so special is the specific way these elements are placed together.

All human beings are 99.9 percent genetically identical, yet no two human beings are exactly alike. There are differences in appearance, preference, taste, personality, demeanor, gifts and talents, and all the little quirks that make you who you are.

The elements are nearly identical, but the unique distinctive emerges in how these compounds are placed together. Every family is made up of a mom, a dad, usually some children, cousins, grandparents, and perhaps a few pets...but the unique characteristics and distinctiveness of the family comes from how these parts relate to each other. The same is true in a business, a school, a team and any number of other organizations.

And the same is true in great churches—their uniqueness is the result of the distinctive features that frame how they're put together. Great churches share major theological doctrines, they may even share values, but how they live them out and put them into practice creates the identity and culture of the church.

> THERE WAS A CERTAIN KIND OF CHURCH HE DESIGNED US TO BE— NOT BETTER, JUST UNIQUE.

Why Does This Matter?

Perhaps the simplest way to explain it is to think of DNA as the code that makes you…you. You didn't write your own DNA and I didn't choose mine. No one asked for our opinion—it was given to us. This is a critical starting point in our culture where well-meaning parents, teachers and mentors tell us we can be whatever we want to be if we want it badly enough. We're told from an early age that our lives are what we make them. It sounds so inspiring, but as you grow up you realize how much pain and disappointment results from this attitude.

The truth is we can't define ourselves.

God gives each one of us our own DNA—as I grow and develop He helps me to discover more and more of who I am…and who I'm not. If I don't know who I am, I'll constantly compare myself with others, try to be something I'm not, fail to be who I truly am or misrepresent myself and create a false sense of expectation in others.

The same is true in an organization. I believe God had Milestone Church in mind long before we showed up in Keller. There was a certain kind of church He designed us to be—not better, just unique.

You might be thinking, *"Jeff, didn't we already talk about this? Isn't DNA another way of talking about your values?"* While they're closely related, it may be helpful to think about our DNA as our values in action—the way we live out what matters most to us. As you read over these distinctives, you'll see how they grow out of our values.

But perhaps the most critical reason to highlight these is to create a healthy expectation for anyone who comes in contact with our community. People often ask, *"Why do you do this?"* or *"How do you feel about this issue?"* or *"When is the church going to do something about that?"*

These eight distinctives frame everything we do. They're the subtext from which we operate. They demonstrate what matters to us and reinforce who we are created to be.

DNA #1: People Matter To God

The first DNA statement is simply, *"People matter to God."*[2] This is basic. It should be self-explanatory but we live in a broken, self-centered world. Living for others and caring about people doesn't just happen. You have to be intentional about it.

This posture isn't natural for us, but it is for God.

He's intimately involved, not only with the details of what's happening in our lives, but our thoughts, our passions, our fears, and our dreams.

I love being outdoors. A picturesque mountain view, rolling green hills, the Texas sky, the waves crashing on a beach...they're vastly different, but the beauty of each one can take your breath away.

For more than 25 years, the Hubble telescope has been capturing unbelievable images of the cosmos. When you look at them, you can't help but feel small but Scripture makes this clear: nothing in all of Creation is as important to God as we are. More than anything else, He loves people.[3] And He made it clear that anyone who genuinely loved God would demonstrate this by loving people the same way He does.

From the very beginning, Jesus modeled this in His ministry. He always moved toward the undervalued, the overlooked and the marginalized to communicate to them how much they mattered to God.

---

2   This concept jumps off the pages of Scripture, but as I cited earlier, the wording is influenced by Bill Hybels.
3   Psalm 8:4-8

The man with the withered hand and the woman with the issue of blood[4]
The Samaritan divorcee He met at the well who was shacked up with another guy[5]
The naked crazy man chained up by a cave[6]
Blind Bartemaeus[7]
The lepers[8]
The tax collectors
The woman caught in adultery[9]
The tax collector[10]
The children[11]
Even the criminal on the cross next to Him[12]

We've tried to build this into our community. Every person is made in the image of God. Sin may have cracked their mirror, but God continues to love them and value them. Like the father in Luke 15, He's looking down the road waiting for His son to come home.

It's not easy. It's not common. It doesn't come naturally, but we're doing our best to see people this way. God doesn't relate to mankind primarily as Judge, Creator, King, Ruler or Enforcer. He is all of those things, but when Jesus described Him, He chose the word "*Father.*"

That's hard for many of us to grasp. Maybe we didn't have a great father. Maybe our father wasn't there for us. When that happens, it's easy for us to project those frustrations and hurts onto God.

---

4   Mark 3:1-6 and Luke 8:43-48
5   John 4
6   Luke 8:26-39
7   Mark 10:46
8   Matthew 8 and Luke 17:11-19
9   John 8:1-11
10   Luke 19:1-10
11   Matthew 19:14—In our suburban world where kids are valued, this doesn't seem like a big deal. But in Jesus' day, kids were treated more like property than people.
12   Luke 23:32-43

////////////////////////////////

I'm reminded of Jennifer, a young woman who serves on our worship team, and her incredible story that played out just earlier this year. Like so many, Jennifer had grown up never knowing her birth father—the relationship between him and her mother was over before Jennifer was even born. Jennifer's only connection to her birth father was her last name. Her mother, with three kids from a previous marriage and a new baby, ended up on welfare and married the man Jennifer would come to call Dad when Jennifer was only eight weeks old.

Though their parents loved them, Jennifer and her siblings grew up in a family struggling through generational issues. It made for a painful childhood. Jennifer's parents were married 28 years until her mother passed away after a battle with cancer at the age of 52.

She had spent a lot of time searching for something that nothing in her earthly life could fill. After giving her life to Christ, Jennifer had started the long journey of forgiveness and healing from the pain and brokenness of her childhood. She found what she was searching for in the unending love of Christ and spiritual family.

Jennifer met her husband, Chris, at another church in our area. They were soon married and began a family. Into their sixth year of marriage, Chris felt the Lord was leading them to relocate. It was unsettling to pick up and move, but they felt like they had heard clearly from the Lord. Through this transition, Jennifer, Chris and their young son landed here at Milestone Church. Jennifer and Chris began to get connected to spiritual family and for more than five years now have been serving faithfully—ministering to other couples in their neighborhood, leading small groups, serving in worship, and laying their lives down daily for His Kingdom.

Just like that, out of nowhere, when you're serving faithfully where God has planted you, He might just rewrite your story. You see, He had been working providentially to write a plotline you could only dream up. Remember, He's in the business of redemption and people matter.

As Jennifer was perusing Facebook one day, she came across a picture posted by a friend of hers, another member here at Milestone Church. In the comment section was a post from a woman with Jennifer's maiden name. Her family was originally from Minnesota, so the likelihood it would end up being any relation was one in a million.

But not in God's economy.

Through some dialogue, Jennifer came to find out that the woman from Facebook was actually married to her cousin—-and not only that, but she had cousins living right here in Keller. Blood relatives living right down the street in her neighborhood, their kids attending the very same elementary school as her son.

And through reuniting with her family Jennifer had the opportunity to finally meet her birth father for the first time.

Jennifer said she was moved to tears to know she looked like someone, to find out the history of her Italian family, to hug her birth father for the very first time. The man that Jennifer grew up with and calls Dad was more than happy to see her be able to connect with that part of her family.

Jennifer wasn't looking for her birth father to make amends or for apologies. She hadn't been waiting around her whole life to see if this one thing could make all the pain go away. The Lord had already redeemed and restored the brokenness in her life. This was just the icing on the cake. We all long to be known by our Father. The Lord was simply doing in the natural what he'd already done in the spiritual.

This is God's heart for all of us. Because we're His children, every one of us matters to Him.

DNA #2 Your Destiny Is Tied To Your Relationships

Life isn't random. It only feels that way from our perspective. Our thoughts, our decisions, our words and our actions all impact the quality of our lives.

One of the most critical factors that many people overlook are the people they choose to do life with. I've said it before and I'll keep saying it—life is all about relationships. I think deep down we all understand this.

In business, Jim Collins tells us one of the most critical factors that causes a good company to become great is getting the right people in the organization. John Maxwell says our lives become the product of the books we read and the people we spend time with.

Every football coach in America at one point or another has said, "*It's not about the X's and O's, it's about the Billies and Joes.*" If you're not familiar, what that means is your players are more important than your game plan.

If we understand God's Word, this shouldn't surprise us. All throughout Scripture we see this pattern—God joins people together for the purpose of doing something great both in them and through them.

Moses and Aaron
Joshua and Caleb
Ruth and Naomi
Hannah and Samuel
Jonathan and David
Elijah and Elisha
Ezra and Nehemiah
Jesus and His disciples
The early church in the book of Acts
Paul and Timothy
The list could keep going and going.

In our world of rampant individualism, this concept can be hard for us. We want our personal space. We want to control our own fates. We want things the way we want them, and if somebody doesn't play nice we take our ball and go home.

This may be our prerogative; an option available to us no one can take away, but it comes at a price. It's why we are more technologically connected but relationally isolated than ever before. There are more people on planet earth than at any point in history and yet millions live lonely, isolated lives.

The Bible is not a story of a bunch of individuals doing their own thing. Rather it's communities of people doing life together.

When we want to give up, God says to get connected. When we cry out and pray for help, God often sends a person to help meet our need. The church isn't a group of disconnected individuals who participate in a religious gathering once a week—it's a community, a family, joined together with intentionality.

In a culture of disposable relationships, finding an environment where people are valued and relationships are prioritized is a unique experience. We're certainly not the only ones doing this—and I'm sure there are others who do it even better—but it will always be central to who we are.

Whenever God has wanted to do something, He's always started with a family. It's the primary way that He distributes His blessing. This doesn't mean you won't get hurt or offended. You will. It doesn't mean the people in the family will be perfect. They won't.

It does mean this is how you were designed to live. At the end of your life, when you look back at what really mattered, it won't be the experiences, it won't be the accomplishments, it won't be your estate that you'll care about.

It will be the people.

One of the key relationships in my life has often told me, "*You find your people, you find your purpose.*" It sounds simple but I believe it's true.

I've seen this play out over and over through a variety of incredible circumstances.

Melissa grew up a Methodist preacher's kid in the central Texas area. Life seemed great—a set of loving parents, two younger siblings and a passion for worship and guitar. After graduating with a degree in Geology from Texas A&M, Melissa started her career teaching Chemistry to high school students in Keller. It seemed like the perfect place to land, considering her dad had just transferred to a church only 20 minutes away in North Richland Hills.

Melissa was leading worship, volunteering with student ministries, teaching, and attending her teenage brother's soccer games (her favorite hobby).

She never could have anticipated what would happen next.

> IT'S COMMUNITIES OF PEOPLE DOING LIFE TOGETHER. WHEN WE WANT TO GIVE UP **GOD SAYS TO GET CONNECTED.**

During Spring Break of her first year of teaching, Melissa's father, Bobby, was diagnosed with an inoperable malignant brain tumor. There was no cure— only treatment to prolong life. It was terminal and it rocked their family to the core. The next year consisted of hospital waiting rooms, chemo effects, and providing rides as her father slowly declined to using a wheelchair. He resigned his role as Senior Pastor after several months of bravely preaching to the Methodist congregation from the seat of his walker.

His brain function finally started to decay. In 2007, 13 months after being diagnosed, Bobby passed away at only 52.

In the two years that followed, Melissa's family attempted to put the pieces back together. Melissa's mother remarried to a stand up guy, her sister graduated from A&M, and her brother began high school. We are all promised trials in this life, but sometimes lightning strikes twice.

In 2009 Melissa's brother, Jonathan, was 17 years old, a stand-out varsity soccer player, a leader in his youth group, and ranked in the top of his class. When he complained of flu-like symptoms and a high fever, just two weeks after completing a deep run into the state soccer playoffs, Melissa's family immediately checked him into the ER.

Jonathan was diagnosed with Acute Lymphoblastic Leukemia…just over two years after his father died.

No way. Not again.

Jonathan went through five months of grueling chemotherapy and suffered several complications of a weakened immune system. He spent 35 days in the ICU, endured more than five emergency abdominal and brain surgeries, suffered bowel perforations, mouth ulcers, and a fungal brain infection that ultimately took his life. October 10th, 2009 Jonathan died…just days after being crowned Homecoming King by his high school.

Melissa's escape from the reality of her family's pain and trials came in the classroom as she continued to teach her students.

By the grace of God, three female students began to make an important connection with Melissa over the years of hardship. Some had walked through similar circumstances, others just saw through her professionalism to her indescribable pain.

I'm so proud to say these girls happened to be a part of our student ministry here at Milestone Church, and in 2010 they invited Melissa to come with them to a service.

Soon Melissa joined a small group and got caught up in the family and community here. She started serving on our worship team and in our student ministry environment and has since been on three mission trips with us.

The healing and redemption she found in the community here came through the providential relationships God placed in her life. He ordered her steps and brought people to intersect her path on the way to her destiny.

The answer to her prayers came through people. God did it—He gets all the glory—but He chose to use people to be a means of healing and recovery in her soul.

> # "YOU FIND YOUR PEOPLE, YOU FIND YOUR PURPOSE."

Now Melissa serves on our staff full-time in a vital role, including providing a good deal of research and support for the book you are reading right now! It doesn't end there. Her entire family has joined us at Milestone, and are continuing to find healing and help through our community.

God's view and value of being placed in spiritual family is so much bigger than the way most of us see it.

The Malone family moved to Keller with me when we started Milestone Church. Our story together spans decades.

One morning a few years ago their son, Randy, was ready to head to the gym. He grabbed his coffee in the kitchen and turned toward the door. His wife, Stephanie had gone back to their screaming infant son's room to comfort him. Randy thought about heading toward the door, but on second thought he knew he never left the house without giving Stephanie a kiss goodbye. He walked back towards the bedroom and saw Stephanie had collapsed in the hall. Her heart just stopped and she was gone.

As Randy described the emotions in that moment, the only word he could find to describe it was *numb*.

"Is this really happening to me?"

"My perfect little world, perfect little box had been shattered."

If you have a spouse and small children, I'm sure, like me, you can't begin to imagine what this would be like.

In Randy's mind he had only two options: give up or press into God. There was a sense of being lost—not knowing what the future would hold for him and his two young sons. Answers weren't easy to find, and as his pastor, I wanted to provide an insight or an explanation, but sometimes there isn't one. In the midst of tragedy, Randy's focus on life changed. He has always been faithful and served in our environments, but life took on a much greater eternal perspective. He began to live intentionally for others at an entirely different level.

This wasn't somehow a covert strategy to find a new wife, but God knew what He needed. In January of 2010 Randy married Vanessa, another member of our church family here at Milestone, and today they are raising his two boys with Stephanie plus three new additions!

In the midst of indescribable pain and difficulty, God provided everything Randy needed through the context of the relationships He'd provided.

We celebrate what God has done for Randy and Vanessa and Melissa and her family—and at the same time we realize they represent untold thousands in need of the blessing of God available through these kinds of relationships.

DNA #3 Character Over Charisma

God gives each of us natural talents and abilities. He doesn't consult us. You may not get the gift you wanted, but God will make sure you have the gifts you need.

He's not asking you to be something (or someone) you're not. But He does want you to honor Him by faithfully developing your gifts so you can use them to bless others and in the process, bring glory to the One who gave you the gift.

Some people are so gifted it's scary. It's not even fair. They're smart, they're persuasive, they can sing, they're creative. From a distance you look at them in awe. Unfortunately, it's really easy to find your identity in and lean on your gifts instead of developing your character. Especially if your gifts are big enough for everyone else to see and people tell you how great you are all the time.

I've found your gifts will open the door of opportunity for you, but only godly character will keep you there. If you never develop your character and only lean on your gifts, sooner or later your life will become a mess. It's tragic—the very thing that creates the opportunity will eventually crush you.

We see this all the time with athletes, entertainers and celebrities. It's easy to look at them and shake our heads, but the truth is, we all face this challenge. Whether you're a student, a business person, a politician, an artist or a pastor—character isn't optional if your goal is long-term success.

I've met a lot of incredibly gifted people through the years who have been blessed with unlimited potential. As my proximity moved closer to their lives, what I realized was their gift was compensating for their character. In the long run, a less-gifted but more dependable person will outlast and outperform an outlier without the internal infrastructure to endure.

A well-known definition of character is *"who you are when no one is looking."* I think this is an excellent way to frame this idea, but it's important to clarify this is bigger than accountability. It's more than whether or not someone is looking. It's about the desires of your heart. People who know someone will be checking on them cover their tracks. There are a lot of guys looking at things on the internet they shouldn't be who simply erase their history on their browsers so they won't get caught.

Character doesn't just modify your behavior, it changes your *"want to"* at a heart level. What you want and desire is molded into the person God created you to be.

You can see this play out in many places in Scripture, but I don't think there's a better example than Saul. He was gifted, handsome, a head taller than his peers, and the guy everyone would have picked first, but he believed his own hype. He always thought he knew better. He wasn't teachable. He didn't take instruction well.

On the contrary, when the prophet came to Jesse's house to find the next king, they lined up all the brothers and forgot about the youngest one. He was an eccentric kid who made up songs while he was watching the sheep. Of course, periodically he would kill lions and bears too.

When the prophet Samuel was sizing up the sons the Lord reminded him: *"Do not consider his appearance or his height, for I have rejected him. The LORD does not look at the things people look at. People look at the outward appearance, but the LORD looks at the heart."*

The reason God chose David and rejected Saul didn't have anything to do with their giftings, it had everything to do with their hearts. David made a lot of mistakes too—more serious and problematic than Saul, but David was willing to repent and change.

A great test of your character is to ask yourself: *"Am I the person God wants me to be in every setting in my life, or are there multiple versions of me? Do I behave one way when other people are watching and another when I feel the freedom to choose for myself?"*

CHARACTER DOESN'T JUST
MODIFY YOUR BEHAVIOR,
IT CHANGES YOUR "WANT TO"
AT A HEART LEVEL.

This simple test is really hard to pass. I'm not trying to make you feel bad, I'm trying to help you see that you are much more important than your gifts. When we fail to realize this, we think God loves us when we perform and He withdraws when we mess up. This isn't an accurate picture of His heart for us. I've always prioritized this with gifted people, and it's not always easy. As a leader, you want to benefit from their gift. But as a pastor, if you really care for them, you've got to take the long view.

This reminds me of one of the most gifted worship leaders I know—Milestone's own Betsy Caswell.

//////////////////////////////

Betsy's music career started as a young girl playing family reunions and talent shows with her brothers—if someone would let them play some down-home Tennessee country music, they'd be there. Over a couple years some doors opened for her band, and eventually Betsy found herself singing in front of tens of thousands of people and opening for several well-known country music artists. But that industry is tough.

She never quite felt like she measured up—never hit the mark and spent years listening to criticism and negative comments. Gradually, Betsy's life became all about insecurities, perfectionism and comparison…and let me tell you, that stuff will start to eat your soul.

The turning point in her life came at age 19. Betsy was asked to make an album and sign a Christian recording contract and through that process actually came to know Christ. Suddenly it all started to make sense—it wasn't about what the industry measured as success.

God wanted to use what He'd put in her from the beginning—He wanted to use her gifts to reveal Himself to people. She hadn't been looking for Him—in fact, she would tell you she had been running from Him. But even in those moments when we have turned the other way, He comes right down in the middle of our world and changes our lives.

This was more than a stepping stone to something bigger or better, this was the beginning of the life she was created to live.

Betsy's record label sent her to Texas to do some shows in the DFW area. She happened to be singing at Brandy's uncle's church and that night she really felt a connection. It was one of the first times she could remember seeing a group of young people passionate about their love for Jesus and she knew God was calling her into something beyond what she had imagined.

She began to sense that God was calling her into the ministry to build His Kingdom, and she realized this would probably mean leaving the incredible opportunities she had in the music industry because of her significant gifts. But Betsy was willing, and she got a job as a receptionist just so she could be part of a vibrant church family. She simply loved being in the presence of God and she began leading worship in several smaller environments.

Derrick Wilson happened to be the youth pastor at this same church at the time and he invited me to speak at an event. It was the first time I met Betsy. Over the next few years, she met her own fiery, young passionate leader named Tyron and they were married. The two shared purpose and vision and could see the journey of their lives lining up—they were both called to full-time ministry, whether that meant living in a hut in Zimbabwe or leading a giant youth group in the suburbs. They were ready for anything God would ask them to do.

This was back when we were in Abilene and we invited Tyron and Betsy to come out and visit us. Brandy and I sat over dinner with this great young couple and shared our heart for the church I felt God had called us to build. I shared the vision God had given me for what church could be—the hope of the world, an authentic community where people were reached, lives were built, disciples were made, and purpose was discovered.

Later they told me that my heart for what the church could be resonated so strongly they couldn't get it off their minds. It was all they thought about for a month. God was doing something bigger than networking. They prayed and fasted and felt like God showed them this was His direction for their lives. Without knowing us very well, they decided to pick up and move out to Abilene. It was one of those divine connections—we all realized God was doing it—and they've been with us ever since.

When Betsy and Tyron came to the church I knew how gifted they both were, and at that point I understood how significantly her skill set would benefit our church. She'd walked away from a lucrative recording contract and a very promising career—her talent was off the charts. But I also knew I'd be doing her a great disservice just to put her on the platform.

That didn't make it any easier.

The girl could flat-out sing the paint off the walls and was comfortable in front of thousands of people, but she had trouble holding eye contact one-on-one. After years of being beaten up by the music industry, her insecurities were rooted in perfectionism and comparison. I knew God was doing something significant in Betsy during this moment so I told her for the next several months I didn't want her to lead worship, I wanted her to serve in the church.

I wasn't penalizing her or benching her—I was investing in her long-term development. She is more than her gift. She was then and she is now. I truly believe people appreciate when you place their heart above their talent. I cared more about the longevity of her ministry than what her talent could give us on a quick fix.

Tyron and Betsy rolled up their sleeves and started serving in any capacity we asked of them. Betsy wiped down counters, sang background vocals, and served in our kids department. Tyron helped build our student ministry starting with twelve kids—his incredible journey is a story all its own!

Here's the win: this couple has experienced over a decade of ministry success with thousands of lives changed, they've led major missions projects around the world and have built a beautiful family. But that's not simply the result of their substantial talents and gifts—it's come through their character—their love for Jesus and each other.

CHAPTER FOURTEEN

DNA PART TWO:

Who We Are At The Deepest Level

There is an unbelievable amount of information stored in your DNA.

The DNA in your cells is packaged in forty-six chromosomes in the nucleus, supercoiled using enzymes so that it takes up less space. There are three billion base pairs in each cell—if you stretched the DNA in one cell all the way out, it would be more than six feet long.

If you did this with every cell in your body, it would stretch approximately twice the diameter of our Solar System...or roughly the length of putting all of Milestone's DNA in one chapter.

DNA #4 The Local Church Is The Hope of the World

By this point, you understand how I feel about the local church. Hopefully, you've also come to see this isn't my idea. I got it from Jesus. I believe He has put all His eggs in this basket. He only promised to build one thing. He only called one thing His bride. The church is His Plan A and He has no Plan B.

At times it makes me nervous. At times I wonder about the logic of the approach, but I can't deny what the Bible makes so clear. Although I didn't come up with this phrase,[1] this belief is at the heart of Milestone Church: *The local church is the hope of the world.*

One man bought the field when he found the buried treasure in it. It makes me wonder how many people walked by that field every day without ever discovering the treasure. They had the same access, the same opportunity as this man. They just missed the extraordinary treasure waiting to be discovered.

This is how I feel about the local church. So many people look at it as an empty field of dirt. On many occasions that's all I've seen, but I've also found the treasure. The treasure men and women have been discovering from the earliest days of the body of Christ. A treasure that is bigger than a denomination or a model.

I love this description of the church from the book of Acts:[2]

> *They devoted themselves to the apostles' teaching and to fellowship, to the breaking of bread and to prayer. Everyone was filled with awe at the many wonders and signs performed by the apostles. All the believers were together and had everything in common. They sold property and possessions to give to anyone who had need. Every day they continued to meet together in the temple courts. They broke bread in their homes and ate together with glad and sincere hearts, praising God and enjoying the favor of all the people. And the Lord added to their number daily those who were being saved.*

---

1   Like I said in the Introduction, it comes from first Charles Spurgeon and then Bill Hybels. Thanks guys!
2   Acts 2:42-47 (NIV)

There are so many great things happening here. There's devotion to one another and to the teaching of the Word. There's a commitment to have meals together. There's an ongoing presence of the supernatural power of God to meet needs. There's a sense of awe and wonder. There's an extraordinary measure of generosity. There's a dynamic sense of worship. And there's a constant influx of new believers.

That's what the church can be.

THE LOCAL CHURCH
IS THE HOPE OF THE WORLD.

Remember—this church wasn't perfect. There were a lot of changes that still had to be made. At this point, unless you were Jewish, you wouldn't have been included. God had to intervene to make that happen.

You can see the fingerprints of Jesus all over this group of people. This was not a religion—it was a way of life. In fact, before they were called Christians, followers of Christ were known as followers of *"The Way."*[3]

When a group of people commit to Jesus and begin to live together the way He's created them to live, it impacts those around them. When you see this first hand, it fills you with a sense of awe.

In his late teen years, Jake Baker became increasingly skeptical. The doubts started with the parade of hypocrites surrounding him in high school. Too

---

3   Acts 9:2, 18:25, 19:9, 23, 22:4, 24:14, etc. Interestingly, the term "Christian" is only used 3 times in the Bible starting with Acts 11:26

many Christians partied with him one night before inviting him to church the following morning. This approach towards Jesus and the church left a sour taste in his mouth.

His intellectual curiosity led him to dig into some atheist literature. After a series of compelling books, he eventually came to a point where he was completely comfortable saying: "*There is no God.*" Jake was studying medicine and felt consistent accepting the scientific idea that when die you simply cease to exist. There is no great objective meaning to life. We have no assurance of being known or loved.

While this view appeared to be intellectually satisfying, it was a lonely and difficult place to live.

Jake's career took off, but even after vocational success he found diminishing levels of joy and fulfillment. He ended up ruining two marriages—his moral compass was completely gone and he just felt dead on the inside. The only escape he could imagine was death.

Jake entered the doors of Milestone Church knowing something needed to change. He wasn't expecting to be persuaded from his skepticism, but he was almost willing to pretend to believe something…if it would help him leave the place he was living. But when the love of Jesus hits you like a ton of bricks, you don't have to pretend—you're genuinely changed.

That day when I asked if anyone wanted to accept Jesus…Jake's hand shot up. He couldn't believe how quickly his heart turned. The depression, the pain, the loneliness was gone.

In a single moment Jake went from death to life, from feeling forgotten and alone to being loved unconditionally by His Creator. There was a peace beyond anything He imagined. He was finally…home.

The message of Jesus helped Jake find family.

The power of family also helped a different Jake find the message of Jesus.

Jake Sowell grew up going to church —it was one of those things you did, but he never really felt connected. Baseball was his life. He played baseball all the way through college, until an injury sidelined him and ended his career prematurely. When that part of his life ended, he felt empty and alone. He followed the path worn by so many others—he partied more and tried to fill the gap in his heart with alcohol. He totaled his truck in a drunk driving accident.

Nothing he was doing had any real purpose to it. Something was missing.

He was passionate about fitness, so he decided to become a trainer for the increasingly popular exercise program, *Camp Gladiator*. Eventually, he realized several members of Milestone were attending his sessions—some in the morning, some at night. Jake said he kept meeting people that were "*just different*"—they had something he didn't. He didn't know they were all from Milestone but he did see that they cared. Not just about their physical conditioning, but about him.

Throughout the day they'd naturally and conversationally share a little bit about God. Over time, gradually, it just started to click—maybe God really did have a plan for his life. Jake came to Milestone for the first time and went to lunch with one of his campers who also happened to be one of our staff pastors.[4] Jake realized that he was passionate about helping people get their bodies in shape, but his soul was unhealthy.

He began to realize that God brought him to the place where he would meet all of these people because He loved him. Ron prayed with Jake in the parking lot of Chipotle that day to receive Jesus.

---

4   Remember Ron from the Harley Davidson story in Chapter 11? That's the one!

There are Jakes[5] all over our communities—people who don't know Jesus, who haven't discovered His purpose for their lives, who feel alone and separated from the people they are meant to do life with.

Every one of these people matter to God. They are on His mind. They are on His heart and His plan to bring them home is the local church.

DNA #5: We Are More Than Servants, We're Sons And Daughters

I've found the average person theoretically grasps the concept of *"serving God"*—meaning, we work really hard to live the most moral and spiritual life we can to please God. After all, He's all-powerful, holy, infinite and eternal. It doesn't take a lot of work to relate to Him as Judge or to see Him as Creator.

Scripture doesn't leave us there. Jesus won't leave us there.

It's exhausting, frustrating and eventually leaves you dissatisfied with yourself and upset with everybody else. That's the Good News of the Gospel. Yes, God calls us to a life of obedience—but not on the basis of our own righteousness—according to the perfect, right-standing of Jesus we could never achieve on our own.

More than Judge, more than Creator, more than Ruler of the Universe, more than King, Jesus called God *"Father."* Through His sacrificial and obedient death on the Cross, as the "Ultimate and Perfect Older Brother," He invites all of us who love God into this same relationship.

The tragedy is many Christ followers never take this step.

---

5   And "Julies" and all kinds of men and women and boys and girls whose names don't start with "J" who are far from God. How will they find a meaningful relationship with Jesus and the people He's called them to walk with? The local church!

Serving a nameless, faceless ruler motivated by fear of judgment doesn't lead to abundant life. It's like an employee who has no relationship with their superior, whose whole approach to their job is not to mess up so they won't get fired. It's hard to find meaning and the motivation to keep showing up.

No matter how hard you try, your heart begins to resent your job. Over time, no matter how talented you may be, you lose confidence and struggle to find any vision for the future of personal fulfillment. You can't leave because you need the paycheck.

This is a massive problem in the workplace, but the same issue exists for many in the church. It's one of the biggest reasons why many people walk away from church or their faith. This perspective leads you to the belief that it's just a dirt field. It makes it really difficult to see the treasure.

God is not building an organization, a movement, a company, a religion or a philosophy. First and foremost, He's building a family.

Let there be no doubt: we are called to serve Him. There's one King in His Kingdom and it's not one of us. But we are more than servants. We have been given the unimaginable privilege of being adopted into the family of God as sons and daughters.

HE'S CALLING

HIS CHILDREN BACK HOME.

The Apostle John spent as much time with Jesus as anyone. He was so close to Him that he actually gave himself the nickname *"the disciple Jesus loved."*[6]

---

6   This phrase shows up five times in the Gospel of John. The first time it appears is John 13:23. And yes, John was the writer of this Gospel and presumably gave himself this name.

Personally, I don't think a man can give himself a nickname—maybe you have had a friend that tried. If you're going to give yourself one, it's a bold move to go with this one. The implication is that there are disciples Jesus *doesn't love*…or at least they weren't His favorite.

Yet a little later in John's life, when he reflects on the extraordinary privilege of being included in the family of God, it's almost too much for even him to process.

"See what great love the Father has lavished on us, that we should be called children of God! And that is what we are!"

Two sentences, two exclamation points. It has the emotional exuberance of a text from a teenage girl, not a pastor in his old age.

When you see what an incredible, unthinkable miracle it is that not only would God save us, redeem us and restore us, but He would also lavish this incredible love on us by calling us His children…you can't help but be overwhelmed.

In the story of the two brothers in Luke 15, they both struggle with this kind of love they receive from the father. It's too good to be true for the younger son who dishonored his father and ruined his life. It's unfair and offensive to the older brother who demanded justice.

That's the wild, life-changing message of the Gospel. God's not calling disobedient workers into His employ. He's calling His children back home.

When you see this, it changes everything. A servant expects nothing more than a job and a paycheck. An heir is invested in everything the family does.

///////////////////////////////

Kendyl is in her early twenties and serves as our Worship Coordinator here at Milestone. She leads teams in multiple environments throughout the week and she disciples many of our up-and-coming, next generation musicians and singers. Aside from her phenomenal voice, she embodies the values of our Milestone family and is growing into an outstanding young leader.

But if you rewind five years you'd find an impressionable, young teenage girl drinking four or five nights a week and experimenting with drugs to numb the pain of a traumatic childhood. Despite the best efforts of her mom, an absent father and an abusive step-father made for a toxic environment filled with dysfunction in her home. Eventually things spiraled out of control.

A professional record label had recognized Kendyl's vocal talents and had signed her to make a country album. They saw what she wanted them to see—a sweet, young Texas girl singing country tunes, but hiding a beaten up and broken soul.

Kendyl described the pivotal rock-bottom moment as one of those confusing times when we ask ourselves, "*How did I end up here?*" It was the kind of moment where you look at your life from a distance in disbelief …never in a million years did you imagine things ending up like this. The brokenness brought her to the point where something had to change.

She went to one of our youth services for the first time in February of 2008 with her friend Emma (you'll hear more about her later). She gave her life to Christ just two weeks later at a weekend retreat. From that moment her story has been an incredible transformation of character and growth.

God divinely placed this young lady at Milestone Church. At her lowest point when she felt all alone, He rescued her and placed her in spiritual family.

Kendyl is not a servant who sings for the benefit of others in order to gain the approval of a disappointed Creator. She's not honing her craft to prepare for a better gig. She's a genuine daughter of God who's been planted in the house. She was saved here, baptized here and placed into family here. She has embraced the process of development, serving as an intern before joining our team, and now in turn, she is developing others.

Her process isn't finished. God is continuously molding and shaping Kendyl to be all He has called her to be, but she's not doing it to make up for her mistakes or to earn the approval of others. The transformation has come as a result of God's love and acceptance that met her when she felt so far away.

This is her story...but it's our story too. We are all sons and daughters.

DNA #6: Generosity Transforms

I live in one of the fastest growing regions of the one of the fastest-growing states in the country. People are moving here from all over the nation—primarily because of the economic opportunities.

Throughout history, the vast majority of people stayed within a couple of hours of where they were raised, but our society is mobile now. We move companies, careers, cities and states. We move to find a better job, a better cost of living, and as a result...a better life.

There's nothing inherently wrong with wanting more. The question is, "Why?" The Bible makes it clear: Everything we have is a gift. We're not owners; we're stewards.

We believe Jesus was telling the truth when He said it was more blessed to give than receive.[7] God doesn't ask us to be generous because He needs our money. Generosity doesn't just meet needs for the one receiving, it also transforms the one who gives.

God doesn't ask us to be generous because He needs what we have. He doesn't want something FROM us. He's after something FOR us. This isn't something for business owners or people with financial margin. It's for all of us—for students, empty nesters, young adults, kids, single moms, business owners, staff...anyone who values a growing relationship with Jesus.

---

7 Acts 20:35

We are never more like God than when we are generous—it's fundamental to who He is.

> # GENEROSITY DOESN'T JUST MEET NEEDS FOR THE ONE RECEIVING, IT ALSO TRANSFORMS THE ONE WHO GIVES.

///////////////////////////////////

George Bullard has been a successful IBM executive in Las Colinas for more than 35 years. But at the peak of his career he found himself empty on the inside. George disconnected from church when he was 14 after his dad died. The pain was so intense, he came to believe living independent and isolated from relationships was a safer approach to life. He never married…and for the longest time he never really felt like he was missing out.

Eventually this gnawing feeling began to grow deep down in his heart. He wondered if perhaps he was missing something. An increasing emptiness that refused to be dismissed by relationships, professional accomplishments, or the large amount of success he was having at work. The void in George's life continued to grow until he knew he couldn't ignore it any longer.

That's when George started planning his Saturdays around commuting to Milestone here in Keller (not exactly a short drive from Las Colinas[8]).

---

8   With moderate traffic you're probably looking at 45 minutes each way. That's a serious commitment. Believe it or not, we have people in our community who drive from an even greater distance! Spiritual family is worth it.

He sensed the wisdom he was gaining through hearing the Word, and the love he was feeling while coming to church began to push back the void he had experienced for so long. George surrendered his life to Christ in one of our services and finally allowed that wall to break down in his heart. As George and I were meeting together one day, he handed me a significant check for the church—it was an emotional moment for him...and for me.

The money didn't create the emotion; it pointed to the incredible change taking place in George's heart. He'd found the treasure buried in the field and where your heart goes, your treasure follows.

George had been transformed by the love of Jesus, and this led to a natural reciprocation through a significant act of generosity. It was more than a financial transaction. He made those every day. Instead, this was an act of worship investing in the future generation.

DNA #7: The Presence of God is Irresistible

The Christian faith is not a series of religious codes. It's not an ancient ideology that when closely followed produces consistent moral improvement. It's not about what we as human beings do to get close to God.

Every other religion is about what man does to make himself more enlightened, more spiritual, more appealing to a Higher Power.

Christianity is none of those things. It's about what God did to get to man.

It's the supernatural, incredible reality that the Creator of the Universe is present in creation because He wants to know and love us.

Sharing our faith is not about memorizing lists of propositions that are intellectually agreed upon. It's about facilitating a new relationship. It's less,

"Here's what you should know about God," and more, "Would you like to meet Him?"

Our confidence is not in the quality of our information. It's in the goodness of the character and nature of our God. We don't follow a dead religion, we serve a risen Savior who is a living God.

> # THERE'S NO WAY YOU CAN ENCOUNTER HIS PRESENCE AND NOT BE CHANGED.

That's why I don't get too freaked out when the latest weird book comes out with all kinds of distorted facts about Jesus.

If our hope in advancing the message of Jesus relied on our ability to control information, we'd be in trouble. When you study history and ask questions about what's happening in the world, you soon discover that the more people try to prohibit the preaching of Jesus—whether in Ancient Rome, Communist Russia or China or in radical Muslim nations—the more He starts showing up in the lives of real people.

There's no way you can encounter His presence and not be changed. It doesn't mean you understand what's happening. It doesn't mean you get the answers to all of your questions. It doesn't mean your problems magically disappear. It doesn't mean you immediately embrace Him but deep down you realize there's far more going on than what you can see. There's something bigger, and deeper, and more real than most of us can even describe.

Antranetta encountered the love of Jesus in a jail cell.

She didn't have a storybook childhood. When she was kicked out of her home as a teenager, for a moment she wondered if it might not be an improvement. She was doing her best to make ends meet, until one day, on her way to work, she was approached by a few women in a car who asked if she was interested in making more money.

With nowhere to go, no driver's license and the possibility of living on the streets looming over her, Antranetta decided to take them up on their offer. She didn't realize what was happening. There were no danger signs to warn her. Before she fully realized what had happened, she'd entered into the world of prostitution.

Though the details differ slightly, similar versions of this story can be heard all over the world. It's one of the most common strategies of the enemy and the results are always the same. It was death—everything on the inside of her just felt dead—in addition to the physical challenges, the emotional pain of the shame and guilt she experienced was paralyzing.

She kept thinking if she could just save up enough money eventually she would be able to get out and escape. Maybe she could find a place to start over, but this world was like a prison.

She was arrested twice and each time spent some time in jail. Not a place a young woman would want to be, but each time she was there she heard the message of the Cross and about the incredible love of Jesus FOR her. No pain, no abuse, no measure of suffering and no prison bars could separate her from this irresistible presence of Jesus. Right there in the jail cell she prayed to receive Christ.

Over the next few months, Jesus began to heal and redeem her heart—the resentment toward her family, the pain of her childhood, the shame of what she'd become—it all began to melt away. Not only did God rescue her from that terrible lifestyle, He gave her a life beyond what she could have dreamed.

Antranetta now has a beautiful family—an amazing husband and three beautiful girls—and a spiritual family here at Milestone. Together she and her husband Nicholas are a part of our internship program, are being developed as leaders, and are investing in the lives of others.

A set of rules couldn't transform her life in such an incredible way, but a living God could. Now her story is helping to give hope and new life to others.

DNA #8: Jesus + Nothing = Everything

Several times each year we gather all of the volunteers together to celebrate what God has done and to look forward to what He has next for us. With multiple weekly services, this is one of the rare times when nearly all of our leaders and committed members gather together in one place. It's always a powerful time.

And in these moments, at some point, I always remind us: *We're doing this for Jesus.*

Not so our dreams will come true.
Not so He'll owe us something.
Not so our prayers will be answered.
Not so our businesses will be blessed.
Not because we're afraid He won't love us.
Not because He's the ticket to what we're really after.
Not so our children will grow up to exceed our expectations.
Not so He'll keep us safe and comfortable.

We do it for Jesus, because more than anything else, what we want…is Him.

Nothing compares to Him. He's what life is all about. The Bible says all things exist for Him and to Him and through Him. There is no life apart from Him. What makes heaven the most amazing place in the universe has nothing to do with gold or angels or clouds.

It's because more than any other place, reality exists the way He created it to exist and right there in the center of it all…is *Jesus.*

Jesus plus nothing equals everything.[9]

It's not Jesus plus the life of our dreams, the home of our dreams, or the spouse of our dreams. It's Jesus plus nothing. We want everything He has for us —and by His divine power He's promised to give us everything we need for life and godliness[10]—but if we only get Him…we're good.

Phil Kraft had only entered the doors of a church 10 times in his entire life before he showed up at Milestone. By most cultural measurements, he was very successful. He was the guy that had all the answers—both at work and in life.

But on the inside there was an emptiness none of the cultural benchmarks could satisfy. Eventually Phil realized God was the only thing that could fill that emptiness. He began spending time in Restore—one of our ministry environments—and within six months he gave his life to Jesus, was baptized and began serving others.

Research tells us it's rare for grown men to make first-time decisions for Christ. Depending on how you interpret the data it's either a statistical anomaly or a genuine miracle. And every time it happens, it has a massive impact on the family.

---

9   We realize Tullian Tchividjian wrote a book by this name in 2011, but we were using that phrase before the book came out. We haven't had much interaction with him so we're not implying anything. I have no idea who said it first, but it's become a common phrase that was passed around, and to Tullian's credit, he was the first one to publish it.
10   2 Peter 1:3

Emma did not grow up in Christian home. The need for God was overshadowed by the American Dream—the successful dad and stay-at-home mom who were happily married, and the son and daughter who were standouts in school. This typical suburban family even came complete with a Golden Retriever.

In middle school, Emma was invited to one our DNOW weekend events for students. Emma gave her life to Jesus and was radically changed. She started attending Milestone and our student ministry (Elevate) and quickly began helping others to give their lives to Christ as well.

When Emma was a sophomore in high school the American Dream her family had enjoyed suddenly began to crumble. One phone call shook the very foundations of their life as her mom was diagnosed with stage three breast cancer.

Months of chemotherapy and radiation would follow. Most days it felt like the white picket fence had been uprooted. Emma is a fighter and when presented with a challenge she wanted to show everyone her strength and faith but when she gave an oral poem reading in English class detailing the challenge, she fell to the ground weeping.

She heard the Lord say *"You have been doing this in your own strength. I had to bring you to your knees in order to help lift you up."*

As the months passed Emma's mom entered remission for her cancer and things started to settle back to normal. Until another phone call would send shockwaves through this already wounded family. Emma's older brother, Eric, had been attending college when some unidentifiable health problems created some concern. He'd passed out on the stairs of his apartment and was rushed to the hospital with congestive heart failure. When the hospital ran tests they discovered Eric also had stage three cancer—but his sickness had already spread to his liver, abdomen, and lungs. He'd dropped all the way down to just 90 pounds. He was withering away.

When the doctors discovered more than 100 tumors and a liter of fluid on his lungs, they told the family the chances were good he would not make it through the night.

But God spoke to Eric and told him he would survive, and He had a purpose for his life. Eric chose to fight. Month after month, and miracle after miracle, Eric began to heal. Their dad ended up giving his life to Christ at Milestone's Easter service that year after seeing all God had done through Eric's life.

During Emma's senior year of high school her mom's cancer returned in her bones. This time, her sickness was terminal. Instead of Friday night football games and friends, Emma spent her senior year shuffling her mom and brother back and forth to hospitals. Eric kept feeling better but her mom kept feeling worse.

> # WE DO IT FOR JESUS, BECAUSE MORE THAN ANYTHING ELSE, WHAT WE WANT...IS HIM.

In the fall, Emma's parents encouraged her to head off to college. In the middle of her first semester, she got a text from her dad that simply read: *"it's time."* She knew. Emma's mom had fought the disease for many years and had now come to the end of her time on earth. Emma struggled with why things were happening this way. She'd trusted God for healing or for the opportunity to dramatically lead her mom to Christ—nothing was happening the way she hoped.

Yet God began to comfort her with supernatural peace. He challenged her to trust Him—He'd been speaking to her mom all along. That wasn't her weight to carry.

If Emma's relationship with Jesus had been a means to heal her mother or to keep her family cancer free, it had failed, but if her hope and joy was in a Jesus whose love is bigger than death and whose message goes beyond this world into eternity, then the entire process was worth it. Not because she got what she wanted. Not because she had all of her questions answered, but because when you have Jesus, you have something cancer, or death or doubt can never take away.

Emma serves on our staff team and her story has inspired many others to find true hope and joy, not in what He provides, but in the incredible person of Jesus Himself.

Jesus plus nothing equals everything.

This isn't my story—it's our story.

This is who we are.

It's the story God is writing through us.

It's such a privilege to be a part of what God is doing.

WHAT IF YOU COULD
GENUINELY IMPACT OTHERS
AND LEAVE A LEGACY
THAT LONG OUTLIVES YOU?

CHAPTER FIFTEEN

CHARISMATIC WITH A SEAT BELT

I spend most of my life surrounded by people—and although it is not easy and it's often messy, I genuinely enjoy it.

I observe people, I listen to them, I watch them, I counsel them and perhaps most importantly, I serve them.

One of the things I learned early on that has only become more obvious over time is this: people are unique. There may be more than seven billion of us in the world, but each of us is a *"one of a kind."* God doesn't use a cookie cutter. We think differently, we talk differently and we have very different reactions to the same experience.

This is one of the things I love most about being a dad. My kids are all so different—despite the fact they come from the same gene pool, they have different likes and dislikes, they give and receive love in different ways, and their personalities are all their own. Yet sooner or later all children have to come to terms with the reality they are one part of a family and they don't always get their way.

That's when the fun starts.

Pastors log a lot of hours in premarital counseling. It's an important part of what we do. God's basic building block is the family and when we help families love and honor God, we create healthy environments in our church, our neighborhoods and our communities as a whole.

When you're working with a couple, one of the things you have to prepare them for is the impending collision of their lives. Most of the early fights in marriage come from the unavoidable tension that results from two separate people coming together as one. Most early fights between newlyweds come down to simple stuff like where you put your dishes, what we buy at the grocery store or what the other person did with the toothpaste.

This conflict is natural, to be expected and perfectly normal. Here's the reason—we are not just unique, we are all a little weird.

The longer we go in life the more particular we tend to become about how we like things. We like what we like. In a world where so many things are out of our control, we tend to cherish the preferences and little things in life so they're just how we like them, but we don't realize it until someone comes along and tries to get us to change.

You see this with food. Some people eat all their fries before they start their burger, others eat them together, and really weird people dip fries in ice cream.[1] Some people go to a buffet and pile it all on—hot and cold, savory and sweet, it's all just mixed together on a giant plate. As you're reading this, some of you are saying, "*Yes! Pile it on,*" while another group is longing for one of those plastic plates with separate compartments.

---

1 Actually...I'm one of those.

We all have our own sense of normal—and this is certainly true when we gather as a church.

Creating Atmosphere, Not Style

There was a time when pews, organs and choirs were normal. If you grew up this way, anything else can feel strange. If you're the kind of person who appreciates consistency, you see deviating from the security of tradition as a violation of biblical principles. For others, these things feel outdated and foreign. All they have known is a contemporary worship experience with a band on a stage, lights and even a little smoke.

I learned a long time ago, when it comes to worship styles, you'll never make everyone happy. This doesn't mean we don't listen and allow people to give feedback, but that's not our primary goal.

Throughout the course of the week we have a wide variety of ministry environments: students, women, men, young adults, small group, large gathering and ultimately our weekend services. The experience in each of these gatherings is adjusted to the context of the group, but the goal in all of them is the same: *we're trying to create an atmosphere where people can meet with God.*

That's the win.

Whenever someone steps on campus and into one of our ministry environments, what we're praying they experience is bigger than an inspiring message or well-executed and uplifting music. Our hope is they hear God speak to them and sense His presence.

By the grace of God, this happens every week, but you can't always tell when it's happening. Like I've been saying, people are unique—some respond by quietly closing their eyes. Others may tear up.

If it is during the message, some people clap, others say, "*Amen,*" while others express themselves more subtly by nodding their heads in agreement.

If it takes place during a song, some people close their eyes, others may sway a little from side to side, and some lift their hands.

The first time you see this, you tend to remember it. Growing up in my church, you only raised your hand when you had a question or if the church was taking a vote. No one ever told me raising your hands as a response in worship was a biblical idea. I guess I just missed Psalm 63:4, 1 Timothy 2:8, Psalm 134:2, Psalm 141:1, 1 Kings 8:54, Psalm 28:2, Job 11:13, Luke 24:50…to name a few. That's not even all of the mentions, but somehow I just missed it.

Let's be honest. There is a wide range of "*hand-raising*" depending on your personality. We don't teach a class and there are no formal rules, but if you watch people like I do, you can start to group people based on what they find comfortable.[2] These are just observations after years of observing people—no matter what group you may find yourself in, I want you to know you're welcome at Milestone.

The anti-hand-raising crowd protests with both arms folded so tightly it's like they're worried an usher is going to come down and force them to join in. The undecided voter is giving a quick glance around to see what everyone else is doing.

Then you have your two beginner-level hand raisers—the first group wiggles their arms at their side or in their pockets and the second, "*Carry the Flat Screen*" (*hands out underhand at your waist*). That's like dipping your toe in the pool.

Once you go waist deep, you're ready for "*Freeze*"—here your hands are out about shoulder high like you got stopped by the cops or "*The Lion King*"—hands upward out in front of you like you're holding up Mufasa at the beginning of the movie.

---

2   Comedian Tim Hawkins has been very helpful in developing my understanding of this practice. You can find all kinds of hilarious images and charts to break this down even further.

If you're a radical hand-raiser you go "*Pick Me!*"—one hand straight up over your head like you want to be chosen or called on and "*Touchdown*"—both hands straight up over your head like your team just put up six points.

I'm being a little silly to ease any tension you might have, but I'm not making fun of anyone. I've enthusiastically done each of these.

Raising your hands doesn't make you more spiritual and it doesn't make God love you more. Like anything else it can become an inauthentic religious duty, but it's clearly a biblical practice and can be a powerful expression of worship.

However they choose to express themselves, whenever people come into an environment that transcends religious duty and gives real people the opportunity to genuinely experience the presence of God—it changes them deeply.

It's hard to describe. Most of us struggle to find the right words to accurately articulate what we're feeling.

Cultural background and experience significantly influence the language we use to frame these emotions. I've heard people say, "*I felt God's presence,*" "*God showed up,*" (and they usually say it like they're surprised!), "*Church was on fire,*" "*The Spirit moved,*" or maybe simply, "*That was awesome.*"

Religion is all the things we do to get God's approval or to become spiritual. But that isn't what this is. It is bigger than a song or intellectually agreeing with a system of beliefs. This is more than talking about God—this is God Himself coming to be with us.

In our every day lives.
Our pride.
Our indifference.
Our pain.
Our deep need.

In this moment, we sense His presence and His unconditional love. No matter where we have been or what we've done, we know He loves us right where we are, but He loves us too much to leave us there. When God meets us with His empowering presence, He calls us into a greater level of trust and obedience.

When that happens, simply calling it *"church"* doesn't seem adequate. So what do we call it?

We've Got Spirit Yes We Do…

When I was first getting started in ministry, the buzzword people used to describe this kind of church was *"Spirit-filled."* People would ask, *"Is your church Spirit-filled?"*

They weren't looking for a denominational identification and they weren't really looking for a theological distinction. The language was a little insider, a little *"Christianese."* It was the kind of the thing where how you answered told as much as what you actually said.

In the purest sense, what they really wanted to know was whether or not people in the church were regularly experiencing the presence of God. Were people going through the motions during worship or was there a prevailing sense that God was somehow present with them as they gathered? Did the preaching presuppose God was speaking in that moment to both the first-time guest and the people who faithfully come every week?

These are critically important questions. Jesus said in Matthew 18:20 that when we come together in His name we should expect Him to be with us. More than hymns versus contemporary tunes or organs versus bands, more than expository versus topical preaching, what causes a church to be Spirit-filled is a deep, abiding trust that God is present to change lives.

Here is what started to happen. This *"Spirit-filled"* discussion started to take on another dimension.

For many, the phrase started to become synonymous with *"Charismatic"* churches. This is not a denominational term but a theological one—at the most basic level, a charismatic church believes, as the Bible says, God gives gifts to His people to encourage and strengthen His body. *"Charis"* is the Greek word for gift and how these gifts are practiced personally and publicly ranges depending upon the church.

Another group of churches, like the church I was raised in, believe God gave these gifts in the early church, primarily to the apostles, as tools to help them until the Bible was finished.[3] The critical consequence of this, is now that we have the completed Scriptures, these gifts were not meant to be utilized the way they were in the early church. These gifts have stopped or *ceased*—this belief became known as *"Cessationism"* and so this group became known as *"Cessationists."*[4]

A mature, reasonable understanding of the historic Christian faith quickly realizes this is not an issue that should determine the authenticity of a fellow brother or sister in Christ[5] but that started to happen.

Remember that old cheer in high school people used to yell at each other, *"We've got spirit, yes we do, we've got spirit…how 'bout you!"* It kind of broke out throughout the body of Christ. Insults were thrown. Accusations were made. Feelings were hurt.

---

3   Here's a little more history on the process because this view, while familiar in our culture is fairly rare historically. The first big division regarding the issue in church history came in 1000 AD between Eastern and Western Orthodoxy. The second division within Western Orthodoxy splits into 3-4 categories around 1833. One third goes the dispensational route, which becomes the predominant view in the Bible belt. Inside of that group is the belief we're discussing, "Cessationism."

4   In this discussion, the contrasting viewpoint is sometimes referred to as not only Charismatic, but also "continuationism" in reference to the belief that the operation of the gifts and the Holy Spirit continue today. This distinction is sometimes preferred because of some of the drama surrounding the wilder type of Charismatic…also known as "Charismaniacs." Hopefully it goes without saying that term is less scholarly and more sarcastic.

5   The historic, orthodox Christian faith calls this "justification"—the act of being made right before God is a gift given to us through the finished work of Jesus on the cross. It's not something we do, it's been done on our behalf. Jesus gives us His righteousness allowing us to enter a relationship with the Father. We don't earn it through our style of worship, our knowledge of Scripture or by our righteous deeds. We receive it by grace through faith.

Enthusiastic Charismatics started to describe the more conservative and traditional cessationist churches as *"dead"* or *"dying."* There's no way to take that as a compliment. A dead church without the presence of God is like a hospital without doctors and medicine or a restaurant without any food.

The cessationist churches called the Charismatic churches *"weirdos"*—sometimes because they were uncomfortable with something different, and other times because things definitely got weird.

Remember—we're all a little weird. We think what we're comfortable with is normal and it's everybody else who is a little "off".

One of the things I appreciate about cessationist churches is their love for Scripture. Their problem with many Charismatic churches was their belief these churches, like the biblical church in Corinth, were out of control. Maybe they saw a weird charismatic church on TV, or they heard about a strange story from the friend of a friend or they actually saw it in person.

The solution, in their mind, is to return the conduct of the church back to a biblical model. I share this approach. We just read the same passage a little differently.

The key text that led to this belief system is 1 Corinthians 13:8-10:

> *Love never ends. As for prophecies, they will pass away; as for tongues, they will cease; as for knowledge it will pass away. For we know in part and we prophesy in part, but when the perfect comes, the partial will pass away.*[6]

Cessationism points to this text as the evidence prophecy, tongues and the gift of knowledge will pass away because they read *"the perfect"* as the Bible. This makes sense when you believe the Bible is perfect—and again, I share

---

6   ESV

this belief with them. But the passage doesn't stop there and this is where the problem comes.

Verse 12 tells us more about this "perfect" the passage is referring to.

> *For now we see in a mirror dimly, but then face to face. Now*
> *I now in part; then I shall know fully, even as I have been fully*
> *known.*[7]

In his instruction to the church in Corinthians, which had some really weird worship services, Paul is describing our inability to understand everything that happens in life. Is the Bible perfect and does it help us to see? Absolutely …but here is the problem. I don't know about you, but even though I love and study the Bible, I can not say I know fully, or to put it more clearly, I do not know God to the degree He knows me.

In his first pastoral letter, the Apostle John gives us a little insight into what Paul is talking about. He is writing to a group of believers who are trying to separate the way they think and interact with the world from those who haven't given their hearts to Jesus. He's describing how, while we are in this process we are not perfect, but we are making progress. God is changing us until we look more and more like Him.

> *Dear friends, now we are children of God, and what we will be*
> *has not yet been made known.*[8]

We are children of God. Through the finished work of Jesus, we have been justified and made righteous before God. We have His Word. We are growing, we're changing, we're being transformed. Historically this ongoing transformation of the believer has been called the process of sanctification but look what He says next.

---

7   ESV
8   NIV

*But we know that when Christ appears, we shall be like Him,
for we shall see Him as He is.*[9]

As we've said, the Bible is perfect; it's a lamp unto our feet and a light unto our path. It's the primary way God speaks to us. Its purpose is to reveal the nature and character of God but it doesn't cause us to be perfect and know everything.

That only happens when Jesus returns, makes us like Him and allows us to know fully even as we're fully known. Unless I missed it, that hasn't happened yet, so as much as I love my cessationist brothers and the way they value God's Word, I can't agree with them on this point. But I will agree with them on another issue—sometimes Charismatic churches get a little out of control.

So what do we do about it?

Don't Hang Out At The Water Table

1 Corinthians 14:1 makes it pretty clear where we should start:

Follow the way of love and eagerly desire gifts of the Spirit...

Believe it or not, 1 Corinthians 13, often referred to as *"the love chapter"* and famously read at weddings is primarily about how we should act in church.[10] If you're following along with me, I'm guessing you're probably thinking now, *"Okay, Jeff, but what does loving other people at church have to do with spiritual gifts?"*

Verse 12 sheds some light on it for us:

*Since you are eager for gifts of the Spirit, try to excel in those
that build up the church.*[11]

---

9 NIV
10 It also helps us understand a biblical definition of love, so keep enjoying it next time you're at a wedding or a marriage seminar!
11 NIV

The purpose of these gifts isn't to build the ministry of an individual or to make people feel uncomfortable. God gives us these gifts to serve others. Paul is really reiterating the point he already made, "*Now to each one the manifestation of the Spirit is given for the common good.*"[12]

The responsibility of our pastoral team is to do everything we can to help the entire body to be built up in love. This doesn't mean we don't challenge or declare boldly the message of the Gospel, but love means we keep the main thing the main thing.

This isn't always easy.

Nearly every week someone new approaches me wanting to express their gift, their teaching, their song or their cause to our church family. In a church without order, there would be no asking—people would just fire away. But I'm responsible to ensure that the entire body, especially those who are coming for the first time, have every opportunity to feel loved and valued…not *weirded out*.

We want people to have the opportunity to use their gifts—in our Growth Track, after you hear about the vision of the church we give you a spiritual gift test to give you the opportunity to start serving others and using your gifts.

It has to be done in a way that is healthy. People ask me all the time, "*Are you a charismatic church?*" It's a loaded question. I realize what I say next could determine whether or not someone will categorize Milestone Church one way or the other and immediately write us off.

I typically answer, "*It depends on what you mean.*"

We absolutely believe God gives gifts to empower His Church to establish His Kingdom and help people be transformed by His power into all they were created to be, but we do not view spiritual gifts as the benchmark of

---

12   1 Corinthians 12:7 (NIV)

maturity. We want to do everything with loving order and we're not necessarily chasing a spiritual experience.

I like to say we're "Charismatic...*with a seat belt.*"

What does that mean? It means we love and practice the gifts, but we're going somewhere and we want to keep everyone safe.

A lot of pastors don't like to spend time in the foyer after the service because things can get weird pretty quickly. A few years back a guy walked up to me after one of the services and said, "*I want you to know, it's good that I'm here 'cause this church is kind of dead, needs some life in it. But don't worry 'cause God wants you to know that wherever I go, revival follows me.*"

No. I'm not making this up. How do you respond to something like that? So I said, "*Umm...okay. Well then I'm glad you're here I guess.*"

Despite this interaction, the next week I'm back in the atrium. During the service our production team had a little mishap and the fog machine went haywire—it was so foggy up there I could have cut a hole in the haze and pulled out a square like a window.

My new friend saw this as a clear sign of the Spirit.

"*The Lord wants you to know He was here today and I saw Him, the shekinah glory was all around you as you were speaking...revival is coming!*"

Now I think of myself as a spiritual man, but I'm also rational. There was a simple explanation, so I told him, "*Actually that was just the fog machine. It's an older model and it got stuck. It wouldn't turn off.*"

In his mind, this had nothing to do with technology or the work of men. He quickly argued, "*NO! It was the LORD! I see things like this all the time. The Spirit was billowing all around you...revival is coming!*"

I'm not sure what happened to him—the Lord must have called him to a church that needed revival a little more than we did.

When the gifts are used biblically, it's amazing the level of encouragement and love they communicate. I've seen years of discouragement, confusion and even sickness supernaturally dealt with in a moment through the biblical, considerate expression of the gifts.

When this happens, the response is overwhelming. If you've suffered with something for a long time and then in a moment God changes your life through a prophetic word or being prayed for and anointed with oil, it makes sense the next time you have a problem you try to recreate the moment.

Before you know it, these gifts or experiences have become a silver bullet. It may not have been your intention, but your Christian faith has now become the chase for the next great experience. *Where's the Spirit moving? Where is healing and prophecy happening? Where is the next great wave of manifestations taking place?*

I've seen people move from church to church, conference to conference, event to event in a constant search for a dynamic, life-changing experience. They believe what God has for them, the best version of themselves or their lives is waiting for them out there, if they can just find it.

That's not how the gifts of the Spirit work.

Several years ago my middle sister asked me to run a half-marathon with her. Now I'm not a huge fan of running, but I like to win. Few contests are more primal than a foot race.

See that guy in front of you? Are you going to let him beat you? GO!!! How could I pass that up?

The race was more than 13 miles long, which sounds a lot shorter than it feels when you're running. About halfway through I made it to one of the stations you may have seen on TV or at a similar event. There's a table filled with cups of water and Gatorade and volunteers hand them to you as you run by. By that point, I was ready for a break.

Deep down there was a part of me that thought, *"This water is so refreshing I think I'll just hang out here for awhile. These guys are really encouraging… maybe we should be friends?"* In that moment, I could have easily forgotten the purpose of the station was to help me keep running, not to get me to spend the rest of the day drinking water.

God has given each of us a race to run. He invited us into His mission to reach people and build lives and to help us along the way He gives us supernatural gifts to encourage, strengthen and refresh us. A church, or a group of Christians, that reduces life down to a series of spiritual experiences is like a bunch of runners who forget about their race in pursuit of the most refreshing cup of water.

God gives us everything we need to run, but He doesn't want us hanging out at the water table.

Underdeveloped In The Spirit

If you want to develop spiritual gifts and experience that sense of God's empowering presence we often sense during corporate worship, a great place to start is to develop your relationship with the Holy Spirit. The truth is, as American Christians, many of us are seriously underdeveloped in this area.

It wouldn't be inaccurate to say we treat this member of the Trinity like a crazy uncle. We acknowledge his existence, we have heard the weird stories about him that get passed around, and we're a little nervous he is going to embarrass us.

In a lot of churches I've been around, the Holy Spirit shows up on their statement of beliefs on their website and He gets the occasional shout out in prayer or in the words of a song, but in day-to-day practice you don't hear much about Him. In some places, the Spirit is referred to as an "it" instead of a "He." This is a critical distinction.

I don't think anyone would argue He doesn't get nearly the same amount of spotlight as Jesus or the Father.

The Bible makes it clear that the Holy Spirit is God—to the same degree as Jesus or the Father. He was present in creation, moved in the lives of people throughout the Old Testament,[13] works in dynamic partnership with Jesus throughout the Gospels, and you could make the case the Holy Spirit is the main character in the Book of Acts.

The Bible doesn't make sense without Him.

As Jesus was coming to the end of His life His disciples were understandably upset. They needed encouragement and comfort—at this critical moment Jesus makes an extraordinary statement. *"Nevertheless, I tell you the truth: it is to your advantage that I go away, for if I do not go away, the Helper will not come to you. But if I go, I will send Him to you."*[14]

Think about that. Jesus chooses the word *"advantage."* Other versions choose the word *"better"*[15] or *"best."*[16]

Clearly Jesus knew that in order for them to go where He was calling them and to do what He would ask of them, they would need the Helper, the Comforter, the Advocate to strengthen, embolden and guide them into truth.

Throughout this passage, Jesus gives His largest and most complete teaching on the power and the role of the Holy Spirit. Jesus describes Him as *"another*

---

13 Most Bible scholars agree He's referred to by a variety of names in the Old Testament including the personalized references to divine wisdom.

14 John 16:7 (ESV)

15 The Message and the Common Bible

16 NLT

advocate," "*the Spirit of Truth*," "*the Advocate*," "*the Holy Spirit*," and "*the Spirit*." He repeatedly refers to the Spirit as "*Him*."

In the Greek the term advocate is translated as "*parakletos*" which literally means to be summoned, called to one's side or one who pleads for another before a judge, counsel and intercessor. John uses this same word to describe what Jesus does for us with the Father.[17]

THE BIBLE DOESN'T MAKE SENSE WITHOUT [THE HOLY SPIRIT].

Jesus tells the disciples the Holy Spirit will help them, be with them forever, live in them, teach them all things, remind them of everything He said to them, testify about Jesus in order to help them do the same, prove the world to be wrong about sin and righteousness, guide them into all truth, speak whatever He hears, tell them what is to come, and glorify Jesus.

When you think about it this way, *advantage* makes more sense.

The Spirit helps us be who God has called us to be and do what God has called us to do by continually bringing us back to Jesus.

He is personal, He lives with us and He never leaves us. He wants to have a relationship with you. You can talk with Him, listen for His voice, ask for His guidance, lean into His comfort and process through your experiences on a daily basis. Even when you don't ask He'll convict you of sin and remind you of what Jesus has said.

---

17   1 John 2:1. This also explains why John 14:16 uses the phrase, "another advocate" meaning more than one.

People often ask me, *"Jeff, how will I know if it's Him or if I'm just imagining it?"* It's a great question. Like any other relationship, trust comes through investing quality time and learning to recognize His voice. When you spend a great deal of time with someone, you can pick their voice out of a crowd even in the midst of other commotion.

This is true in our relationship with the Holy Spirit. The Bible makes it clear that He will never say anything that goes against God's Word, no matter how strong our feelings may be.

If what you're hearing causes you to love and trust Jesus more, there's a strong possibility it is Him and even if it's not, when you are willing to listen with a teachable heart, even misunderstanding what the Spirit is saying helps strengthen the relationship more than completely ignoring Him.

What's your relationship like with the Holy Spirit? Do you hear His voice? Do you think about Jesus and what He said throughout the course of your day?

If I stop for a moment and think about an issue, passages of Scripture begin to come to my mind. It's not because I have a photographic memory or because I'm a Bible trivia champion. I am not that good, but I have invested in my relationship with the Holy Spirit and so when I am carefully considering something, He does what Jesus said He would do—*He leads and guides me into truth.*

He will do the same for you.

Honestly, the biggest obstacle any of us have is our own level of expectation. I promise you, if you will simply keep your ears open and believe the Holy Spirit is present with you to help guide and instruct you, you WILL hear His voice. It may not be how you expect it or even what you want to hear, but He won't hold back. He'll lead and guide you into all truth and remind you of what Jesus said.

Think about how this could change your daily life.

- If you are a student, expect the Holy Spirit to speak to you in between class, on your way to school, or on your lunch break. And yes…even during that exam you didn't study for. I am not promising He will give you the answers. He may speak to you about your study habits though!
- If you're a mom, expect the Holy Spirit to speak to you as you fold laundry, discipline your toddler for the 27th time this morning, or as you drive around the seemingly never-ending carpool routes. He is present with you to encourage you and to remind you of the significance your faithful service can make for His Kingdom.
- If you're working a job that feels unspiritual—not necessarily bad, but removed from what God cares about—you may be surprised to find He has many things to say to you. Both the work you do and the way you do it reflect what you value. Ask the Holy Spirit to show you how to glorify Jesus through the way you serve others and become excellent in your craft.

This help, this guidance, this comfort is available to any follower of Christ at all times.

Wait For The Power

These descriptions of the Holy Spirit from Jesus came before He was arrested, crucified and raised to new life. After these events take place the disciples are more than a little rattled by it all. Jesus lovingly tells them, "*I tried to tell you!*"[18] And then He opened their minds so they could understand the Scriptures before returning to be with the Father.

Before He leaves, Jesus hands over the responsibility of the mission of His Kingdom. This is the parallel passage to the Great Commission Jesus gave

18   My paraphrase of the end of Luke 24

in Matthew. But in Luke He explains, "*...repentance for the forgiveness of sins will be preached in His name to all nations, beginning at Jerusalem. You are witnesses of these things.*"[19]

You may have heard the process of sharing your faith in Jesus with others referred to as "*witnessing.*" This is where that expression comes from. But Jesus has more to say about how He would help them do this. "*I am going to send you what my Father has promised; but stay in the city until you have been clothed with power from on high.*"[20]

[THE HOLY SPIRIT] LEADS AND GUIDES ME INTO TRUTH.

Remember the condition of His followers at this point in history. They were still in shock. When He was arrested and crucified—it devastated them. They scattered. His inner circle went back to fishing.[21] Even after He started reappearing, some of them doubted.

Basically Jesus tells them that they're going to preach this message all over the world, starting right here in their own backyard.

It makes way more sense to us today than it did to them. They weren't exactly the most obvious "*church planting,*" "*global missions,*" "*Gospel preaching*" candidates. But the story doesn't end there.

---

19   NIV
20   NIV
21   That's right...John 21. Maybe you can tell it's one of my favorite passages.

The book of Acts is a continuation of the Gospel of Luke. Acts 1:8 provides additional insight into why Jesus believed they could preach His message and take His Kingdom to every nation.

> *But you will receive power when the Holy Spirit comes on you; and you will be my witnesses in Jerusalem, and in all Judea and Samaria, and to the ends of the earth.*[22]

The disciples were already Christians, they had already been born again, the Holy Spirit had already entered their lives, they knew what they had seen, they understood the Scriptures and the message of the Gospel and yet Jesus decided they needed to wait until the power came to go be His witnesses.

That's exactly what happens next. In Acts 2, they're all gathered together when the Holy Spirit comes on them at Pentecost. He fills them with power and by the time we get to verse 14, Peter is no longer the same guy. The same man who denied Jesus three times to strangers, the same guy who was so discouraged he had gone back to his old job of fishing, is now boldly preaching to a crowd of thousands of his Jewish peers.

He finishes his first sermon with the not-so-seeker-friendly line: "*Therefore let all Israel be assured of this: God has made this Jesus, whom you crucified, both Lord and Messiah.*"[23]

When the crowd heard this they didn't say, "*You're lying Peter!*" or "*That's your opinion,*" or even, "*That may be true for you, but not for us.*" The Bible simply says they were "*cut to the heart.*" In other words, his message challenged them so profoundly they simply said, "*Brothers, what should we do?*"[24]

What happened? How do we explain this incredible change in Peter? The promise Jesus made to them from the Father was the empowering presence

---

22 NIV
23 Acts 2:36 NIV
24 Acts 2:37b NLT

of the Holy Spirit. Led by the Spirit, Peter had an authority and a boldness he didn't have on his own.

Now you might be saying, *"Okay Jeff, but that's what God gave Peter. What does that have to do with me?"*

It's a great question…but I don't have to answer it for you.

More than two thousand years ago, under the inspiration of the Spirit, Peter answered it so definitively nothing more needs to be said.

> *This promise is for you and your children and for all who are far off—all whom the Lord our God will call.*

The Bible goes the extra mile to communicate how all-inclusive this promise is—*you, your children, all who are far off*…and if you're still not getting it… *all whom the Lord will call.*

You don't need to know Greek to understand what *"all"* means. This isn't a promise for the disciples or this unique group of people at Pentecost. It's available to anyone of any age in any place. The promise of the gift of the Holy Spirit, this empowering presence and power to be His witness, is available to all of us.

Four Guiding Principles

You were created to live a Spirit-filled life. Not on the basis of your moral performance or unique wiring. It's not something you add to your spiritual to-do list. It's not a religious obligation. It's not for a select few. *You* can do this.

I realize your past experiences or the perspectives of others can create confusion in this area so I want to give you some basic, biblical guidelines as you continue to grow in this area. They won't answer every detail of every question, but they should give you some anchors to help you develop both a greater understanding and a new measure of this empowering presence in your life.

1) THE HOLY SPIRIT IS A GOOD GIFT

Hopefully by now we can agree that the Bible is unanimous in its assertion that the Holy Spirit is a gift from God, He *is* God and He was given to us. Now the question becomes what kind of a gift He is.

> WHEN JESUS IS STRESSING THE LOVING GENEROSITY OF THE FATHER TO LAVISH HIS CHILDREN WITH GOOD GIFTS, **HE CHOOSES THE GIFT OF THE HOLY SPIRIT TO MAKE HIS POINT.**

Unfortunately for many, the gift of the Holy Spirit has been like a gift card someone gives you to a store where you don't shop. You can't think of a reason to use it so it gets tucked into a drawer and forgotten about.

God doesn't give unwanted gift cards. When Jesus was teaching the disciples how to pray,[25] He repeatedly emphasized God's desire for His children to ask Him for anything they need. Finally He asks the fathers in the audience if their children ask them for a fish, do they give them a snake? Or when they ask for an egg, do they give them a scorpion? This whole setup sounds a little strange to us. (I don't know about you but my kids aren't regularly asking for fish and eggs—it's usually more about sleepovers and money to hang out with their friends.) But that's not the point.

---

25   Luke 11 & Matthew 7

Jesus has to work so hard to make this point because so many of the people in the audience had trust issues with their fathers. This is still true in our world today. Over the years I've heard countless, heartbreaking stories of neglect and abuse on the part of men who failed miserably in their roles as fathers. This has a huge impact on the ability of these children to believe in and trust the goodness of a heavenly Father. This is one of the reasons I'm passionate about serving single moms and their families.

Even an absent, selfish dad wants to give something good to his children at some point.

> *If you then, though you are evil, know how to give good gifts to your children, how much more will your Father in heaven give the Holy Spirit to those who ask Him!*[26]

Don't miss this. It's incredibly significant. When Jesus is stressing the loving generosity of the Father to lavish His children with good gifts, He chooses the gift of the Holy Spirit to make His point.

It's not a small thing. It is a treasure that is often buried in a field, overlooked and undervalued, but it doesn't have to be that way. Be grateful for this gift. Celebrate it. Put it into daily practice. Develop your relationship with the Holy Spirit on a daily basis.

2) The Gifts of the Spirit are not a Sign of Spiritual Maturity

The church in Corinth was one of the more memorable churches in history. When you read Paul's letters to this early group of believers, this becomes clear. As you become more familiar with what was happening, it's easy to focus on their challenges and mistakes, especially if you're a leader or if you like to solve problems.

---

26   Luke 11:13 (NIV)

I would love it if the Apostle Paul came to Milestone Church as a consultant and told us what he told them: "*...you do not lack any spiritual gift as you eagerly wait for our Lord Jesus Christ to be revealed.*"[27]

Think about that. They weren't lacking anything. Not many churches can say that.

However, as I am sure you are aware by now, Paul's assessment did not end with this remark. In classic coaching form he started with affirmation before coming back around to correction. Here is something I would definitely NOT want Paul to say about our community.

> *Brothers and sisters, I could not address you as people who live by the Spirit but as people who are still worldly—mere infants in Christ.*

Don't miss this. It's huge. It's a fascinating dichotomy—on one hand they lacked no spiritual gifts, but at the same time, they weren't people who lived by the Spirit. They were mere infants. Development wasn't happening. They had gifts, but they weren't participating in the process of sanctification—the ongoing, empowering presence of the Holy Spirit that makes us look more and more like Jesus. Paul tells us in Galatians 5 that true spiritual maturity is measured by the fruit of the Spirit, not the gifts.[28]

Many people in the body of Christ mistake the gift for the individual. God gives spiritual gifts to people to love, build up and serve others. Often this becomes clear with a public gift like preaching or singing—the person appears one way when they're using their gift, but when you spend time with them it becomes quickly apparent their lives don't match up with their gift.

God doesn't take the gift away because the individual didn't earn it. His primary goal is not to make people think highly of the individual but to serve the body of Christ. Unfortunately for the gifted individual, it is not a sustainable approach.

---

27   1 Corinthians 1:7 (NIV)
28   Galatians 5:22-25

The Bible says your gift will make room for you. It can create opportunities and a measure of success, but only the continual, development of mature character through the process of sanctification will allow you to finish your race.

As a leader, if you lean on someone's gift without encouraging and challenging them to develop their character, you're not *loving* them. You're simply *using* them.

Tragically, I have seen many individuals foul out of the game—not because they were not gifted, but because they never developed the kind of character necessary to sustain their gift.

This is the reason that from the very beginning we have prioritized character over charisma.

3) DISCOVER AND DEVELOP YOUR GIFTS

Don't hear what I'm not saying. I want to you to step out in faith and trust God to show you how He has uniquely wired and designed you. The fact that gifts are not a sign of maturity is not meant to devalue their worth. God gives them to us for a reason.

The cautions and qualifications don't exist to discourage you but to allow you to passionately go after them without worrying about potential drawbacks. "*Follow the way of love and eagerly desire gifts of the Spirit, especially prophecy.*"[29]

Spiritual gifts are described throughout the New Testament, but when they are mentioned it is less like an exhaustive list in a catalog and more like relational conversation based on the particular audience. In other words, there is no passage in Scripture that says: "Here's the list."

Instead, under the inspiration of the Holy Spirit, we find multiple mentions with some repetition. 1 Corinthians 12 describes the *word of wisdom, the word of knowledge, faith, healing, miracles, prophecy, discernment, tongues*

29   1 Corinthians 14:1 (NIV)

and the interpretation of tongues, helping and administration. Romans 12 mentions *prophecy, serving, teaching, encouragement, giving, leadership and mercy.* 1 Peter 4 adds *hospitality* and reiterates *speaking, preaching and serving.*

Peter's posture is essentially this: use whatever gift God has given you as a *"faithful steward of God's grace in its various forms."* I love this. We're back to the idea of being a faithful steward. We didn't give ourselves these gifts—God has entrusted us with them and He's going to ask us what we did with them.

In other words, *a spiritual gift is any ability you have that supernaturally benefits someone else in a way that causes them to love and honor Jesus more.* For example, intercession doesn't show up in any of these specific lists, but there's clearly a biblical precedent for this gift.

There are all kinds of spiritual gift assessments and lists out there and the range of the total number of gifts can span from as few as around 25 to as many as 80. This is not the main thing. The primary goal is to be pursuing and faithfully using whatever gifts God has given you.

Our pursuit of the spiritual gifts typically lines up with our personality but don't miss those last two words Paul gives us—*especially prophecy.* Why would the Holy Spirit lead him to phrase it this way? I think it's for the same reason chapter 12 ends with *"Now eagerly desire the greater gifts."*

Some gifts are more accessible and acceptable than others. It's one thing to pursue hospitality, administration or serving—and we need all of those—but it takes a little extra push, a little extra faith to go after prophecy, word of knowledge, healing or miracles. It's out of our comfort zone. It feels a little different or even strange, but I've seen every one of these gifts used for the greater good in ways that weren't weird or strange.

I genuinely believe God gave us these gifts for a reason. For example, a healthy, powerful prophetic word can do something unique in the life of a believer.

Can it be weird? Sure, but do not let that ruin it for you. Remember, we're all a little weird and we need each other.

We should be secure enough in Jesus to spend some time around people who are gifted differently than we are without freaking out. If we continue to value the Word as the final authority we can trust the Holy Spirit to lead us and guide us into all truth.

I don't have to agree with everything someone else in the body of Christ believes to genuinely benefit from their gift.

How will we know if we have these gifts if we never step out and try or spend time around those who are walking in them?

4) You Need The Power of the Holy Spirit

Hopefully this is obvious by now and I don't mean it like, "*Hey, you should have five servings of vegetables every day and stay away from donuts.*" That's one of those highly aspirational and seriously unlikely suggestions.

This is more vital than that.

Like…*without the power of the Holy Spirit, you will not become who God created you to be and do what He has called you to do.*

Will God still love you without it? Absolutely. Will you still go to heaven? Certainly. Justification is not on the basis of what we do or don't do—it has been done completely on our behalf through the atoning death of Jesus, but why would you want to stop there? I have never met anyone who has seriously postured their life in a way that communicated, "*I want everything you have for me Jesus,*" who came back and said they regretted it.

They didn't always understand.

It wasn't always easy.

But in the end…it was *always* worth it. They found a greater value.

This discussion is often framed in the context of whether or not there is a subsequent work of the Holy Spirit. At times in the past, the enthusiasm for the ongoing work of the Holy Spirit has created a perception of insignificance in the initial work of God in the life of a believer. I don't believe this.

However, when you look at the book of Acts, you see disciples experience multiple encounters with the Holy Spirit after their initial conversion. We've already described what happened to the disciples at Pentecost, but then we see this again in chapter 8 when they discover disciples in Samaria who believed in Jesus but hadn't heard about the Holy Spirit. Peter and John go and lay hands on them and they receive such a dynamic power, Simon the sorcerer tries to buy it from them. A similar instance takes place with Paul in chapter 19 when he comes upon a group of disciples who believed in Jesus but hadn't heard about the Holy Spirit.

The point of this is not to classify some Christians as Spirit-filled while others are not. Each of these examples demonstrates the posture I'm encouraging you to take. "I love Jesus, I want to give Him my whole life, and I want whatever He has for me." That is what the process of sanctification is all about.

In Ephesians 5 Paul describes this attitude of the heart. "*Do not get drunk on wine, which leads to debauchery. Instead, be filled with the Spirit…*"[30] This is not an evangelistic letter. The entire theme of the Ephesians is about who you are in Christ. Already. Past tense.

The key word in the passage is "*filled.*" It's an ongoing process. Paul's contrasting what happens when you are filled with the Spirit to what happens when you are intoxicated with wine—you come under the influence of it. Wine was the centerpiece of celebrations and gatherings. Paul is describing

30   Ephesians 5:18 (NIV)

what the presence and ongoing filling of the Spirit produces. When you come under the influence of the Holy Spirit he says we speak to one another with psalms and songs from the Spirit, giving thanks to the Father in the name of Jesus.[31]

The empowering presence of the Holy Spirit is a subsequent experience, but it is so much bigger than a second filling. It's about a third, a fourth, a thirty-fifth, a 239th and if we live long enough a 1,457[th] filling. He can do this whenever He wants.

I also try my best to be open and attentive to the leading of the Spirit on a daily basis, but at key moments, I'll get away and create space for Him to speak to me.

The Holy Spirit is not weird. He is not spooky. He is not something to feel weird about. He is a good gift.

He is our comforter, our advocate and our helper who reminds us of everything that Jesus said.

He empowers us to be a witness for God.

He gives us gifts to serve and love others.

You and I desperately need Him.

---

31   see Ephesians 5:19-20

Chapter Sixteen

THE STORY CONTINUES...

I preached my first message when I was 16 years old. By the time I entered my 20s I started speaking nearly every week and I haven't stopped since. I have preached in different cities, different states, different countries in different languages to all different kinds of people. Styles come and go. Methods change.

One thing has never changed. People love stories.

After I preach I like to talk with people. No matter how hard I try to keep it to three simple and memorable points,[1] most people have a hard time recalling what I said by the time they reach the parking lot, but they remember the stories.

I have never met someone who said, *"You know what, I don't think I ever need to hear another story again."* We have an insatiable appetite for stories.

---

1   Even when I get really tricky and bust out alliteration (all points start with the same letters) or an acrostic (the first letters of each point spell a word: Faithful Available Teachable).

We will fight traffic, stand in line and overpay for popcorn and tickets at the movies all for the chance to experience a great story. Often times we leave the theater disappointed, but even when that happens, we don't give up on stories. We come back again later.

It's why we read books, watch TV and follow sports. When we are with a group of friends and one of them is in the middle of a story, we lean in and hope we can catch up.

It's in our makeup. Stories communicate progress in relationships between people. They deliver meaning in a way we can understand. They carry a narrative forward and demonstrate purpose and significance.

Stories capture our imagination. They transcend age, background, gender and ethnicity. They're fundamental to the human experience. They demand to be retold. They grow in meaning and value over time.

There is a reason that when God became a man and walked among us, He told stories. He hasn't stopped. God is writing a story through your life, my life, and the lives of the people of Milestone Church.

How do you live a great story?

Great stories have a few things in common. They always include great characters (complex, nuanced and flawed), a journey, conflict, and consequences. If you take away any of those components, something essential is lost.

What I have discovered is that it is easier to hear a great story than to live one.

It is one thing to escape for a few hours to experience a thrilling adventure, but it is something completely different to live through it. An audience borrows the emotion of the moment but the characters feel the full weight of it.

For the character, the journey, conflict and consequences simply mean things are going to change. For most people, change is difficult. It is scary. It's threatening. It requires us to do things that when left to ourselves, we wouldn't initiate but when we embrace this process, we become a better version of ourselves.

We grow closer to the person God created us to be.

The American Dream is a story many people have gravitated towards—work hard, pay your dues, succeed, get comfortable and retire to a life of leisure and comfort. You might be thinking to yourself, *"That sounds pretty good."*

People come from all over the world to achieve this dream. In many cases, they sacrifice their integrity, their friendships, their marriages, their families and often multiple business partnerships to get it.

Unfortunately, most people discover this dream can't deliver on its grandiose promise. For all the comfort and safety this goal produces, it fails to satisfy the deep longings of the soul. Many high-powered, *Type-A personalities* don't know what to do with themselves in retirement.

They end up bored.

And those are the ones who made it.

Without a cause, without conflict, without a mission, they wander. Hebrews 11 lists a whole series of great and familiar stories—Noah, Abraham and Sarah, Moses, Gideon, David, Samuel and the Prophets. When the author of Hebrews is summarizing these stories, here's how he describes these people: *"who through faith conquered kingdoms, enforced justice, obtained promises, stopped the mouths of lions, quenched power of fire, escaped the edge of the sword, were made strong out of weakness..."*[2]

---

2   Hebrews 11:33-34

Notice there is no mention of a guy named Joe who just wanted to sit on the couch and eat ice cream. There is nothing about Mr. and Mrs. Jones retiring early so they could play golf every day. I did not notice the inclusion of a teenage girl whose dream was getting the perfect "*selfie*" or a young man who gave all his passion and energy to playing video games until 3am every night.

Those aren't great stories.

God loves you too much to allow you to settle for ordinary. He has a unique story for you. It won't happen on your timetable and it won't be easy. It will take you on a journey filled with conflict. It will stretch your faith, remind you of your limitations, and force you to change. It will cause you to trust Him when everything else tells you to give up.

I can promise it won't be boring.

Embrace Your Season

I've found one of the greatest challenges we face in living the life God has for us is all about timing. We wait for something great to happen. We look back to the way things used to be. We feel like everybody else's life is moving forward while we're stuck in neutral. Some days we wish life would speed up—in other moments we wish we could slow things down.

When you watch a movie, the music always cues you in to what is about to happen. If it's eerie and suspenseful, something bad is about to happen. If it is peaceful and melodic, you can expect good news. If it is building towards a crescendo, you may suddenly get something dusty in your eyes.

We don't even realize it, but it is always the music that makes you cry. I mean…if you're the sort of person that cries at movies. Not that I would know.

But life's not like a movie.

There is no soundtrack that clues us in to what is happening. So much of life feels like we are waiting for something significant to happen. It can be very difficult to realize a life-defining moment when we're in one.

Yet the Bible makes it clear it is possible to live this way. 1 Chronicles 12 describes the sons of Issachar as people who *understood the times and knew what to do*.[3] The third chapter of Ecclesiastes starts with a well-known poem: "*There is a time for everything, and a season for every activity under the heavens.*"[4] The implication is simple and yet so critical. As a follower of Christ, a significant part of enjoying life depends on recognizing and living in the season you're in.

This isn't strictly an Old Testament phenomenon either. Paul adds his typical urgency when he weighs in on the subject. "*Look carefully then how you walk, not as unwise but as wise, making the best use of the time…*"[5] Wise people embrace the season they're in.

> # GOD LOVES YOU TOO MUCH TO ALLOW YOU TO SETTLE FOR ORDINARY.

If we struggle to properly identify the place and the moment God has prepared for us, we end up frustrated and stressed out. It's like wearing a sweater and a beanie in the summer or flip-flops and shorts on the coldest day of winter.

Singles can't wait to get married. Married couples long to have children. And parents with kids can't wait for them to walk and get potty trained!

---

3   1 Chronicles 12:32
4   Ecclesiastes 3:1 (NIV)
5   Ephesians 5:15-16a (ESV)

If you have small children and you're expecting to enjoy the same personal freedom you had when you were single and in college…you're going to be miserable and your family is going to feel neglected and unappreciated.

I've seen guys kill themselves working 80-hour weeks to provide enough financial margin so their kids can have everything their heart desires. They often find out too late what their kids really wanted was to spend some quality time with Dad.

Both our culture and the enemy tell us that we deserve happiness at all times and in any way we desire it. Anyone or anything that prevents us from the longings of our heart becomes our enemy. The problem is that our hearts are fickle—we want something until we get it and then we realize it wasn't what we really wanted after all.

When Jesus was entering Jerusalem towards the end of His life, He wept over the city because He felt their pain and the unsatisfied longings of their souls.[6] The moment they had waited centuries for had come and they missed it. Not only were they without peace—they didn't even know where or how to find it.

Like so many other things in life, this issue comes down to trust. God is not trying to frustrate us. He doesn't give us desires only to taunt us by reminding us of what we don't have. Abraham and Sarah never stopped longing for a child, but it wasn't promised until he was seventy-five years old and then they waited another agonizing twenty-five years…but their parenting journey is one of the most well-known and celebrated stories in world history.

They didn't know what was happening in the moment. They just felt left out.

Yet you know there had to be moments in the middle of the night when Isaac wouldn't sleep, screaming like crazy, his ancient diapers smelling awful when Abraham thought to himself—"*I kinda miss the old days…*"

---

6   Luke 19:42

We all come to those moments where we believe God's promised something and we just can't see it happening. We want to trust Him and believe He's going to do it but it hurts to be disappointed over and over. We've all been there.

And in that moment, we need to remember the difference between "*no*" and "*not now*." Just because something is not happening now, does not mean it will never happen. The problem isn't the desire—it is the timing.

When your kids are small, it is really difficult for you and your spouse to wake up, leisurely grab a cup of coffee, read the Bible and peacefully pray together each morning. If your house is anything like mine, it feels like each morning is exploding with noise, motion and activity.

If you can relate, we have to remind ourselves that these moments may seem mundane and ordinary, but they are critical. Every morning we have the opportunity to send our kids into their day with the blessing and presence of God. If we do this long enough, it will become normal to them. It will become the pattern they walk in the rest of their lives. Once that window is closed, once the season is gone, there is no going back.

I'm not saying you prioritize your children over your marriage—but I am saying you have to prioritize people above your own schedule preferences. Invest in your marriage, pray together, study God's Word—just realize in order to do this, you will have to be flexible and intentional.

I could literally repeat examples like this for every season of life. We never outgrow this. Remember—a great story includes a journey, conflict, and consequences. And God has a great story for you.

Everyone is looking for a shortcut, the killer app, the life hack that allows us to quickly move ahead to the next thing. I only know one. It's a proven method. It's the stewardship approach.

If you want the next thing God has for you—be faithful and responsible with what He has already given you.

The same principle is true for organizations. If you have ever started your own business, you know it is not a 40 hour per week gig. It takes as long as it takes to get momentum rolling, but as you are faithful with the customers, opportunities, and projects you are given, you gain more. Once you become established, you still have pressure and challenges, but in a new season you have new opportunities and freedoms.

What's Next For Milestone?

This is a question I am asked regularly—and I realize there is usually a question behind the question. What they really want to know is, "*Are you going to get weird?*" They never come right out and say it, but when I do, it breaks the tension and they laugh and exhale.

I'm not looking to upgrade from being a local church pastor. In my heart there is nothing higher to move on to. I'm not waiting for the moment when the church gets big enough for me to get a wig and a pinky ring.

I'm sorry if that is what you're hoping for.

I get tired and I feel stress, but honestly, when I wake up every morning I can't believe this is what I get to do with my life. I love my job. I love our church. I love the people I'm doing life with. And I love Jesus more today than ever before.

In an era where critics are saying organized religion in general and Christianity in particular is dying off, we're a growing church community where people are continuously giving their lives to Jesus. Atheists. Californians. New Yorkers. Students. Empty nesters. The "*dechurched.*" Religious people.

The kinds of people some missiologists call *"unreachable"* and most sociologists argue are unwilling to consider the claims of Christ. They call them statistical anomalies. God calls them His sons and daughters.

It is miraculous and yet it's happening all the time. New believers are getting baptized, inviting their friends, and being developed into leaders.

Every week hundreds of volunteers are serving the people in their community because of their love for Jesus. We have never built around personality or individual gifts and talents.

God is doing this—and I'm so grateful to be a part of it.

Jesus is making good on His promise to build His Church in order that the manifold wisdom of God would be made known in the heavenly places.

It is not without its challenges. It's not easy. But *it's worth it.*

Here is what's next for Milestone Church: We are going to keep living our values. We're going to keep growing into more and more of who God created us to be. We're going to keep reaching people and building lives.

As we continue to grow, in the days ahead, we believe there will be more campuses throughout the DFW area. We will plant churches. We will develop church planters and leaders. We'll continue to train interns and develop people for what God has NEXT for them.

When I look into our future, I see a church where a husband who reluctantly comes for the first time tells his wife: *"Unfortunately, I liked it. I want to go back."*

- A church where a Dream Team member greets an unsure, nervous person who doesn't feel like they belong only to have their lives radically changed by God.

- A church where the entire congregation cheers and wipes away tears watching the latest baptism video.
- A church where a 40-year-old focused on their career has their heart captured by the mission of God and begins to passionately give resources to reach others.
- A church where a 55-year-old catches a vision for their legacy and begins to invest in eternal initiatives that will far outlive them.
- A church where a 19-year-old comes in angry and disappointed only to be overwhelmed by the love and the goodness of God. Within a year they're leading small groups and going on missions trips. Within five years, they've recognized the call of God on their lives and within another year or two they're leading from the platform as a pastor.

As we continue to faithfully handle the responsibility God has given to us, we know He will give us more. It's what He has done from day one. More freedom, more resources, more opportunities to advance His Kingdom and impact not only our generation, but the generations coming behind us.

Measuring the success of Milestone cannot be done in our lifetime. We will learn how well we have built according to our pattern after we are gone.

What's Next For You?

You may be saying, "*Okay Jeff. We're finally coming to the end of the book. What is it that you want me to do?*"

I want for you the same thing I want for my own children.

I want you to live the story God has prepared for you.

I want you to leave rules-based religion and inauthentic relationships behind.

I want you to find the treasure buried in a field.

I want you to discover the kind of divine relationships only available through spiritual family.

I want you to experience everything God has for you.

I want you to invest your gifts, your talents, and your resources into a legacy that will make a historic impact for the cause of Christ.

And here's the great news: *I genuinely believe you can do it.*

Not because you're perfect. Not because you won't make mistakes. Not because it is common or easy—but because God will give you the power to live this way. If you want it, no one can keep you from it. It won't just happen. You will have to choose it and receive it by faith. It's not a quick fix and it won't happen overnight.

Some days it will feel like you have waited forever and then all of a sudden you will look back at what God has done and you will be amazed.

If you are ready to say yes, here's what you will need to do:

1) PRAY AND GET A REVELATION OF WHERE GOD HAS PLACED YOU

Remember, Milestone didn't invent spiritual family, God did. We don't choose a church based on convenience, location or personal preference. It's got to be a stronger connection than, "*I like the preaching,*" "*The worship is good,*" or "*They have quality kids' programs.*" If that is how you see it, you won't experience the quality of life God intended for you. We do not just join—God places us in a body as He sees fit.

Many times people come into Milestone and think, "*Where did they find all these friendly people?*" What they are experiencing is real, but it is more than friendliness. That is not the recipe for the apple pie. What they are sensing is the value of divine relationships and spiritual family. It is not easy, it is not without its challenges, but once you experience for yourself, it's really hard to go back.

We believe this placement is both in a local body, but also in the larger body of Christ. We need each other. Jesus said the world would know we belong to Him because of the way we loved each other. I think we all would agree we have some work to do in this respect.

It is such a privilege to live in a part of the country where there are so many great churches, led by true fathers in the faith. I honor them—I don't compete with them. The DFW area may be the brass buckle of the Bible belt, but we've got a long way to go in extending the Kingdom of God in our communities.

2) TAKE A NEXT STEP—AND THEN ANOTHER AND THEN ANOTHER

This is the heart of development, the process of sanctification, the thing that separates intellectual mental ascent to genuinely following Jesus. Don't get too comfortable on the bench. Being a disciple isn't about sitting in the stands; it's about getting in the game.

Get in the Growth Track, join a small group, lead a small group, invest in the lives of people, pray, give, serve, lead, etc. We don't do this so God will love us—we do it because He already loves us. He loved us when we were unlovable. He has proven His love over and over again in our lives.[7] This is a massive distinction.[8] Trying to take enough steps to earn God's approval will leave you hurting, angry and frustrated. Taking steps in response to the continual love and encouragement will stretch your faith, but it will draw you closer to Him.

---

7   If you're still not convinced, remember Romans 5:8 "But God demonstrates His own love for us in this: While we were sinners, Christ died for us," and 8:32 "He who did not spare His own Son, but gave Him up for us all—how will He not also, along with Him, graciously give us all things?" (NIV)

8   Remember, this is the difference between sanctification and justification.

Discipleship isn't a class or a program—it is a lifestyle. A disciple is an apprentice—someone who does the stuff. Look back and find someone earlier in their journey and encourage them to take a next step too. Disciples don't make themselves—God calls us to go and make them.

We never outgrow steps. I'm right there with you. Let's keep putting one foot in front of the other as we all grow closer to Jesus.

3) MODEL THE VALUES

Everything that's healthy grows—not wild in every direction, but pruned according to the values that make us who we are. If this is your home, if you're a part of this spiritual family, model the values. Help us to ensure they don't become aspirational, existing only on a website or on a wall. Be a living stone, a living epistle and carry the DNA of this spiritual family. We're not better than anyone else, but we are proud of who God has called us to be.

If this is not your family, commit to the people God has placed you with. If you are a leader in another environment, help the people in your family by clearly articulating your values. They shouldn't have to dig and search for them—they should be on display—not on a website, but in the lives of your people.

4) FIGHT FOR UNITY, NOT UNIFORMITY

Historically the church—the ecclesia of God—have been known as *"the called out ones."* When the Bible describes heaven, it always includes people from every nation, tribe and tongue. A vibrant, dynamic church consists of different ages, different backgrounds, different ethnicities, and different socio-economic groups gathered together in Jesus.

If you've ever been part of something like this, it is nothing short of supernatural. Even the most irritable critic struggles to find a chink in this armor. It is powerfully compelling. They can't believe it and they don't understand...

331

but it creates a hope in their heart that says, *"If this is genuine…it's worth it. I would be part of something like that."*

We don't have to dress the same, talk the same, vote the same, like the same music or the same food. There is freedom in Christ. But we must be willing to fight to preserve and maintain a unity of heart and vision. This is why values are so important.

Jesus prayed for His followers to be of one mind and one heart. In Philippians 2 Paul gets really dramatic as he begs the people to make his joy complete by being of one mind and one spirit.[9] In Ephesians 4[10] Paul says God gave pastors, prophets, evangelists and teachers for the equipping of the saints so the body may be built up. From Jesus, the whole body holds together, grows and builds itself up in love and becomes mature as every part does its work.[11]

God hasn't given up on His Church. He still believes it is a treasure buried in a field. Some people only see dirt…but when you've experienced it like I have, you know it's worth it.

---

9   *Therefore if you have any encouragement from being united with Christ, if any comfort from his love, if any common sharing in the Spirit, if any tenderness and compassion, then make my joy complete by being like-minded, having the same love, being one in spirit and of one mind Do nothing out of selfish ambition or vain conceit. Rather, in humility value others above yourselves, not looking to your own interests but each of you to the interests of the others.* Philippians 2:1-4 (NIV)

10   Ephesians 4:11

11   Ephesians 4:15-16

ACKNOWLEDGEMENTS

I may have signed up for this pastor thing thinking it would be Sundays, Wednesdays and a little golf mixed in...but the bottom line is, with the demands that I have as a husband, dad, leader, pastor, and weekly communicator, I could not have produced this book without the help of an incredible team of people, who not only functionally saw this project to completion, but live and breathe these values with me every day.

The real heavy lifting of this book was done by Jed Walker. Jed and I have been friends since our early twenties, and he serves as Associate Pastor on our teaching team. Over a several-year period he and I labored over this book together, and his partnership has helped see this project go from just an idea to the book you now hold in your hands. Jed truly owned the heart behind this book as not just a teaching, but a desire to communicate heart and passion—and heart and passion truly represent who Jed is. He is one of the smartest people I know and is a great teacher and pastor. My wife and I are so honored to serve with him and his wife, Sara, and I want to say "thank you" to them for their sacrifice in this book.

Tiffany, my executive assistant, makes everything in my world happen—she truly has one of the greatest gifts to move projects and initiatives down the field. Her drive, dedication, patience, and gift set helped carry this project over the finish line, and I couldn't be more grateful for what she does on a daily basis for my family and me.

Pat Brown, our Executive Pastor of Communications and Creative Arts, weekly helps me communicate the heart and vision expressed within the pages of this book. I'm so grateful for the countless hours he spends creating atmospheres for people to encounter Jesus.

Blake Campbell, our Pastor of Worship and Creative Arts, is a walking example of these values lived out. Blake shares my burden to keep telling the stories of everyday people and the life-transforming power of Jesus. His investment of time and talent in the entire creative process has been invaluable.

We couldn't have completed this book without Melissa Baggett who invested so much time researching for and laboring over this final product.

Steve Chesnut, Ron Stegall, and Meghan Genard are the trusted friends and voices that helped review the manuscript and assisted me in communicating the heart and values of our spiritual family.

Thank you to Jon Essen, for helping manage the final stages of production and carrying the project to completion, Venicia Carroll for editing and proofing the manuscript, and Ryan Boone, for all the incredible time spent on layout and design.

To the overseers of Milestone, Steve Robinson and Jim Laffoon—many of the concepts that I have lived out in the pages of this book I received from the impartation of these men. I am one of the most blessed pastors in the world with the men who speak into my life.

To the Elders, Lead Team, Pastors, and Staff of Milestone—I am partial but I believe I get to work with some of the most talented, gifted, authentic people on the planet. Their love for Jesus and heart for people every day are what is poured out onto the pages of this book.

To my wife, who has lived this vision with me and has been willing to say "yes" to Jesus at every turn. I love you with all my heart and am passionate about seeing and sharing in the values in this book in our kids Hannah Grace, Caleb Scott, Lauren Elizabeth and Laney Kate.

SELECTIVE BIBLIOGRAPHY

1. Coleman, Robert E. *The Master Plan of Evangelism.* 2nd ed. Westwood, NJ: F.H. Revell, 1964.
2. Collins, James C. *Good to Great.* New York, NY: HarperBusiness, 2001.
3. Houston, Bobbie. *Heaven Is in This House.* Castle Hill, NSW: Maximised Leadership Inc., 2004.
4. Hybels, Bill. *Courageous Leadership.* Grand Rapids, MI: Zondervan, 2002.
5. Lencioni, Patrick. *The Advantage.* San Francisco: Jossey-Bass, 2012.
6. Lewis, C. S. *The Screwtape Letters.* New York: Macmillan, 1943.
7. Majernik, Jan. Joseph Ponessa, Laurie Watson Manhardt. *Come and See.* Steubenville, OH: Emmaus Road, 2005.
8. Rath, Tom. *Eat Move Sleep.* Missionday, 2013.
9. Sanders, J. Oswald. *Spiritual Leadership.* Chicago: Moody, 1994.
10. Stanley, Andy. *Deep & Wide.* Grand Rapids, Mich.: Zondervan, 2012.
11. Willard, Dallas. *The Divine Conspiracy.* San Francisco: HarperSanFrancisco, 1998.

ITSWORTHITBOOK.COM

#ITSWORTHITBOOK

Questions? Comments?
Email itsworthit@milestonechurch.com

VISIT US ONLINE

MILESTONECHURCH.COM

@milestonechurch

FREE RESOURCES
FOR YOUR CHURCH